Making the Right Decision

Ethics for Managers

Making the Right Decision

Ethics for Managers

WILLIAM D. HALL

Retired Partner
Arthur Andersen & Co, SC

John Wiley & Sons, Inc.

New York ■ Chichester ■ Brisbane ■ Toronto ■ Singapore

ISBN O-471-58632-3 (cloth)
O-471-58633-1 (paper)

10 9 8 7 6 5 4 3 2 1

CONTENTS

PREFACE

Lawrence A. Weinbach
Managing Partner—Chief Executive
Arthur Andersen & Co, SC

Over the past several years, much attention has been focused on what some have called an "ethics crisis"—a breakdown in behavior deemed to accord with accepted ethical norms. Some people perceive the malaise to be societel in nature, impacting business, governmental, and personal behavior alike.

Others, however, speculate that human frailties are probably no worse than before and that growing instances of publicized wrongdoing are a factor of intensified media scrutiny—plus the media's willingness, bordering on compulsion, to expose lapses of conduct once considered off-limits to public view.

And still others maintain the "true issue" is really not so much the deliberately unethical behavior that grabs headlines. Rather, it is the increasing complexity of business and society and the demand for greater accountability to different publics with different interests that makes it more and more difficult to differentiate "ethical" from "unethical" behavior.

All of this comes at a time when there is near-universal recognition that ethical behavior is a basic in the exercise of credibility and trust in all manner of business activity.

As an organization committed to the free flow of commerce, the partners of the Arthur Andersen Worldwide Organization underwrote in 1987 a $5-million, five-year Business Ethics Program designed to integrate ethics more fully into the curricula of the nation's business schools. Its objective was to encourage and facilitate the understanding and teaching of business ethics to future business leaders. An Advisory Council on Business Ethics—consisting of scholars, teachers, and business executives—designed, conducted, and monitored the program.

Since the start of our effort, some 1,120 faculty members from almost 300 colleges and universities have participated in conferences addressing the subject of business ethics at the Arthur Andersen & Co., SC Center for Professional Education in St. Charles, Illinois. Our program design was basically to inform the teachers about inculcating principles of ethical business conduct among their students.

An independent research firm, retained in Fall 1990, has evaluated the program. Telephone interviews with randomly selected participants have affirmed the need for, as well as the efficacy of, the initiative. Ninety-one percent of the teacher respondents reported they had changed their courses of study after attending the Business Ethics Program; 86 percent had greater confidence in teaching business ethics. Using every measure we can identify, the program has been successful—even beyond our original high expectations.

Although I am gratified about the long-term impact the program will have on students after they graduate and continue with their careers in business, my partners and I looked for some vehicle that would expand on the immediate direct benefit that has influenced students of business during the five years of the program. Our goal was to capture the lessons learned about business ethics for transmission not only to future generations of business leaders but also to those now in business who had minimal or no exposure to teachings on business ethics.

We decided that a book, based in large part on what had been learned from the program, would, at the least, be a first step in perpetuating ethical behavior in business as a topic of consideration and instruction.

Bill Hall, a retired partner and an involved member of our Advisory Council on Business Ethics from its inception, was our choice as author. Prior to his retirement in 1984, Bill had served as chairman of our Committee on Professional Standards, whose responsibilities included establishing and monitoring professional ethics in our worldwide practice. He has also authored numerous papers and articles during his long career.

Bill's approach to his assignment has more than confirmed the wisdom of our selection. Initially, he contemplated a somewhat straightforward treatment of business ethics written from the viewpoint of recognized business ethicists that would also draw from the vast storehouse of data developed in our conferences over the past five years.

But as Bill pursued his task, he came to believe that the world was not crying out for another conventional textbook on business ethics. In fact, many such texts, authored by students of business behavior and philosophers alike, already exist.

And although the same is true also of conventional casebooks, Bill felt strongly that "real life experiences"—the stuff of which case histories are made—were most compelling in creating and retaining interest and in communicating experiences. He ruminated that some of the most effective lessons one can find on ethics are related in fiction that explores the human condition, with all the dilemmas, the shining moments, and, yes, the lapses that mark the trail of a person's life journey. He recalled the solution to a nagging problem that came to him as he read George Eliot's *Middlemarch,* and the lessons he clearly remembers from William Dean Howells's *The Rise of Silas Lapham,* sometimes described as the first novel to deal with modern business.

The result is this book, written as a real-life fictionalized extended case study—or perhaps more accurately, a series of related case studies—centered on a medium-sized manufacturing company in a small city. Most of the cases are developed conversationally, through dialogue, artfully facilitating the presentation of multiple (and most often conflicting) points of view. The debates are sharp, the atmosphere is real, and a sense of urgency is always present.

Indeed, as I read the manuscript, I came to feel close to the company and its people and to emphathize with their problems. Time and time again, I felt compelled to make the decision myself.

That says a lot about Bill Hall, about his book, and, I hope, about the experience you are in for when you read *Making the Right Decision: Ethics for Managers.*

ACKNOWLEDGMENTS

Making the Right Decision: Ethics for Managers evolved from the five-year Business Ethics Program of Arthur Andersen & Co, SC. An Advisory Council, composed of leading professionals and others in the field of business ethics, helped design, conduct, and monitor this program. I was fortunate indeed to work closely with all of them, first as a consultant to the program and then as a Council member. These informed, dedicated individuals increased my awareness of the complexities inherent in ethical dilemmas and introduced me to the skills one can use in applying moral reasoning to their resolution.

Three members in particular provided essential help as the book began to take form, as I wrestled with what to include and how to present it, and as I worked on the finishing touches. At the outset, Dr. Robert A. Cooke counseled me on format, encouraging me in the use of the case study approach; he also pointed me toward source material and reviewed the earlier chapters. Later, Dr. Peter Madsen gave invaluable guidance as I tried to resolve the more complex issues that surfaced when I was trying to tie up loose ends; then he served as a friendly critic in reviewing the final manuscript. And John E. Swanson's insight, as an executive who has devoted much of his career to implementing a business ethics program in his own company, offered practical suggestions and concrete examples that helped bring the ethical concepts to life.

The first Council chair and a man widely recognized as *the* pioneer in the field of business ethics, Dr. Clarence C. Walton, provided inspiration and guidance through his leadership in meetings and in his writings. Other Council members included Clarence's successor as chair, Dr. Patricia H. Werhane, and Don G. Baker, Dr. Norman E. Bowie, Dr. Edwin M. Epstein, Dr. John E. Fleming, Robert L. May, Howard L. Siers, and Dr. Manuel Velasquez. Each of them, in one way or another, offered insights that found their way into the book.

G. Robert Baechle, a fellow retired Arthur Andersen partner who served as director of the program, provided able and willing counsel and backup as I labored to bring the book into being. Bob suffered through the reading of more chapter drafts than I—and, I am sure, he—like to recall. He did not even let a heart attack, one from which he is fortunately recovering, stand in the way of helping—clearly support above and beyond anything that could be expected. And his able assistant, Barbara Bunning, was always there, ready to be of assistance or to find someone who would fill the bill.

Robert Mednick, my successor at Arthur Andersen, had recommended me as the author when the notion of this book first arose and had gently "leaned on" me to accept the challenge. He offered his valuable support throughout, including careful reading of many drafts. Our long and warm friendship not only survived the stress of my authorship and my demands on Bob's daunting schedule, it prospered.

Recognizing that most of those whose counsel I had sought during the writing were mature professionals and executives with considerable experience, I wanted to see how the effort would "play" with persons just beginning their business or professional careers. My youngest sons, Alex, a 1986 MBA involved in real estate, and Andrew, then just one year out of law school, agreed to read drafts of some key chapters. Their comments generally encouraged me in the direction I was taking, but their criticism (which has always been frank, sometimes uncomfortably so) caused me to sharpen the focus of some sections and even to add some material. Perhaps the money spent on their education was not entirely wasted!

And finally, I wish to acknowledge the contributions of my publisher, particularly Jeffrey Brown and Erika Heilman. After reading the manuscript, they offered only a few, but very perceptive, suggestions. Although these suggestions were seemingly simple and easy to implement, the result gave the book the focus it needed.

As is customary in acknowledgments such as this, I appreciate all the help offered me—help without which the writing of this book would not have been possible—but I alone am responsible for the way in which this help has been interpreted and used.

What This Book Is About

Decision Making: The Art of Management

The ability to make sound, timely decisions is an art, one could say *the* art, of management. Identifying a problem where action is required. Obtaining and evaluating pertinent information from diverse, sometimes conflicting sources. Weighing alternatives and assessing priorities. Reacting to late-breaking developments. And then making the decision. These are all important components of the decisions, from the more trivial to the most complex, that individuals in business make daily.

This book deals with decision making, and how ethics plays a vital role in these decisions. The successful manager is one who can make decisions quickly and usually be right, all the while dealing with many, varied issues that demand immediate attention. And the responsible manager is one who reflects ethics in this complex decision making. Michael Rion, who has been actively involved in business ethics both as a manager and as a consultant, captured the essence of this in a few words:

> Managers are . . . faced with the sheer rapidity of the decision process and the necessity to act. Individual managers typically handle this complexity with quick decisions. There are simply

too many simultaneous issues and demands on their time to allow for deliberative consideration in every case. Indeed, a critical skill for managers is knowing when to stop the process for careful deliberation; it cannot be stopped every time. The manager who slows down the process too often will in many cases miss the opportunity to decide and will ultimately fail to carry out the managerial task.[1]

Earlier, Rion had written:

From education and experience, a person brings a repertoire of skills, models, and perspectives into rigorous interaction with unique problems and thereby discovers new directions. [This] model fits well the lived reality of managers who cope daily with complexity and ambiguity. Their ethical decisions come not from application of moral absolutes, but from the interplay of values, concepts, experience, and immediate realities.[2]

In this book, these characteristics of real-life decision making come to life through such true-to-life dilemmas as:

■ Pressure on a board of directors to make a fast decision on a relocation that affects the viability of an important product line, millions of dollars of the shareholders' investment, the jobs of hundreds of longtime employees, and the well-being of a community.

■ The mental tug-of-war of a purchasing agent, having to reduce orders of a certain item by 25 percent and trying to decide how to allocate the cut between a local, longtime supplier that may not be able to survive without the business and a large company that has offered a price incentive if it can retain or increase its level of orders.

■ The soul-searching of a promising young manager confronted with a nagging suspicion that the study he had made,

---

[1] Michael Rion, *The Responsible Manager: Practical Strategies for Ethical Decision Making* (San Francisco: Harper & Row, Publishers, 1990), 37.

[2] *Ibid.*, 36, discussing the views of Donald Schon, *The Reflective Practitioner: How Professionals Think in Action* (New York: Basic Books, 1983).

one on which the company has based a critical decision, may be seriously flawed.

Each of these decisions has ethical dimensions. But managers and others, confronted with dilemmas like these, do not ordinarily stop and consciously, deliberately, apply a conceptual framework of ethics to their decision making—even if they are familiar with such a framework. Possibly they might do so on infrequent, very important decisions like the proposed relocation. Normally, though, especially in individual situations, they cannot afford that "luxury."

This does not suggest that a sound basis in moral reasoning is irrelevant. Indeed, the very need to assimilate relevant factors and reach a decision quickly emphasizes the importance of a grounding in basic principles—such a grounding that their application becomes almost reflexive. In dealing with complexity and ambiguity and a wide range of problems simultaneously, a person needs far more sophisticated guidance than lessons learned as a child, at home, at school, and in church.

Ethical Issues Can Be Complex

Answers to ethical questions are clear, at least we normally think they are, regarding flagrant violations of the law. The transgressions of an Ivan Boesky, perhaps. Or a Michael Milken. But common sense and experience tell us felonies like theirs were not committed in isolation. We know about those associates, closely involved, who were granted immunity to testify against the leaders. Beyond those, there were bound to be many others who, perhaps, broke no law but knew or suspected something was amiss—who said they were only following orders . . . who looked the other way . . . who said, "That's how business is."

Ethical concerns, however, are not limited to situations in which people are involved, directly or indirectly, in illegal acts. *Ethics is broadly concerned with how persons or organizations act, or should act, in relations with others.* Although takeovers that enrich a few persons while jeopardizing the savings or livelihoods of thousands may not be illegal, they can pose as many ethical questions as illegal insider trading. And so can some of the golden parachutes crafted for a few favored executives just before a threatened takeover.

Even some necessary actions, such as the closing of a plant that, despite the best efforts of the owners and management, has continued to drain resources desperately needed elsewhere, have ethical implications. Although loss and suffering for innocent people may be unavoidable, ethics calls for reaching and implementing decisions in such way as to minimize harm. And that involves identifying and dealing with competing claims of those affected—attempting to balance myriad rights and obligations.

The well-known ethicist Manuel Velasquez points out that ethical issues in business involve three levels—that of *society*, that of the *organization*, and that of the *individual* within the organization.[3] At the societal level, business is part of a social system that includes various economic, legal, and political institutions; this macro level may be concerned with broad questions of the ethical rightness or wrongness of the system itself, for example, the ethical basis of capitalism or other forms of political and economic structure. Although this book addresses all three levels, it focuses at the societal level only on how the organization impacts the society of which it is a part.

A Company Faces a Tough Plant Relocation Decision

A reader can learn from messages embodied in concrete examples, situations to which he or she can readily relate, far more easily than from abstract discussion. The chapters that follow, therefore, take the form of a story, a case study—or, more precisely, a series of interrelated case studies involving a single company. As the situation develops, the book uses the dilemmas posed to draw out

---

[3]The discussion of the three levels in this introduction is based on a paper that Dr. Robert A. Cooke, Director of The Institute for Business Ethics at DePaul University, prepared for the author.

ethical issues and then to point toward ways in which they can be resolved. It relies heavily on dialogue, frequently argumentative, sometimes heated, occasionally humorous.

Our story opens with first the chair, George Hauser, then the board of directors, of Hauser-Moore Manufacturing Company coping with a sudden, unexpected proposal for the relocation of a major product line—a move that would cost hundreds of long-time employees their jobs and that would traumatically affect other local businesses and the community at large. As the directors of this medium-sized company, long a major part of the community, debate the proposal, they are torn by economic arguments, ethical questions, and personal concerns. It becomes apparent that they have no common agreement on what ethical issues are present—or, in the case of several, whether ethics is even involved. But they must make a decision—and reluctantly they do.

Here, we are at the organization, or company, level referred to earlier. At center stage are the ethical aspects of company decisions that affect others. For example, when the management of a company considers relocating a plant, what may appear to be a basic economic decision has consequences for other individuals or groups that usually have no voice in the decisions. A concern at this level is corporate structure and corporate culture. Does the structure or culture help or hinder ethical decisions? If roadblocks to ethical behavior exist within the organization, what can be done to remedy the situation?

A month after their difficult decision, Hauser and Michael Lerner, another director, discuss what took place:

> "As I see it," Hauser said in response to a comment by Lerner, "we didn't have an ethics problem—except possibly for the involvement of Dick's brother in the plant purchase. We just had one hell of a big management and PR problem."
>
> "I disagree, George," Lerner interjected, "and that, I believe, is one of our problems in addressing ethics. Too many people think there's no ethics issue unless someone is caught with his hand in the till. Ethics is the way in which people behave toward one another; as a result, it is intertwined with

many decisions we make, business or otherwise. What happened at our meetings was full of ethical implications."

Identifying Issues: Finding Answers

There we come up against a major, not uncommon, problem—a difficulty in identifying ethical dilemmas under our very noses. The fact that ethics is so pervasive, so intertwined with the economic and other facets of many decisions, personal or business, tends to make the questions it raises difficult to recognize.

Another problem in dealing with ethical dilemmas is their inherent, almost intractable, ambiguity: They do not lend themselves to pat answers. And that frustrates many people. They would like to deal with ethics solely as a matter of right or wrong. That is fine as far as it goes, but that is only the beginning. As Carl Iverson, a consultant later retained by the Hauser-Moore board to assist in developing a corporate ethics program, stressed:

"Ambiguity is at the heart of ethical dilemmas—that's why they are dilemmas. You run into competing claims, mutually exclusive but each with a valid, persuasive argument for its selection. With many ethical issues, there isn't a simple right answer. Two or more alternatives, mutually exclusive, may be 'right.' So you can't have the luxury of reaching a comfortable right answer that will satisfy everyone."

And later, in pointing out the need for a conceptual framework in addressing ethical dilemmas, Iverson said:

"Human existence is not always made up of clear-cut right and wrong actions. We've seen that in our brief initial discussion about the conduct of the board deliberations on the relocation matter. As a result, we need to have conceptual guidelines for our behavior—ones that go beyond the lessons sometimes referred to as 'ones learned at our mother's knee.' "

Those conceptual guidelines are addressed as the story goes on, with a focus on two models. One, the utilitarian model, looks at costs and benefits. A result is deemed to be ethically sound if it produces what is sometimes characterized as "the greatest good for the greatest number of people." The other model, based on rights and duties, stresses attention to the rights, sometimes conflicting, of those affected by a decision and the duties of decision makers to consider those rights. One might say that the first model assigns primacy to the end result while the second looks at the means.

Theories, of course, are of limited usefulness without the means to apply them efficiently and consistently. As the case develops, Iverson introduces Hauser-Moore to a structured, seven-step analysis that facilitates the integration of ethical concerns with economic factors in reaching sound business decisions.

How Do Individuals Cope Within the Corporation?

Our reference to the case thus far has been at the level of the organization. As the story proceeds, it addresses the third level, that of the individual within the organization. The decisions facing any person in business are subject to the same ethical constraints, the same conceptual rationale, as underlie company decisions; but they raise a host of unique questions that need to be recognized by both the individual and the organization. Clashes may occur between individual moral standards and corporate policies. How should a person react if asked to do something that violates his or her ethical beliefs? Does the individual have certain basic rights that are protected from company decisions or policies? And what rights does the company have in cases of conflict?

As Iverson later points out, "There are knowledgeable critics who believe that addressing ethics as an individual matter is an exercise in futility. People, they claim, must operate within the constraints of their environment." But, one manager argues with some heat, carrying that too far can be "nothing but a copout. It's the same wooly thinking that leads some people to say that criminals aren't responsible for their own acts, that they are unfortunate individuals who were abused as children, suffered from poverty and so on. I'll admit," he goes on, "that it may be hard sometimes, but people have to take responsibility for what they do, not pass the buck to someone else."

The book focuses generally on these concerns—the role of individuals within the corporate environment. Among others, the following cases highlight the discussion:

■ An area manager of shopping centers who is wrestling with the implications, economic and ethical, of leasing vacant space to a major company that would compete against, possibly even drive out, a good longtime tenant that has recently renewed its lease; and

■ A supervisor deciding what to do about a previously conscientious employee with 32 years of service, now within two years of normal retirement, who has become increasingly undependable since the death of her husband.

The importance of sound company policies and a sensitive management in dealing with such problems becomes apparent.

In Hauser-Moore, we find an up-and-coming young employee agonizing over his role in the study that supported relocation of the product line. He has come to suspect that he accepted too easily some estimated costs that may have been understated; if so, the study's recommendation, and the company's decision, may have been wrong. Should he tell his supervisor of his suspicion? He senses he should, but what's to be gained by stirring up a hornet's nest now? After all, plans for a move have been made, notices have gone out to employees who will be terminated, and contracts have been let—isn't it too late? And possibly his fears are ill-founded; the study may be all right after all. If it is wrong, perhaps no one will ever find out. As the story unfolds, we get a chance to examine the roles not only of the employee who made the study but also his supervisor, the manager who gave him the suspect figures, the friend in whom he confided his fears, and even the chair. There is a sharp focus on the interrelationship of individual behavior and the corporate environment.

A Company Ethics Program Is Essential

General exhortations about ethical behavior fall short, and there is a rapid falloff without a well-conceived, well-organized ethics program within a company. The latter part of the book looks at the elements of such a program. As part of that consideration, the appropriateness, nature, and effectiveness of training in moral reasoning skills receive close attention.

First and foremost, however, is the company's ethics environment. The tone at the top is paramount. Body language, if you will, is important. A sensitive management, establishing and abiding by a soundly based program, creates a climate in which employees feel comfortable with the way in which they are expected to behave.

The story goes on to address other, more specific, elements of a comprehensive ethics program—for example, the role of a company code of ethics, the desirability and function of ethics training, a "hot line" for handling ethics inquiries, and the structure of ongoing oversight. At the end of the book, a conclusion entitled "How to Get an Ethics Program Started" provides practical guidance that a company can follow in designing and implementing an effective ethics program.

But Is Ethical Behavior Worthwhile to a Company?

And finally, our story turns to the question: Is business ethics worthwhile? For the company? For the individual? Readers will undoubtedly surmise that the conclusion is yes; otherwise there would be little point in the book. But the reasons may not be obvious.

The answer is something that only reading the book will reveal. We hope it will be persuasive.

PART ONE

Ethical Issues From a Company Perspective

CHAPTER ONE

A Board's Painful Decision

The meetings had been difficult—not at all what the directors of 70-year-old Hauser-Moore Manufacturing Company were used to. Frustration was evident, and most of the directors left irritated and dissatisfied with a decision they felt had been forced on them. The problem was behind them, at least they thought, but they felt used, not too pleased with themselves.

An Unexpected, and Unwelcome, Dilemma

The problem—the cause of unhappiness and dissatisfaction at the board meetings—had begun a couple weeks before when the president and chief executive officer, Richard Bentley, sent board chair George Hauser a report, just completed, on a cost study. The study related to facilities needed for the manufacture of a new line of small, two-cycle engines to replace an outdated product line—the company's Series F models—whose sales had been falling off badly. In a brief note transmitting the report, Bentley had said that he wanted Hauser to see it first, and to discuss it with him if he wished, but that he considered it important that it be sent to each director and put on the agenda for action at next week's board meeting. There was almost an implication that review and approval would be little more than a formality.

Hauser had been generally aware that the study was under way, but he was stunned at the implications when he read it. Perhaps, he thought with a sense of guilt as well as anger, he had let himself get too isolated from developments. To expand the existing facility and retool here in Janesboro, the report said, would cost about $3.5 million more, on a present-value basis, than the proposed alternative—to build a new plant in Hendersonville, another small city about fifteen hundred miles away. And, if the study could be believed, the advantage from relocating would probably become greater as time passed.

Hauser and others in management had known that the company's labor costs in Janesboro were high. Transportation costs were also a problem. Perhaps he should have reacted to those problems earlier. Maybe he had let himself get lulled into a belief that the established order, a comfortable way of doing business he had long taken for granted, would never change. Some changes, he acknowledged to himself, were inevitable.

But he could not dismiss the fact that Hauser-Moore was a fixture in Janesboro. Even though most of the company's operations would remain, the move of the one product line would cost 300 people their jobs, to say nothing of the impact on local suppliers, many of whom had long been closely tied to the company. And the loss of tax revenues would exacerbate an already serious budget problem for the city. This was not something, he thought, that should be decided quickly on a strictly dollars-and-cents basis. Also, he felt the need for more information than appeared in the report, so he told Bentley to meet him, in his office, the first thing next morning.

A Long Identity with the Community

As Hauser sat in his office the next morning waiting for Bentley, he fiddled impatiently with papers on his desk. Lost in thought, he glanced from the papers to his father's portrait on the far wall, first abstractedly, then—for the first time in months—with eyes that really focused on the familiar picture. What, he wondered, would his father think of this development?

Rising from his chair, he strolled over to the window that looked out over Hauser-Moore's facilities and part of the city beyond. Although he had viewed the same scene often, probably thousands of times, over the years, this morning he studied it more closely. It came to him that he had always thought of his family, the company, and the city as inseparable. Certainly there had been occasional stresses, some serious, as during the unionization drive 15 years ago, but he had never thought of the company being located anywhere but in Janesboro—or of his having to choose, perhaps, between them.

Cofounded by the late Henry Hauser and Edward Moore just before World War I, Hauser-Moore had grown and diversified over the years. Today it was the major employer in Janesboro. Some 20 years after its founding, Moore had suffered a severe heart attack; with no family members likely to become involved in the business, he had sold his partnership interest to Hauser but had remained active as a consultant. When Hauser incorporated the company a few years later, he had asked Moore to serve as a director and had continued the old name, both because of friendship and because of his respect for tradition and continuity.

After Hauser's death 25 years ago, his only son George, who had been groomed to take over, became president and chief executive officer. He had earned the respect of business associates and the company's employees over the years, both for his qualities of leadership and for his fairness and integrity. Although somewhat reserved and, at least in the view of some, demanding in his expectations of others, those who had worked with him and for him over the years always found him accessible, open, and candid. His honesty, someone had once said, was almost painful.

It had appeared that the family's identity with the company would be perpetuated when George and Jessica Hauser's oldest son, named after his grandfather, showed a flair for the business and was named executive vice president six years ago. George's dream of continued family involvement ended a few months later, however, when young Henry was killed in a freak automobile accident, leaving no heirs. Neither George's other two children nor his sister's only daughter had an interest in joining the company; one was a history professor at the state university, one a writer and sometime poetry editor in New York, and the other a successful attorney with a Los Angeles law firm.

Seven years ago, the company had gone public, but the Hauser family still owned 22 percent of the company's stock. The company's earnings had started slipping about four years ago, not dangerously but enough to cause concern. There was a sense that the company might be drifting a bit—inbred, perhaps, and not keeping up with new developments. And George Hauser's age and health following heart bypass surgery were a worry, especially since there was no obvious successor within the company. On his own initiative and with the encouragement of the company's investment bankers, he had continued as chairman of the board but had brought in a new president and CEO, Richard Bentley, from a larger, out-of-state company. Gradually, Hauser had begun spending less and less time at the office.

With the help of a board committee, Hauser had found Bentley through an executive search agency. Bentley appeared to have the right credentials: He was 37, with an M.B.A. degree from Harvard and a record of identifying solutions and turning around lagging operations at his previous company. Bright and personable, he seemed a perfect answer to concerns about Hauser-Moore's parochialism. True, he had changed jobs twice in the last 13 years, which raised questions about his commitment, his loyalty. And he was not steeped in the company's traditions, a fact that bothered some local board members, but Hauser and others chose to view this as more a plus than a problem. Since Bentley had taken over, complaints surfaced from time to time that he was in too big a hurry, not sufficiently sensitive to people, but earnings had stabilized, and Hauser liked many of the innovations Bentley had introduced. Also, he tended to discount criticisms of the new president as what one would expect when a new person takes charge of an organization that has become somewhat set in its ways. All in all, Hauser had been well satisfied until quite recently.

As Hauser looked beyond the company's facilities and focused on the city, he reflected that his interests, and those of the Hauser family, had never been limited to Hauser-Moore. Beginning with the first Henry Hauser, the family had always played a major role in community affairs. Henry Hauser had been the driving force behind the art museum. During World War II, he had led the city's bond drives. A longtime trustee of Trinity University, a renowned college on the outskirts of Janesboro, he was serving as its chairman when he died.

Twenty years ago, George Hauser had served two terms as mayor. He had succeeded his father as a trustee of Trinity and had twice headed the United Way. His wife Jessica was still a member of the school board and president of the art museum. And his sister served on the boards of several charities. Many of the city's philanthropic and civic organizations looked to the Hauser Foundation as a major source of their support. Indeed, to many people, the names Hauser and Janesboro had become virtually synonymous. As one of the city's business leaders had said a few months ago at a ceremony honoring Hauser for his many years of service to the United Way, "George Hauser's success in business is second only to his commitment to doing the right thing—in his company, in his family, and in our community of which he is so much a part."

An Unsatisfactory, Tense Discussion

Hauser acknowledged Bentley's arrival in his office rather curtly, inviting him to sit down but without the usual genial smile, small talk, and offer of coffee. Without wasting any time, he told Bentley that he was upset that matters had gotten to the point they had before he was told. "Don't you realize," he asked, "what would happen if people would hear, without advance warning, what you are suggesting? Even that the matter is under consideration? There'd be hell to pay.''

Bentley seemed rather taken aback by this reaction. ''George, the board has frequently, even at the last meeting, agreed that we have to do something to update or replace that obsolete line of Series F engines. The drop-off in sales is accelerating—it not only hurts earnings but gives our distributors problems. I know the engines perform well, but frankly, they look old-fashioned. Maybe it has little to do with performance, but customers want something that looks more modern. And the Series F models aren't as easy to install, or to repair, as what our competitors are pushing.

''Also, we have known that our costs are out of line—that something has to be done. Part of this comes from local wage scales, and part from design problems. Because of the old Series F design, the engines require more labor to produce. I told the board that we had a new product on the way—also said, and no one seemed to disagree, that eventually some of the company's operations might have to be moved elsewhere. I believe that it was Mike Lerner who said he'd been thinking the same thing. Don't you remember? The fact that the new line of engines will require a drastically changed layout and retooling makes this an obvious time to look at alternative locations. It all seems to tie together.

''Perhaps,'' he acknowledged, ''I should have kept you better informed on the progress of the study. But I thought we were generally together on what had to be done and I hadn't wanted to bother you with any details until something definitive was available—that hadn't come until the completion of the cost study a few days earlier.''

''Dick,'' Hauser shot back with obvious irritation, ''we see each other every day that I'm in—which is at least three days a week. With something this important, it would have been only natural to keep me posted. Or did you think I might cause a problem if I knew?''

''Of course not, George,'' Bentley exclaimed hotly. ''That's not fair. I wouldn't have done anything like that, and it wouldn't have made sense anyway. The board would never approve something if you're against it. Maybe I was wrong in not saying something earlier, but I wasn't deliberately keeping you, or anyone, in the dark."

"Sorry, Dick," Hauser apologized quickly. "I shouldn't have said that—it sounded personal, and I didn't mean it that way. But this is important to me—more, probably, than just business. And surely you had a feel for how the study was going a good while before you sent the report to me?" Bentley looked a bit embarrassed, then admitted that he had had interim oral reports on the progress of the study, beginning a month or so ago. He went on to say, though, that these had been too preliminary and tentative, in his opinion, to provide a basis for any discussion. From the look on his face and the way he said it, it was evident that he recognized that this was a rather lame excuse, and he let it drop.

"Putting all that aside," Hauser said, "I can't help wondering if you and the others put as much effort into finding ways to keep costs down here so we wouldn't feel the need to move as you did in planning for a new plant. Most of the creative thinking seems to have gone into making the move cost-effective and attractive."

Seeing that Bentley was about to protest vehemently, Hauser held up his hand and continued in a more conciliatory tone, "Look, Dick, I'm not suggesting that you were consciously biased—and Lord knows we all have our biases. Some of mine are showing now. But let's be frank: Is it possible that you are so convinced that a move is in the company's best interests, maybe inevitable, that you thought more about planning for an all-new plant, miles away from here, than you did about ways to make staying here economical?"

"George, I can't deny that I think moving some of our operations will ultimately be necessary," Bentley admitted, "and now might be a good time to start. But I didn't let that influence the study, consciously or, I am sure, unconsciously. I even had our people redo the cost to expand and retool here twice because Joe Hendricks, the manager of manufacturing operations, and I found ways we could cut costs if we were to retool here. The reductions we came up with were substantial.

"And even more important, you must have noticed that the study reflected almost $6 million of savings for wage concessions we might be able to get from the union and some tax reductions the city might agree to if we were to remain. If we hadn't included those possible savings from staying here, the present value of the benefit from relocation would have been $9.5 million. I told the people making the study to treat this information very confidentially, to put it in on my say-so, without any detailed support.

"Frankly," he continued, "I am not at all optimistic we could get those savings—they represent about a 10 percent average pay cut. They are a little higher than what you and I talked about as a possibility when we were reviewing the Series F operations some months back—you know, before any question of relocation had come up. We'd probably have a real fight on our hands to get anything near that, but I thought we had to put something into the study on an estimated basis; then, if the answer had favored staying here, or even been close, we would have had to go to the mat with the union and city to see what we might actually get. As it turned out, though, even with those potential savings included, the study showed a significant net advantage—about $3.5 million—for relocation. So there was no need to open that can of worms."

"I'm just as glad," Hauser said, almost with an air of resignation. "I don't think we could have limited such discussions to just the old engine operations. I have no idea where it might have ended—and it might have been even more traumatic than what you are proposing. Still, though, I can't see why you are trying to rush this so fast. What's the urgency? The Series F engine situation is not a new problem—it has been a long time in the making. Why is it suddenly necessary to spring a long, detailed report on the directors just a week before the meeting and to expect them to react that fast? It doesn't make sense."

Acknowledging the problem, Bentley admitted he should have explained what made timing so important before sending Hauser the report or should have delivered it in person and discussed what was involved. "Happening on an opportunity a few weeks ago to get a good building cheaply is what cranked up the timetable. The real estate consultants," he said, "found a partially completed plant at the proposed location in Hendersonville—one where construction had stopped. A major company had acquired the company that was building it and then decided to relocate all its operations to another city. They're stuck with the building and want to unload. It's a tremendous break for us.

"We can utilize most of what has been done with little change," Bentley continued enthusiastically, "and the price, as you can see in the report, is very good. In fact, that is a major reason that the cost comparison so strongly favors relocation. When I visited the location to evaluate it personally, I heard that other possible purchasers were interested, and I hadn't wanted to risk losing the opportunity. I took it on myself to put down $25,000 on the spot, a relatively small option payment under the circumstances, I thought, to hold it until after the meeting."

Although Hauser wondered why Bentley hadn't at least called him before making the option commitment, he could understand the rationale and went on to the next point, the one that probably concerned him the most. "What consideration," he asked, "have you given to the impact on employees who would be terminated and on the community generally? You know that we aren't just another company as far as Janesboro is concerned."

Bentley hurriedly pointed out that this was reflected in the study. It included the cost of termination payments required under the union contract and a round amount, one he thought ample, that would be used for various purposes such as job counseling, a payment the company might wish to make in lieu of taxes the city would lose for the next couple years, and a few other items. "I have asked the human resources people," he continued, "to develop some ideas that I will bring to the board meeting, but I haven't pushed on this in the interests of getting the cost study done and ready for distribution first."

This upset Hauser—that Bentley had regarded the impact on employees and the community as a secondary issue. "Nobody likes profits better than I do," he interrupted, "but Hauser-Moore is not—never has been—run solely for the bottom line. We're dealing with people—real, live people—and in a town where I've spent my whole life. I see them on the streets . . . in many cases, knew their parents. These people helped build Hauser-Moore.

"I will let discussion of the proposal go on the agenda for the meeting, but I want more than generalities on what the company will do to be a good citizen in making this difficult transition—if, that is, the board approves relocation. And," he warned Bentley, "you will probably be in for a rough going over by some of the other directors."

An Oral Report to the Board

It's a week later, and the board meeting is under way. Besides Hauser and Bentley, the seven-member board includes:

- Janice Freeland, senior partner in the law firm that serves as Hauser-Moore's general counsel. A calm, thorough, objective person, Freeland has been a director for nine years.
- Lawrence Albertson, president of one of Janesboro's two largest banks. Albertson, who has served on the board for more than 20 years, is outspoken—some would say opinionated—but with sound business instincts and a feeling for what will go in Janesboro.
- Stuart Andretti, a longtime friend of the Hauser family and chair of the board—formerly CEO—of a company with headquarters in a town several miles away. A widely-read person with a broad range of interests, he has been a director almost as long as Albertson and is sometimes referred to, only half in jest, as the conscience of the board.
- Blair Shanley, a representative of the investment banking firm that had handled Hauser-Moore's initial public stock offering seven years ago. He joined the board a year later, and is the only member from outside the immediate Janesboro area.
- Michael Lerner, a respected economist who has been president of Trinity University for the last six years and a Hauser-

Moore director for four. Because of the broad perspective he brings to the board's deliberations, Hauser has come to rely heavily on Lerner's views, especially where his area of expertise is involved.

After disposing of some preliminaries, Hauser had introduced the matter of the possible relocation, noting that each director, he assumed, had received a copy of the report that Dick Bentley sent out. Observing rather pointedly that he hoped each had had an opportunity to read it in the short time available, he said that Tim Saunders, who had made the cost study, and his boss, Harry Burns, would be called in first to explain what they had done and to answer any questions. Then, after those two had been excused, Bentley would explain the background of the study, including the reasons for wanting a quick decision, and then make his recommendation. He went on to say that he wanted to hear the reactions of others before reaching, and expressing, his conclusions.

Saunders and Burns had just completed an oral presentation and answered questions. Now they had been excused, and Bentley leaned forward and started speaking:

"I owe you an apology, I know, for what must seem like too short a time to consider such an important matter. Perhaps I'm too close to the situation and assumed that the rest of you were operating in the same time frame I was. I'm sorry if this has made any of you feel pressured—the last thing in the world I intended.

"As you know, we have been discussing the need to do something about the old Series F engine line for some time, and we have recently developed the prototype of a replacement that we are quite excited about. It will require significant changes in the manufacturing operation, however. So I asked Harry Burns, whom you just heard, to conduct a cost study to see what would be involved in the change. Should we revamp the present facility here in Janesboro or would it be cheaper to relocate in Hendersonville, an area I'm familiar with that has many advantages? It has good labor at a lower cost than here . . . reasonable taxes . . .

very good transportation, with closer access to most of the present and prospective customers. All matters reflected in the cost figures you've seen.

"The study was completed just a few weeks ago," Bentley went on, "and the cost advantage of relocating looked favorable enough that I made a fast run there to look the situation over personally. While there, I learned about something that for me was a clincher—a partially completed facility that could be bought at a bargain price and completed quickly . . . one that would just fill the bill for us. The only problem was that others were looking at the building and it might not be available long. So, as I told George, I made a fast decision to put down a $25,000 option payment to hold it until a few days after this meeting. That's what is behind the urgency."

After pausing a moment, Bentley continued, "As to the decision itself, once I saw the results of the study, it seemed so conclusive that I hadn't thought there could be any question but one of implementation. We've all been concerned about our somewhat stagnant earnings level, and the present Series F line has been a real drag—something that, we all agreed, had to be addressed. And the new product looks very promising. I'll admit that I was surprised that the study so strongly indicated relocation, but I can't see any alternative.

"I don't intend to go into more details at this point, since the study pretty much speaks for itself, but I would like to answer any questions. And then, if you see matters as I do, I'd certainly like your approval of going forward with the move. This should be an exciting period for Hauser-Moore."

Differences in Views

Several directors tried to speak at once, but the rest gave way to Lawrence Albertson, who was flushed and appeared upset. "I came in hot under the collar—I still am—but I decided for once to listen before getting what bothers me off my chest," he said. Turning to face Bentley, he continued, "Look, Dick, I don't question the study, and if some of my questions can be answered, I'll probably support relocation. But I certainly don't like the way this has been handled. You haven't lived here long, but I have, and I know how word gets around. I don't know the source of the leak, but one of the bank's big customers called me yesterday to ask what I knew about Hauser-Moore's moving out of Janesboro. Quite disturbed, he was, and figured that, as a director, I would know what was going on. I sort of danced around the subject. Since much of the company would remain here even if the old engine line moves, I felt no compunction in saying that Hauser-Moore does not intend to abandon Janesboro. But I felt as if I'd been sandbagged by all this. It hasn't been handled in a businesslike manner at all, and the company—and its management and directors—won't come out of this looking very good. I'm very unhappy about all this."

Before Bentley could respond, Janice Freeland broke in, "Another thing, Dick, is that I think the directors have been subjected to unfair time pressure. I hear all you've said, and part of it, at least, makes sense, but springing this option on the board really puts everyone on the spot. I have an advantage over most of the others because you have reviewed the legal aspects with me, but I'd feel lost without that background. None of us wants to be a party to letting $25,000 go down the drain, especially if the building is such a good deal, but I feel as if I've been given no alternatives and too little time to think of any. That's just the way business is, you can tell me, but I am uncomfortable and feel that this rush could have been avoided."

"How, Janice?" Bentley asked. "I certainly didn't intend the option to be pressure, and I resent being put in a box as much as any of you, but I didn't see how I could let this opportunity pass. I'd be the last to minimize the importance of $25,000, but I felt we had to risk it. Right or wrong, I just made a business decision.

"Frankly," he continued, turning to Albertson, "I'm more concerned about the leak you spoke of. I can't figure where it could have come from. I hope it wasn't someone in the company who doesn't want to see the move and thought they might back us into the corner where we'd have to deny it. Whatever we decide today, I think we have to get a release out immediately to scotch rumors and to tell people what we are doing."

Blair Shanley, who had been quietly listening up to this point, spoke up, "It seems to me that Dick needs some support, and I'm going to give it to him. Maybe some mistakes have been made in how this has been handled, but the important thing is that Dick has come up with a plan that should help the company's earnings. I'm willing to be pressured if we can achieve that. After all, we have another public offering planned for late next year, and nothing could be more helpful than to have an upward earnings trend. In fact, it's essential."

A Strong Disagreement

"Just a minute," Stuart Andretti broke in. "I hear you Dick, and Blair, too, but I think this whole discussion is out of focus. Sure we're interested in earnings—we won't last long if we aren't. But there's such a thing as keeping our priorities in order. What about the 300 people who will lose their jobs? Many of them have spent their whole lives with Hauser-Moore, and I'd hate to think that we're adding human beings to a throwaway society. Maybe we'll have to relocate, but I'm not going to sit here and listen to these people treated like just an incidental cost.

"And," he continued, "what about the suppliers? Has anyone considered them? Have you thought, Dick, about what kind of notice they're entitled to in order to prepare for this shock? I don't need to tell you that I'm most unhappy about what I've seen and heard today. This doesn't sound like the kind of company your father started, and that you have built up, George."

"Before you jump to conclusions, Stu, let me tell you what we have in mind," Bentley interrupted. "We mentioned, of course, that we had looked at the union contract and are prepared to pay any required termination payments. I've had Janice look into that—she can explain in a minute.

"But we don't propose to stop there. As George and I agreed when we talked about this yesterday morning, we plan to make a two-year payment in lieu of the taxes Janesboro will lose if we relocate. And we intend to continue the company's support to the United Way at the current level, both in terms of money and in the people we make available.

"Also, we plan to offer a whole battery of services—out-counseling and even job training. Maybe other things. These are details we haven't worked out yet but will."

"Dick," Andretti retorted, "I don't mean to be on your case, but you've just proved what I'm concerned about. Here you've had a detailed study of the dollars-and-cents costs of staying here versus relocation, but how we treat hundreds of faithful employees is, as you put it, a detail that hasn't yet been worked out. Entirely aside from the moral implications of that, it's a horrible public relations gaffe. As Larry mentioned, word is apparently out on the street that Hauser-Moore is going to relocate, but when someone asks what will happen to the people, we'll only be able to say, 'Trust us. That's a detail we haven't addressed yet, but we'll get to it.' I may sound sarcastic, Dick, but I'm not at all happy with what I've heard. We have an obligation to these people. We can't—"

Debate over Obligations

"Just a minute, Stu," Albertson broke in. "I was with you until the last thing you said. I agree that this thing has gone out of control. We have a PR disaster on our hands, one that will affect our image in the city and our relations with employees at the locations that aren't moving. They'll wonder if they have just heard the first shoe drop.

"But I don't like that word 'obligation' that you used—not one bit. I'm not hard-hearted, I hope, but business is business. I guess you can put me in camp with Milton Friedman, who says that a company's only obligation is to its shareholders. That probably produces the best answer for all concerned; otherwise we get into never-never land—acting like a philanthropic organization. I believe Hauser-Moore has to do something for the employees, and probably the community, but because it's good business, not because we owe them anything. If we pay the employees what they earn and honor all the terms of the union contract, we have fully discharged our obligations.

"Don't you agree, Janice?" Albertson continued, turning to her. "You're our lawyer and the authority on our obligations. Dick said you had looked into the situation, and I see that you've been trying to get a word in edgewise while Stu and I have been philosophizing."

"It's more than philosophizing," Andretti shot back. "It's damn real. But go on, Janice."

"You're probably right about obligations, Larry," Freeland agreed, "if you restrict yourself to legal obligations. I've had our people start looking into the proposed relocation, and the study we received has recognized all the liabilities we've identified. Of course, we're not through yet, and we may uncover something else, but I can't imagine we'll find anything major that we don't know about.

"You and Stu, though, are using the word 'obligation' in different senses. Stu is thinking of moral obligations, and I think many of us would agree that we can't stop with just the letter of the law. We have other obligations—call them moral obligations—although I'll admit I can't define where they begin or end."

"Exactly," Albertson snorted, "you can't define them because these other so-called obligations are like so much smoke, something you can't get a hold of. When we observe them, we do so because it's good business. Period."

"You can't be serious," Andretti came back heatedly. "Just because they aren't spelled out in a signed contract doesn't make these obligations any less real. All of us have obligations to a lot of people that aren't on paper."

"I hear you as far as our personal lives are concerned, Stu, but I'm with Larry when it comes to business," Shanley spoke up. "It sounds heartless when put bluntly, but I don't believe it is. We end up with nothing if we don't keep our eyes on the bottom line. That doesn't mean we act like Genghis Khan—we behave humanely and show compassion, but we can't let sentiment get in the way of business."

"Blair," Michael Lerner came in for the first time, "You're contradicting yourself. Either you say, as Larry does, that Hauser-Moore has no obligation to anyone but the shareholders, that anything it does for anyone else is strictly business-motivated, or you say along with Stu that the company has obligations to employees and others that it should honor. When you talk about being humane and compassionate, you really get into an area that has no definition. Do you mean to be generous, even sentimental? Or do you mean that you would give them a warm smile, and maybe a watch, when you give them their pink slips? I'm not trying to be funny, but I'm trying to highlight the dilemma inherent in your position. We have to know where we're coming from."

"I may have gotten tied up in semantics, but I know where I'm coming from," Shanley shot back. "Some of you may think that it's easy for me to say, since I don't live here and don't get personally involved. Maybe I'm fortunate in that respect, but my answer would be the same if I did live here. We've got to make money—and get the trend headed up faster. We sold stock to people a few years ago who assumed the company was honest, reputable, but beyond that didn't give a damn what it did as long as dividends increase from time to time and the earnings per share keep improving. That's why I'm on the board, as you well know. Sure, we can't become a pariah in the community—we have to act responsibly—but we can't let sentiment get in the way of taking care of our shareholders."

"Do you mean, Blair, that we don't worry about the people that our decisions affect—maybe hurt irreparably?" Andretti asked.

"Stu, you know me well enough to know that I worry about them. But maybe that's all I can do, or should be expected to do. We're running a business. We play by the rules—no corner cutting. But beyond that, we spend money only for what helps earnings, now or over the long run. Some of that may look softhearted—

when we support the United Way, for example, or when we give generous severance payments. That's what I meant earlier when I said we should behave humanely. But I know why we do that: because it's good business. And I suspect that, in your own hearts, you feel the same way. I may spend my own money when there's not a payoff, but I don't intend to do that with the company's."

"Hear, hear!" Albertson said with a smile. "I couldn't say it half as well."

Hauser broke in, "Mike said we should know where we're coming from. It's clear in your case, Blair. And yours, too, Larry—as if I ever had a doubt. But I'd like to have Mike tell us where he comes from on this."

"I'm closer to Stu than anyone I've heard. I believe we have obligations that extend beyond the law and the shareholder group, although I suspect I might take a bit longer view than Stu. But that's just a guess because I'm not sure how he'd implement his sense of obligation."

"What do you mean?" Andretti asked. "Isn't an obligation an obligation?"

"Sure," Lerner replied, "and I guess I owe it to you to be more explicit. I may be oversimplifying your position, but I got the impression that you would throw obligations to present employees, suppliers, perhaps other local merchants and the city, measured in some subjective way, on one side of the scales and the obligations to shareholders, weighed by the cost study we received, on the other and then see where the balance lies. That may be drawn too simply, but is that the idea, Stu?"

"Maybe—I'm not sure, but go on. What would you do differently?"

New Factor Introduced

"Only that I'd try to look further down the road," Lerner resumed. "The cost study appears to be fine, as far as it goes, but it is narrowly focused on the immediate future. It does not address the whole picture, even as far as economic benefits and costs are concerned. We should put our decisions in a broader context."

Leaning forward, he continued, "A big problem in this country today is the excessive attention to short-term results. Our Business Research Bureau at Trinity has been studying the economy of this region, and they believe that the future of this area is high tech, not basic industry like Hauser-Moore's. I had planned to mention this to George and Dick soon so that they could evaluate the implications for the company. I don't want to extrapolate too far from such incomplete information as we now have, but it suggests that expanding and retooling in Janesboro for the new engine line might only be postponing the inevitable. We might be wasting the company's money and jeopardizing its future by expanding into the wrong kind of business in the wrong place. Hendersonville might be a far better place to put the new business even if the cost study that we have seen had favored staying put."

"I hear what you say, but I don't get the flow, Mike," Freeland interjected. "You indicated at the beginning that you were close to Stu in your thinking, but now it sounds as if you're saying the dollars lead you to Dick's recommendation. How do you reconcile this?"

"That's easy, Janice, for two reasons," Lerner replied with a smile. "First, I'm not against being prudent financially. I want Hauser-Moore to make money—but over the long term. I'm saying, I guess, that from a strictly financial perspective, I would suspect that Dick's study may have understated the advantage of relocation. Whether the company makes more money the next year or so from staying here or from moving is only part of the story, and maybe not the most important part."

"It is if we're selling stock," Shanley interrupted.

"I understand—and we have to look at that," Lerner came back, "although an undue emphasis on that factor may be part of our problem. But I'm not limiting my reaction to just money, short term or long term. If we were to expand here, I'm afraid we'd be laying the groundwork for a more traumatic decision involving the company and others a few years down the road—

one that might even be forced on us. We might find that we had created false expectations, that we had to relocate a few years after expanding and then had to face laying off even more people. I wouldn't want it to get out of this room, but I wouldn't be too surprised if, 10 years from now, we find that Hauser-Moore's entire manufacturing operation is gone from Janesboro. That is a matter we should start thinking about now, not letting it sneak up on us as this situation has."

"Mike, are you sure you're not getting carried away on this?" Albertson asked. "I don't mean to poke fun at you economists, but you know your profession's record on predictions isn't always much better than that of weather forecasters. I'll admit I've been a bit uneasy seeing some slowdown in the growth of our heavy industry here, but it may only be temporary. After all, we've had a few new manufacturing businesses start up the last year. I'd hate to see us give too much weight to an economic study that is still incomplete."

"You're absolutely right," Lerner responded, smiling, "and your crack about economists doesn't offend me—I have a bunch of economist jokes that I use in speeches and at meetings. But let me get to specifics. Yes, the study is incomplete, but I have gotten into it in enough detail to be satisfied with the reasonableness of the overall answer. Sure, there may be fine-tuning as the work is buttoned up. And, like any forecast, it may not prove to be entirely accurate. Timing and the extent of the impact may change. Without more work, I would not want to rely on it if it were the only basis for a decision. Since it reinforces other factors we are considering, however, both economic and ethical, I have no hesitation in giving it some weight in our deliberations."

A Summing Up

"Well," Hauser said, rather unhappily, "maybe you haven't all had your complete say yet, but I think I have the flavor of your views. I've sat back, hoping I might hear a solution, but I'm afraid I haven't heard one that I like. You can guess, I'm sure, how hard this is for me. And Mike's views, relevant as they may be to this decision, certainly don't give me any personal comfort. If we hadn't gone public a few years back, I'm sure that my family and I would say, 'The cost be damned; we'll stay here.' We've grown with this city. Many of these employees are third generation with Hauser-Moore. I know them by name. My father must be turning over in his grave to hear the discussion we're having.

"Maybe we have no choice, but I wish we'd approached this differently. We should have studied the impact on the employees, suppliers, and others before getting ourselves in the position where we feel the need for making a fast decision. This is a hell of a way to run a railroad. Dick, you may think we've found a pot of gold, but I'm not sure we haven't fallen into a pothole instead."

"George," Bentley urged, "we aren't committed. Perhaps I got things out of order, but we can put all this on hold. We are at risk for $25,000, but maybe I can even negotiate an extension on that. I'm convinced the move is right, but it's no good if you don't agree."

"I wish I could see it that way," Albertson said, shaking his head, "but I believe it's wishful thinking. If the word is out on the street, we can't just hold everything in limbo while we thrash about. I would be surprised if the union president hasn't already got a call in to your office, Dick—and probably to yours, too, George. All the employees will be nervous and unhappy, including those in facilities that are not involved, and a lot of the good people may even start thinking about leaving. The matter has gotten out of control, and I'm not a bit happy about it; however, the study speaks for itself, together with Mike's comments, and I see no advantage to procrastination. We'd better move fast and exercise damage control."

"You're right, Larry, that we shouldn't drag this out," Andretti agreed, "although I don't think the study says it all, not by a long shot. But I don't want to be a party to jumping out of the frying pan into the fire. This has all been too rushed, and I don't think any of us has had a chance to sit back and think it through. Even today, something new—Mike's forecast about the area—has come out, and who knows what someone might think of if we took a few days to digest this? I suspect we have the answer, and that it's inevitable, but we'd be irresponsible not to give this a few more days."

"But what about the plant and the option payment?" Shanley asked.

"To hell with the option payment," Hauser said, "and I'm not used to talking that way about $25,000. This decision, though, is probably a lot more important to Hauser-Moore than twice that amount of money. I agree with Stu—we shouldn't get stampeded. Maybe Dick can get a few days more; if not, I'd rather risk losing the plant than to do something we might all regret later. Dick, why don't you call the realtor in Hendersonville and see what you can do? We'll take a break while you do."

Fifteen minutes later, Bentley returned, reporting that, for $15,000 more that could be applied on the purchase, the seller would be willing to extend for ten days. Hauser polled the directors and got unanimous agreement to extend the option and to have a special meeting at which they would reach a final decision in one week. As they broke up for the day, Andretti said, "I imagine we'll end up approving a move—but if we do, we'll have had more time and information, and we'll be more comfortable with our decision. My only plea, Dick, is that you push as hard developing a program for easing the transition as you did making the cost study for relocation. That's where I'm still unhappy, very unhappy."

"I agree," said Hauser heavily. "We'll all feel better if we know more about that. You may not have all the details, Dick, but be sure to have a better picture of the transition plans for us when we get together next week."

A Second Meeting

A week later, the board met again. The directors had had time to study the report, and Bentley had sent them, by courier, a comprehensive summary of the steps that the company would take to ease the relocation, both for the terminated employees and for the community. After a thorough discussion, the board authorized relocation for the new engine line.

"I'm not sure what," Hauser said, "but I hope we can learn something from this—all of us. I'll speak frankly. Dick, you aren't blameless; you unloosed the tiger. You were too impetuous, not sensitive enough to the problems of other people. Much of this, of course, I told you before last week's meeting.

"But I bear at least as much responsibility—and that's what really bugs me. We'll stumble into more of these situations if we don't agree on our priorities. That is something I should have been thinking about. And something all of us had better start thinking about. For one thing, we'll have to look at the economic study that Mike's people are making and see how it might affect our plans . . . decide where we want to be 10 years from now and how that affects everyone involved.

"Now don't get me wrong," Hauser continued. "Planning won't solve all our problems. We'll make mistakes. But at least we'll have tried, which would make me feel much better today, and we'll have avoided a lot of problems along the way. For now, though, I'm prepared to put this behind us and support the relocation."

They all agreed, but they didn't leave particularly happy.

CHAPTER TWO

The Role of Ethics in Company Decisions

A month later George Hauser and Michael Lerner were having lunch at the Janesboro Club.

"I'll admit," Hauser said, "after three years it's hard to climb back in the saddle and run the company. I certainly hope that it won't take us too long to find a new CEO. And so does Jessica. We've had to cancel next month's cruise, one she'd been planning for almost a year."

A Sudden Departure

"I understand," Lerner returned. "It must be a blow, especially with no warning. George, would you please fill me in on just why Dick left—and so suddenly? I know you'll report to us at the board meeting, but I'm curious—and concerned. There are a lot of rumors floating around."

"That's perhaps the worst part," Hauser sighed, "and it was all so unnecessary. Frankly I hated to lose Dick, but I didn't try to change his mind. It was probably past the point of no return.

"He came to me the other day to tell me that he had just received an offer for an opening in his old company—one that would probably lead to the president's job shortly and one he didn't think he could pass up. He had to make a fast decision and wondered if it would upset me if he would take it and leave soon. I asked if unpleasantness lingering from the board meeting and all the adverse publicity around town was behind the decision. He said no, but he wouldn't deny that what had happened probably impaired his image and effectiveness, at least for a time. He went on to say, though, that he would have preferred to stay and prove himself, other things being equal."

"Did he say anything about the rumor that the move to Hendersonville had been rigged, that his wife had wanted to end up in their old hometown and that his brother was getting a commission on the plant purchase?"

"Yes and no," Hauser responded, "and really, Mike, I don't place much credence in those stories—at least, that there was anything dishonest about what he did. Maybe that's where his wife would like to go, but just putting the new small engine plant there wouldn't have led to their moving. That's certainly not where they're going now, and besides I don't think he'd be dumb enough to jeopardize his future by putting the operation in the wrong place. I didn't care to get into such petty stuff with him, although I must admit that one advantage to his leaving is that we'll be rid of his wife. People can say all they want about the inappropriateness of companies' looking into the behavior of spouses, and generally I agree, but that woman liked the country club too well and talked too much after a few drinks. You'd have thought she was the president of the company.

"But Dick did volunteer that his brother would be getting a commission on the plant sale and admitted that he should have told us that at the outset. He said that it was coincidence, had nothing to do with his recommendation, but that he was afraid that mentioning it might raise questions and queer the deal. He claimed he was so sold on the move that he didn't want anything to get in the way."

"Maybe so," Lerner acknowledged, "but it still doesn't quite smell right. He said that the availability of the plant came up toward the end and that he flew to Hendersonville at the last moment to see it and that he then put the option down. I've been wondering the last few days how it happened that the study used the figure for that plant, although the study, or at least that part of it, had been completed several days earlier.

"I won't say that Hauser-Moore isn't getting a good deal," Lerner continued. "Or that there's anything wrong with the study. But I think Dick was less candid with us than I would have wished. It's probably a matter of the appearance of a conflict of interest rather than the reality. Someone in Dick's position, though, should be sensitive to the importance of appearances—not let himself get into a position where he has to explain and people are likely to smile knowingly. You know what I mean. I'm not sure that we aren't better off to have lost him, along with his wife.

"But that, George, isn't why I asked to meet with you."

"You don't need a reason, Mike. Why, though, since you've brought it up?"

Desirability of Ethics Training

"You may remember," Lerner said, laying down his fork, "that we talked some time ago about the desirability of some ethics training for Hauser-Moore's people. I told you then that I knew a good man for it—Carl Iverson, a professor who has conducted a lot of ethics training for corporations of all sizes around the country. He's very much down to earth, practical, so you wouldn't have to be concerned that he'd turn off your people, including some board members, by preaching at them. You were interested, but—as with many things—all of us got busy, and nothing came of it.

"Some recent developments suggest that perhaps we should put this on the front burner now. For one thing, as I understand Janice Freeland has mentioned to you, the recently revised Federal Sentencing Guidelines used by Federal judges to levy fines against defendant business organizations increase managements' responsibility for 'white collar' crimes of employees or agents. At the same time, they offer a reduction in fines, which can be quite significant, if an effective prevention program is in place. Such a program focuses heavily on a company's values, as well as on its policies, procedures and controls.[1]

"Now I know that we don't expect anyone in Hauser-Moore to commit acts that would subject the company to fines for criminal behavior, but such things can and do happen in even the best-run organizations. Besides, the steps required to reduce the chance of improper behavior—to say nothing of evidencing the company's good-faith measures to exercise proper control and supervision—introduce a healthy discipline and make good business sense in any event.

"That would be reason enough for an ethics program, but then we had the problem at our recent board meetings. The way we stumbled into the relocation problem without even thinking of the ethical issues involved told me that the time is ripe to consider establishing a company ethics program. Carl's coming to Trinity in a couple weeks to run part of our executive training program, as he has the last couple years. I don't know his schedule or commitments. Perhaps it wouldn't work out, but I'd like for him to meet with our board, maybe at the next meeting, so that they could size him up and decide whether Hauser-Moore should start an ethics training program and whether he's the man for it. That is, if you think it's a good idea."

"I like the idea, Mike, except for one thing," Hauser replied, "and that's the emphasis you put on what has happened recently. I've been reading what Janice gave me and had already concluded that the initiation of an ethics program—in fact, a general review and tightening up of our policies and procedures—would be a good idea. That would provide us with some insurance and, as you observed, makes good business sense anyway. But I don't see where what happened at our recent board meetings has any relevance to that. As I see it, we didn't have an ethics problem—except possibly for the involvement of Dick's brother in the plant

---

[1]The Federal Sentencing Guidelines are discussed in more detail later in the chapter.

purchase. Certainly no one committed any crimes. We just had one hell of a big management and PR problem."

"I disagree, George," Lerner interjected, "and that, I believe, is one of our problems in addressing ethics. Too many people think there's no ethics issue unless someone is caught with his hand in the till. Ethics is the way in which people behave toward one another; as a result, it is intertwined with many decisions we make, business or otherwise. What happened at our meetings was full of ethical implications, and I think reviewing that is the best possible way to get into the matter of ethics training."

"What do you mean, Mike, that the meetings were full of ethical implications? I sure didn't see them."

"Let me give you just a few for starters," Lerner responded. "Dick hadn't even considered the employees and the community—and at least two of the other directors seemed to think that was all right—unless, that is, there might be an adverse business fallout. Now it may be that that is what the majority of the board believes, but I don't think it's a foregone conclusion we should come to so cavalierly. Many people today would agree with Stu and me that the impact on others in a situation like this is a matter of ethics as well as business. That, in itself, is enough for me to be convinced that we need some ethics sensitizing, at least.

"And what about the inadequate time given us to consider such an important matter?" he continued. "A basic principle of ethics is to respect others' rights—put in old-fashioned language, to treat others as we would like to be treated. I'm sure Dick wouldn't have wanted to be treated the way he treated us with those reports.

"Also, honesty is the basis of ethics. I don't want to make a scapegoat out of Bentley, but I don't think he was completely up front with us on when the plant we've now bought came to his attention."

"But Mike," Hauser interrupted, "most of your concern is about Dick. He's gone, so aren't we beating a dead horse?"

"Not at all. Just look back over the meeting right after we got the cost study, and you'll find most of us were floundering around with a decision, not even asking ourselves if there were moral issues in the first place and then, when we did spot one, dancing around the issue. I think that you would find that Iverson could tell us a lot in just a few hours."

Hauser pondered, then said, "Well, Mike, I'm still not sure, but I have a lot of respect for your judgment. You certainly seem convinced. And regardless of that, I agree that it would be a good idea for the company to have some ethics training. See if you can get him to join us for a session the afternoon and evening before our next board meeting."

Ethics Training—An Orientation for the Board

Lerner made the necessary arrangements with Carl Iverson, and Hauser scheduled the meeting to start at 3:30 at the Janesboro Club.

After introducing Iverson to the directors, Hauser said that he wanted to make a few introductory remarks. He reminded the board that the matter of ethics training had come up some time back but had gotten lost in the press of other matters—matters seemingly more urgent at the time. In the light of recent developments, he now wondered whether their priorities had been right; be that as it may, he said that he now wanted to give the matter the attention it deserved.

Hauser continued, saying that Mike Lerner had told him Carl Iverson was in town, handling a portion of Trinity's executive training program, and had filled him in on Iverson's broad background in business ethics. In addition to teaching and consulting with companies on ethics, he had been the full-time director of the Joyce Company's ethics program about 10 years ago—a role that involved him for more than three years in training and in consulting with the company's management and employees on ethical dilemmas faced in their worldwide activities. This seemed, Hauser went on, to be the right time for the board to hear what a knowledgeable outsider like Iverson might have to say about company ethics programs, including ethics training, and he was delighted that this meeting could be arranged.

Larry Albertson broke in, "Excuse me, George, but before we get into details, would you tell us what the recent developments are that make this particularly timely now? I'm not against the right kind of ethics training—in fact I think we should do it, but I'm in the dark as to why it is suddenly a hot item."

"There are really two reasons," Hauser replied. "First, the U.S. Sentencing Commission has recently issued revised Federal Sentencing Guidelines that can significantly affect businesses. While placing greater responsibility on managements for acts of their employees and agents, these guidelines identify measures companies can take to lessen the likelihood of business crime. And if companies implement appropriate programs, judges will take this into consideration when handing down sentences for violations, and resulting fines may be substantially reduced.

"None of us, of course, expects Hauser-Moore to get into this kind of trouble, but it can always happen—such matters as vendor kickbacks, improper gifts, conflicts of interest, to cite just a few. As you know, we bend over backward to avoid these risks, but we can always be at the mercy of some overly eager, unscrupulous, or dishonest employee or agent. I've asked Janice to outline the implications of the Federal Sentencing Guidelines before turning the meeting over to Carl Iverson; it all ties in with what he's here for."

"You mentioned two reasons, George. What's the other?" Stuart Andretti asked.

Hauser paused a moment before replying, "I'm not as sure on this. Mike Lerner thinks that our recent meetings in which we dealt with the relocation issue revealed some uncertainty, perhaps even some insensitivity to the ethical dimensions of what we were considering. And I must admit that what he said made some sense, although I still have problems identifying what aspects involved ethics and what were strictly business. I agreed, though, that it would be a good idea to hear what Carl might have to say, since consideration of an ethics program makes good sense anyway."

"It's hard to object to something before I hear it, but it sure makes me uneasy," Albertson said, shaking his head. "I can almost feel what's coming.

"Certainly I think we ought to take every step necessary to see that Hauser-Moore runs a clean operation—one that observes the letter and the spirit of all our legal obligations. I'm all for any program that is aimed at the type of compliance that would help us if we should ever run into a legal problem. I want to hear what Janice has to tell us, but beyond that I would caution everyone here to move very cautiously. I certainly don't want you to take this personally, Carl, and it may not even apply to what you're going to tell us. You can be on notice, though, that I question whether a lot of the Pollyanna preaching about ethics and what is loosely termed 'corporate social responsibility' I read about in the paper and in magazine articles has any place in business. I sure don't want to participate in turning a good, well-run business like Hauser-Moore into a public welfare agency.

"I'll get out of the way, though, for now, George," Albertson concluded, turning to Hauser, "so we can hear what Janice has to tell us."

"This will be pretty brief," Freeland said, "since the principles involved are pretty straightforward, and I doubt if the board wants to get into a lot of details. As George said, the new sentencing guidelines stress the importance of company programs for crime prevention and offer substantial incentives in the way of reduced fines for companies that have taken appropriate measures. I'll pass around a sheet that summarizes the seven elements that are identified as elements of an effective program.

"The application of the sentencing guidelines is rather complex, and I doubt if you want me to go into any details. The substance is that the judge starts with a base fine for a particular crime—say, noncompliance with some tax law. Then he or she enters a 'culpability base score' for the crime and either adds or deducts points to recognize the level of the company's program, the quality of its performance, with respect to the seven elements. The result is called a 'total culpability score.' A statutory multiplier

1. Establish compliance standards and procedures to be followed by company employees and other agents.
2. Assign specific individuals at a high level within the organization to oversee compliance with these standards and procedures.
3. Ensure that substantial discretion and authority have not been delegated to individuals who the organization knows (or should have known) have a propensity to engage in illegal activities.
4. Communicate the standards and procedures to all employees and other agents through training programs and/or printed materials.
5. Develop systems to achieve compliance with company requirements, e.g.:
   - Install monitoring and auditing systems to detect criminal conduct.
   - Install and publicize a system for reporting criminal conduct.
6. Reinforce standards consistently through appropriate disciplinary mechanisms.
7. Respond appropriately to reported offenses and take action to prevent recurrence.

is applied to that score, and the result is a maximum and minimum fine range.

"Now all this sounds pretty mechanical and complicated—and it is, although judgment does enter into the way a judge assigns points for the quality of a company's program. The important point is that the quality of a program—its design, maintenance, monitoring, and response to violations—can have a big impact on the fine assessed for a violation. I saw one hypothetical case that started with a base fine of $2,000,000. The fine that would result, however, dropped to an $800,000–$1,600,000 range where there was an effective program. On the other hand, it increased to a $4,000,000/$8,000,000 range where there was a weak, virtually nonexistent program. If nothing else, having an effective program amounts to good—I'd even say necessary—insurance coverage against some lapse that could get the company in serious trouble.

"George, I know you just wanted a short briefing at this stage, and I believe I have covered what is involved and its significance. I would be glad, though, to answer any questions."

"Thanks, Janice, that gives us what I wanted, providing additional background for why I think Carl Iverson's presentation deserves our careful consideration. Although these guidelines are important in themselves, I'll ask everyone to hold questions on them until dinner, since we don't want to cut into the time needed to hear what Carl has to say. If it's all right with you, Carl, we'll run to a good breaking point around 5:45 to 6:00, have dinner, and then resume for an hour or so."

"Thanks, George," Iverson began. "And Larry, I'll keep your concerns in mind. It may be that our differences are not as great as you fear. On the other hand, I'm sure I'll say some things you'll take exception to. That's OK—I'd rather be argued with than ignored.

"I can well understand if some others of you—not just Larry—wonder whether I have anything to offer, either in discussing what you went through in your recent relocation decision or in the broad ethics training program I understand you may be considering. In view of the harsh, occasionally one-sided criticism that some members of the academic community have directed at business from time to time, you may fear that I will approach any ethical problems you may have with an antibusiness bias. Some of you may question whether an academic who doesn't have to meet a payroll can understand the bottom-line issues that people in business must face in reaching bread-and-butter decisions each day. Despite the three years I spent in business 10 years ago, you may wonder if they are too far in the past for me to have retained any feeling for real-life decisions.

"Let me assure you, though," he continued, "I won't engage in business bashing. I understand, and am sympathetic to, your difficulties in addressing complex issues—issues where vital dollars-and-cents considerations are commingled with ethical demands. I don't intend to second-guess your recent decision or how any of you got there—although you may read a personal preference into some of my comments as we go along. And I don't intend to preach. As we'll discuss, ethics is often too complex a matter for easy, simplistic answers. My role, I hope, will be to give you some useful, hands-on tools that will help you deal with your decisions—and make you feel more comfortable in doing so.

"To get started, please let me ask a question: Does anyone want to define ethics?"

The directors looked at one another, smiling uncertainly; then Blair Shanley spoke up that ethics, he guessed, is a matter of right or wrong. Lerner came back, "Fine. But what is right or wrong?" Several board members ventured their views. After a few minutes of discussion, revealing rather wide differences of opinion, Iverson said, "That's good for now. You can see what I wanted to get you to focus on—that ethics is not quite as easy to define or to understand as some of you may have thought."

Continuing, he said, "I think a good, nontechnical definition for our purposes might be: Ethics is the way people behave toward one another. Giving it a normative twist, which I think is appropriate for our purposes, ethics can be considered the way in which people *should* behave toward one another."

"Aren't we back to right or wrong?" Janice Freeland asked. "Ignoring for the moment what we might consider to be right or wrong."

"No," said Iverson with a smile, "ethics is more than a matter of right or wrong. People, unfortunately, often tend to think of ethical issues only as ones involving possible acts of dishonesty or something flagrant. That is not true. Often there is no clear-cut line between what is ethical and what is unethical behavior. Good people have to deal with ethics—as much as do those whom we might consider evil."

"Why?" two or three directors asked at the same time. "I don't follow that," one of them added.

"Because," Iverson answered, "as we shall see, ambiguity is at the heart of ethical dilemmas—that's why they are dilemmas. You run into competing claims, conflicting responsibilities, mutually exclusive but each with a valid, persuasive argument for its selection. With many ethical issues, there isn't a simple right answer. Two or more alternatives, mutually exclusive, may be 'right.' So you can't have the luxury of reaching a comfortable right answer that will satisfy everyone.

"Ethicist Peter A. Madsen calls these 'quandary decisions.'[2] One example he characterizes as 'the lesser of evils quandary'—an individual must choose among alternatives, none of which would be considered desirable. Take, for instance, the choice that government regulators must make where protection of the environment is involved—on the one hand, imposing costly conservation measures, some of which might bankrupt businesses, lead to job losses, even destroy communities; on the other hand, risking long-term, perhaps irreversible, damage to our air, water, or soil, devastating the quality of life, and even threatening the health of present and future generations. Whatever the decision, someone will be hurt.

"Or, continuing with Madsen, another type of dilemma involves 'the quandary of ethical alternatives.' As examples, he cites abortion and the right to choose, euthanasia and the right to die, gun control, art and obscenity, justifiable war, capital punishment, free speech issues, affirmative action, and on and on. With these, of course, he is addressing public policy questions, but similar quandaries involving ethical alternatives arise in business; for example, fair returns for shareholders—even the word 'fair' opens Pandora's box in this context—and job security for employees. We'll get into such matters in a more organized manner later—I'm just trying to set the stage now.

---

[2]Peter A. Madsen, "Moral Mazes: Quandary Decisions," an introduction to *Essentials of Government Ethics*, Peter Madsen and Jay M. Shafritz, eds. (New York: Meridian Books, Penguin, USA, 1992).

THE WALL STREET JOURNAL

A.BACALL

"This is quite an ethical dilemma. I discovered an endangered species of caterpillar that can survive only by eating an endangered plant."

From the Wall Street Journal—permission, Cartoon Features Syndicate. This permission does not extend to revised or subsequent editions of the work.

"I'm passing around a cartoon that, perhaps, illustrates what I'm trying to say in a better way than a lot of words.

"That's good, perhaps, for laughs," Iverson said. "Sometimes, though, I'm not sure it's too farfetched as I read some of the environmental debates that keep appearing in the paper. But it illustrates what we mean by ethical dilemmas. And your relocation decision is right on point: It posed a dilemma for which there was no clear-cut right answer. You might consider it a 'lesser of evils quandary.'

"That is why, George, when we were setting up this dinner meeting and you said that you weren't sure you could see many ethical issues in your strictly business decision to relocate a plant, I disagreed . . . because it involved people—people with whom Hauser-Moore had a relationship, arguably some obligation. Let me read you what John J. Nevin, a well-known CEO, had to say on that very subject." Pulling a file toward him, Iverson took out a paper and read slowly and with emphasis:

You can't close a plant without an awareness that it is having
a god-awful effect on a lot of people who aren't responsible
for it.[3]

"If you think about it," he continued, looking around the group,
"doesn't that say it all?"

Albertson spoke up sharply, "No, it doesn't say it all if you
are implying from that that we were wrong to approve Hauser-
Moore's relocation of the engine plant. That's where I was afraid
this ethics discussion might lead, and it bothers me—that we get
so tied up worrying about what happens to everyone that we forget
this is a business."

"But that's not what I was suggesting," Iverson responded
with a smile. "All I meant, and I'm sure all Nevin, who's a practical
businessman, meant, is that putting people out of work may be
regarded as an ethical issue to be addressed. It doesn't mean that
having to terminate people is wrong, unethical. It may be necessary. And it certainly doesn't imply that I am critical of your
decision to relocate—frankly I don't know enough of the details
to have an opinion. Does that explain what I meant?"

"Perhaps," Albertson said grudgingly. "I see what you're
driving at, and I'll admit it's hard to argue against being aware
of the effect of what we do. And I noticed that you said that
relocation *might be* an ethical issue, not that it *is* an ethical issue.
I'll probably have a chance later, if I wish, to lock horns with you
on that.

"My only concern at this point is that I am afraid of where
all this may lead. Some of your comments a few minutes ago
implying that perhaps consideration of the shareholders' interests
was just one of the responsibilities of business, possibly not even
the main one, got close to the nerve as far as I'm concerned. Go
on, though—I want to hear more."

"OK, Larry, I promise that you'll get your chance to debate
that, or any, issue. Tonight, of course, we can't do much more

---

[3]As quoted in R. Edward Freeman and Daniel R. Gilbert, Jr. *Corporate Strategy
and Search for Ethics* (Englewood Cliffs, NJ: Prentice Hall, 1988), 156.

than scratch the surface. Let me tell you how I propose to approach matters—if you agree that it makes sense. And please, now and all during our discussion, don't hesitate to stop me if you have a question, disagree with what I say, or want to add something."

"I'm sure Larry will be relieved to hear that he can speak up," Stuart Andretti said, turning to Albertson with a smile.

A Critique of the Board Meeting

After a moment's pause to see if there were any comments, Iverson resumed, "Now, to bring a few ethical issues into focus, I'd like to run fast through some problems that surfaced in the way your recent meeting was conducted—as I understand what happened based on a summary I was given of the meeting and what George and Mike have told me in answer to my questions. At this point I don't intend to get into the substance of the meeting, just the way it was set up and run. Much of this will sound—no, will be—critical of Bentley, which in a sense isn't fair since he's not here to defend himself. But we can't escape that because he was, perhaps, the lead performer.

"The first thing wrong that I see is that you weren't given enough information to make an informed decision. That is something you are entitled to, and you didn't have it."

"Just a minute, Carl," Hauser broke in, "we certainly didn't have enough time, but I can't see that we were shorted on information."

"Didn't you ask, George, for the impact on the employees? And on the community? I think you told me you did. And didn't Bentley act rather surprised and say that it wasn't quite done before your first meeting? Whether you consider the treatment of these other people an ethical issue or not— and we'll get into that later—most of you agreed that that was information that was relevant to a business decision. But you didn't have it, and what's more Bentley didn't seem to think that was important."

"But Carl," Andretti broke in, "I am probably one of the most disturbed about what happened, and I think that the treatment of these people is an ethical issue. In many business decisions, though, we don't, indeed can't, have all the information we would like to have. You surely aren't saying that we're immobilized if we don't know everything."

"No, Stu," Iverson came back, "perhaps I haven't put this well. And I don't want us to get hung up on this point. All I'm saying is that the treatment of the employees and the community was an important piece of information, whether from the point of view of ethics or business, and I am sure Bentley knew this but he didn't acknowledge it when he brought the proposed relocation up. At the very least, he should have said that he hadn't had time to do all he might have wished on that but that he thought reaching a decision promptly was overriding, too important to wait. That would have been honest." A couple directors nodded their agreement.

"Turning to another matter," Iverson continued, "the leak of information that got out soon after the proposed relocation study was completed . . . you probably don't know where this originated, and it's not my role, or my desire, even to start talking about that. One could speculate that someone who wanted the relocation to go through thought that making the information public would lock in the decision. Or someone might have had an opposite thought—that letting the cat out of the bag would start such an outcry as to quash any action. Another scenario, a more probable one, is that someone just talked too much. Whatever the reason, disclosure of confidential information is a serious ethical lapse."

"You're suggesting one of us is guilty?" Shanley asked.

"Hardly. I'm reaching no such judgment," Iverson said, "and anyway, Blair, that is not germane to my point. I'm sure, especially with the study having been made by company people and all the information-collecting that went on, the leak could well have come from someone else."

Pressure for a Decision

"But let's address another point, one raised earlier—the pressure put on you for a decision. Maybe Bentley regarded it as unavoidable; sometimes events outrun us, and we're forced to act faster than we want to, than would normally be prudent. I think Stu suggested that a few minutes ago. But I want to make the point that it is unfair to people, and therefore unethical, to force them to act too fast if it can be avoided. I can't prove it, but I have a suspicion that Bentley, in this case, was not unwilling to use time to his advantage. I'm not implying that there was anything underhanded in his desire to see the relocation approved, but I don't think he was averse to putting you on the spot."

"That's what I suspected," Albertson asserted. "I think what he wanted to do was in the company's best interests, but I resented the way he put us under the gun."

"Exactly," Iverson replied. "And now for the last point I intend to raise about the conduct of the deliberations—if you can call them that. I know there are others, but I don't want to spend too much time on this aspect. My final point deals with the fact, which I think all of you now know, that Bentley's brother was to receive a commission on the plant deal—in fact, I guess, has received it. Now there's nothing inherently wrong with that. And from what George tells me, I imagine that there was nothing disadvantageous to the company in the transaction. What was wrong was Bentley's not being up front with you and disclosing this. People cannot always avoid conflicts of interest in this complex world we live in, but they have an unequivocal obligation to disclose them in situations such as this.

"That's all I intend to bring up about the conduct—not the substance—of the meeting unless one of you has a comment or question. Anyone?"

"Yes, Carl," Janice Freeland said, "and I hope you won't take this personally, but I feel as if we've been sort of beat over the head for the conduct of a meeting that wasn't a whole lot worse than many I've been at. Maybe the subject matter makes it more sensitive, but we're talking about how it was conducted. Don't you think you're being rather judgmental, with the benefit of hindsight?"

"A fair point, Janice," Iverson acknowledged, "and I'm not offended; I've been accused of a lot worse things. And I'm sorry if it looked as if I was piling on, particularly in a rather sore situation. From personal experience, I know your meeting was conducted as fairly as most, far better than some. And I know full well that people who live in glass houses shouldn't throw stones; as I'm sure Mike will confirm, the way academic meetings are conducted isn't always a model of ethical sensitivity.

"What I was trying to do, and will again later, is to make my observations relevant—to make them seem real to you. All the abstract discussion in the world doesn't drive something home like being able to say to yourself, 'Yes, that's what we did. Now I understand.' Does that explain what I was trying to do?"

"Yes," Janice replied, "and maybe I was just too sensitive. Also, I guess that what we're trying to be is not just like everyone else, but better. We can hardly do that if we don't admit to any shortcomings. Please forget what I said, and go on."

"I'll go on but not forget. You probably spoke for others, as well, and I should bear in mind how my comments may sound. Now, though, if you'll permit me to shift gears, I'd like to describe how we'll proceed from here. To begin with, I want to discuss the ethical concepts that I believe have particular relevance in dealing with a company's business decisions. From there, I want us to focus on what's unique about the business environment, why we must look at ethical issues in business somewhat differently from the way we would in personal situations. After that, I shall run through the way in which we can identify stakeholders, a term we academics use for those affected by and having a legitimate interest in decisions under consideration."

After a brief pause while he poured himself a glass of water, Iverson resumed, "I don't, though, want the whole evening to be just an abstract, ivory-tower lecture on my part. That is seldom, if ever, productive. As I mentioned earlier, George and Mike gave me a summary of the discussion you had at the board meeting. After dinner, I'd like to critique that with you. And, if you don't mind—and your agreement is important in the light of the discussion Janice and I just had—I'll be specific, using names. This is something I'd never do if someone involved had taken an indefensible position so that a critique would be embarrassing, but that wasn't the case here; and being specific will make the things I want to say more real. Any problems?"

Hearing no objections, he continued, "OK, we'll proceed on that basis. And finally, after the critique, I'll try to tie together the threads of what may sometimes become a rather untidy, rambling discussion as we explore the issues."

Getting into the Nature of Ethics

"As we discussed a little earlier, everyone believes that he or she knows what ethics is, but when asked to define it many people flounder. In the broadest sense, it involves the relationship of people or groups with one another . . . their behavior toward others, if you will. A basic mandate of ethical behavior is: Do no harm to others. Put in simplistic terms, ethics requires us not to lie, not to cheat, not to steal. Not to do bodily harm, of course. And a whole lot of other 'thou shalt nots.'

"But it is more complex, goes far deeper than that, since human existence is not always made up of clear-cut right and wrong actions. We've seen that in our brief initial discussion about the conduct of the board deliberations on the relocation matter. As a result, we need to have conceptual guidelines for our behavior—ones that go beyond the lessons sometimes referred to as 'ones learned at our mother's knee.' "

"I never thought there was much wrong with those," said Albertson with a bit of a twinkle in his eye. "Of course, though, I guess they didn't alert me to conflicts between endangered insects and endangered plants, or tell me what to do about a plant relocation."

"Are you trying to play straight man for me, Larry? That's exactly the point," Iverson came back smilingly. "The mother's-knee precepts are fine as far as they go—telling us not to lie, cheat, steal, all that. Very important teachings, these are, but they don't deal with the complexities of competing rights, the grayer areas that are the most difficult."

Consideration of Ethical Theory

"Ethicists over the years, from the ancient Greeks to the present, have developed theories to deal with ethical dilemmas. As an ethicist, I'd love to discuss these with you. And I think you'd find some of the discussion more interesting, more mind-opening, than you would ever guess.[4] But we don't have time for that. What I will do is to discuss two theories, one that I don't think we should try to use for most business decisions and the other that I think we should use."

"If you don't mind my asking, Carl," Stuart Andretti inquired, "why waste time on a theory you intend to reject, at least for our purposes? That may be interesting but if, as you indicated, time is limited, isn't that a waste?"

"I don't think so," Iverson responded. "In the first place, even though we haven't time to delve deeply into ethical theory, I'd feel that it was improper not to give you a glimpse of at least one recognized model other than the one I recommend for your use. You should feel that you have a basis for your choice. My second reason is that the two theories are, in some ways, contrasting; it enables me to do a better job of describing the one I favor for your use if I can compare some of the aspects."

"Do I understand that you're telling us," Albertson broke in, "that with all the high-powered attention to ethics over hundreds, even thousands, of years, we have two accepted the-

---

[4]For a good discussion of these and other theories, see Manuel G. Velasquez, *Business Ethics: Concepts and Cases*, 2d ed. (Englewood Cliffs, NJ: Prentice-Hall, 1988), 65–140.

ories—maybe more—that might give different answers? If so, how much reliance can we place on all this?"

"Larry, I said they were contrasting approaches, not theories that give different answers," Iverson replied. "But now that you've brought the point up, the answer is yes, they may give different answers. What you're facing is an uncertain world . . . complexity and human fallibility. Think of it this way: If there were a single right answer that I could explain to you in an afternoon and evening, there wouldn't be any ethics problems to worry about. But this uncertainty, this ambiguity, isn't limited to ethics; we have contrasting theories in many areas. Take economics, for example."

"You take economics," Albertson retorted, glancing with an almost malicious smile at Lerner. "If the ethical models don't give more reliable results than their economics counterparts, we may be wasting our time. But I see that some of my fellow directors want me to quit needling you so we can get on with it. And seriously, I want to hear what you have to say."

"OK," Iverson resumed with a smile. "One model focuses on consequences, the impact of a decision on others. The other model addresses the decision making itself. With some oversimplification, we might say that the distinction between the two is the primacy of the end or the means.

"Although I do not intend to subject you to an Ethics 101 discussion tonight, at the end of the evening I shall pass out a paper that summarizes and contrasts the two theories, and I shall be glad to discuss the matter in more detail at a later date, if you wish. For now, I shall give you enough of a brief summary to provide a basis for our discussion."

Focus on End Result

Continuing, Iverson explained, "The theory I would reject for our purposes, one that focuses on consequences, is utilitarianism, concerned with the greatest good for the greatest number of people. It is probably best exemplified in your experience by cost-benefit analyses. Whether or not recognized explicitly as such, this theory is widely employed in governmental studies. Some applications of the theory are restricted to economic costs and benefits; others include intangibles such as health, happiness, pain, and so on. The theory calls for looking beyond immediate results to the effects on down the road."

Hauser interrupted, "I can imagine that there could be many difficulties in application, but I can't see why you are rejecting it. Conceptually doesn't this theory address what we should be concerned about? Aren't we primarily interested in the end result?"

"That depends," Iverson responded, "on what you consider the end result. And for whom. The principal criticism of utilitarianism, other than the practical measurement difficulties you mentioned, is that it tends to ignore the individual. The dedicated advocate of this concept would opt for maximizing the overall good even if this meant depriving some people of even their needs. Let me read to you what one supporter of utilitarianism has to say." Pulling a book toward him, Iverson found the page he had marked and started reading:

> If a utilitarian is given the choice of two actions, one of which will give 2 units of happiness to Smith and 2 to Campbell, and the other of which will give 1 unit of happiness to Smith and 9 to Campbell, he will choose the latter course. It may also be that I have the choice between two alternative actions, one of which gives -1 unit of happiness to Smith and $+9$ units to Campbell, and the other of which gives $+2$ to Smith and $+2$ to Campbell. As a utilitarian I will choose the former course . . .[5]

"A few pages later, the same person continues, 'Utilitarianism . . . is ready to contemplate some sacrifice to certain individuals (or classes of individuals) for the sake of the greater good of all, and in particular may allow certain limitations of personal freedom . . .'[6]"

---

[5] Excerpted from J. C. C. Smart, "Distributive Justice and Utilitarianism," published in *Justice and Economic Distribution*, edited by John Arthur and William J. Shaw (Englewood Cliffs, NJ: Prentice Hall, 1978) as included in W. Michael Hoffman and Jennifer Mills Moore, *Business Ethics: Readings and Cases in Corporate Morality*, 2d ed. (New York: McGraw-Hill, Inc., 1990), 49.

[6] *Ibid.*, 51.

"A very cold theory, isn't it?" Freeland observed.

"A valid comment. Carried to an extreme, utilitarianism could produce results that, to most people, would be unpalatable.[7] Some utilitarians would modify the theory, calling into play tests of fairness and justice. Others, possibly to ameliorate their discomfort at the seeming harshness of their position, claim that the end result of applying the theory not only results in the greatest overall good to society but is also generally beneficial to the most people, taken individually—although they would admit that this latter result is fortuitous, not built into the theory as a requirement."

"Then you don't think there's any place for this theory, at least in business?" Lerner asked. "Is there any problem other than conceptual?"

"Oh, there's a definite place for it, although I would question its use in most business situations. One problem for business, entirely aside from conceptual objections, is practicality. Despite the claim that utilitarianism can, or should, recognize costs and benefits other than monetary, doing so is a difficult task. I want you to stop and think how you could have developed any usable measures had you chosen to apply this model to your relocation decision. For a theory to be useful in business, it must be practical to apply. As to where it might be used outside of business, I'd prefer to wait and cover that after we discuss the other theory."

A Look at Rights and Obligations

Glancing around the room, Iverson asked, "Shall we go on to the other model?"

"Yes, as long as we'll get a chance to go back if a question occurs to us," Hauser said.

---

[7]See the discussion in LaRue Tone Hosmer, *The Ethics of Management* (Homewood, IL: Irwin, 1987), 100, concerning the example in Dostoevsky's *Brothers Karamazov*. He asked what should be done if the happiness of the whole human race, forever, could be brought about by the sacrifice of only one person, one completely innocent child, who would have to be tortured to death.

"Fair enough," Iverson replied. "The other theory focuses on the means rather than the end. It could be called the rights and duties theory; it concerns itself with the rights of the stakeholders and the duties or obligations of the decision maker. Like love and marriage in the old song, rights and obligations go together like a horse and carriage. For every right, someone else has an obligation to observe that right. Let's look at some of the features in layperson's terms, basing what I say largely on what is called the 'categorical imperative,' formulated by the 18th-century philosopher Immanuel Kant.

"First, for one to have a right, it must be universally available for all persons in similar circumstances and must be reversible. Now what does that mean? An example: I can't assert a right, or act as if I have a right, to drive on the shoulder to get around a traffic jam unless I am willing to acknowledge that all other people in the jam have the same right. And that, if carried through in practice, we can see would be self-defeating. All we'd do would be to extend the traffic jam to include the shoulder."

"Would you mind running through that again?" Freeland asked. "It sounds good, sort of like the Golden Rule, but I am not sure I have all the implications."

"And you probably never will have," Iverson responded, smiling. "I haven't. Although it sounds deceptively simple, I find that nuances I'd never thought of keep emerging. Let's get down to earth and illustrate it with an example nearer home—Hauser-Moore's relocation decision. If you consider the decision to relocate the Series F engine line ethically proper (and I'm certainly not suggesting it isn't), it means that you would have to believe that it would be ethical for any other company to do the same thing under similar circumstances . . . even, to bring the analogy home, if it meant that your 52-year-old brother who'd worked there for 28 years would lose his job. It doesn't mean you'd like the answer some other company might come to, it doesn't mean you'd agree that they'd made the right business decision, but it means that you couldn't fault them on the ethics of the decision. Do you follow?"

"Yes," Freeland said, "and I can see that the concept is intriguing, challenging. I want to think about the implications. Please go on."

"The other aspect of the categorical imperative is that we should respect others as ends, not only as means. We should treat them as human beings, worthy of consideration."

"Please explain what that means," Albertson said. "I may just be lost in the words."

"It means that people are not just tools, something we can use without considering their needs; we shouldn't deceive, manipulate, or take advantage of them. Now a person may be a means; for example, he or she may be your agent or employee. There's nothing wrong with that as long as you recognize that the person is also a human being with rights that should be respected."

Continuing, Iverson said, "One of the beauties of this rights theory is that it fits in nicely with most people's views of what is morally proper. It mirrors, you might say, our better instincts."

Limitations of Rights Theory

"Didn't you suggest earlier that there could be problems with the rights and obligations model? What are they?" Hauser asked.

"The problem with this theory, as we have previously discussed and noted in the cartoon I passed around, is that there can be conflicts among stakeholders' rights. Let me give you an example from real life—one that affects good people on two sides of a knotty issue. Just before coming over here, I was reading a magazine article about the conflict between environmentalists and Hispanic land-grant sheepherders in New Mexico that clearly focuses on that issue. I'd like to read from a key paragraph:

> The question [the sheepherders] raised, in essence, was whether indigenous people in a poor area have a right to use public land or land they once held in common for their own sustenance, even when that land has been set aside for the unarguably commendable purpose of preserving wildlife and biodiversity. It is a debate certain to escalate as the question

is asked in Africa, South America and elsewhere. Which is the greater good? Can the two be reconciled?[8]

"In a situation such as this, each party may have a claim that is conceptually as valid as another, and this theory gives us no clue to assigning priorities."

"What do you do about that?" Andretti asked.

"In big situations—the location of an interstate highway, the construction of a dam—this is where utilitarianism, or some other form of the consequentialist model, fills a role. There are too many interested parties to be able ever to identify, to sort out, their rights, even stratified in groups. And even if you do, someone is going to have to lose. In that type of situation, the best course, I believe, is to try to find the greatest good for people as a whole.

"Take the water situation in California that we have been reading so much about. From what the papers say, some farmers have long-standing water rights stemming from the times that dams, reservoirs, and aqueducts were built many years ago—rights that permit them to take water that is now so precious at such a low cost that there is little disincentive to uneconomical use—uneconomical, that is, from the public interest point of view. Quite a bit of water, I gather, is wasted.

"At the same time," Iverson went on, "many residents are limited in the ability to take baths and can flush toilets only once a day. Industries are stifled. Possibly—and I say possibly because I do not have adequate firsthand information to know—the greatest good for the most people might suggest some curtailment of individuals' rights. This is venturing into an area that makes some people uneasy, but it isn't a new notion; otherwise the eminent domain concept wouldn't exist."

"But how do we handle competing rights in a less global situation. For example, a company decision—our relocation, say?" Andretti asked.

---

[8]Donald Dale Jackson, "Sheepherders, Wildlife and Compromise," *Smithsonian* (April 1991), 44.

"There's no pat answer," Iverson answered. "We use the rights and obligations approach, but we have to weigh these subjectively. This is something that, if you'll bear with me, will become clearer later—after we consider the corporate environment. That is what I want to get into now. But please, Stu, make a note of your question, and bring it up later if you do not feel that we have addressed it adequately.

"Ethical concepts," Iverson continued, "are of no use if we don't know where to apply them. In other words, we must know whose interests we must consider in applying our theory. And that requires us, in my view, to look at the nature of the corporate entity, since that affects the interests to be considered. Before we turn to that, however, I'd like to take five minutes, if you don't mind, to rest my voice—and perhaps your ears."

The Corporate Environment

Resuming, Iverson said, "As I noted before our break, I think we need to start from here by defining the business environment. In doing this, I shall use the terms 'corporation' and 'corporate,' which fit for you; however, I'm using them in a generic business sense, and most, possibly all, I have to say would apply equally to any business entity—for example, a partnership or even an individual proprietorship.

"You'll hear people say, 'Ethics is ethics. Why focus on business ethics? Or on the corporation?' True, ethics is ethics. But a corporation operates in a restricted, a defined area, and this affects the way in which ethical issues are addressed."

"That's what I tell people," Albertson broke in. "People try to act as if a business is a person, and it just doesn't work that way."

"Well, yes and no," Iverson rejoined. "You're right, but perhaps not entirely in the way you're thinking. Let's look at it. Legally, of course, a corporation is a person, but it's a very specialized person—not a human being, certainly. It doesn't experience emotions. No corporation ever risked its life to defend its country. It doesn't fall in love. What it does, and the reason society sanctions it and the reason people create it, is to operate a business, within accepted norms, to make a profit.

"You may wonder, 'What is the significance of that?' It is this: The nature of a corporation affects whom we identify as stakeholders. A stakeholder, as I mentioned at the outset, is someone who is affected by another person's actions and—I want to emphasize this—someone for whom that person has some identifiable, reasonable responsibility. Virtually every action anyone takes can conceivably have an effect on an almost limitless number of other persons—almost a domino effect. Remember the old saying that runs something like this: For want of a nail the shoe is lost, for want of a shoe the horse is lost, for want of a horse the rider is lost. Especially in today's complex society, we never know all who may be affected by our actions. So I believe that we must define stakeholders as persons for whom we have an identifiable responsibility that can be reasonably attributed to us—something we'll discuss shortly.

"I would say that there is a basic level of stakeholder identification that every person, human or corporate, should observe. To me, that level includes those sufficiently proximate that one can see, feel, know the impact of his or her decision and those to whom one believes he or she has an obligation, legal or moral. Many human beings go beyond that. They feel an obligation to the homeless in their community, possibly to the homeless everywhere. They may feel an obligation to starving children in Africa, in Haiti. You see what I mean; they go beyond what most of us would consider to be a direct responsibility. It comes from their emotions, their consciences—from the qualities, if you will, that make them human.

"A corporation," Iverson continued, "doesn't have, I'd say can't have, that extended sense of responsibility. That takes human emotions, an ability to go outside oneself. Now I know there are people who say that a corporation can have a personality, even a conscience.[9] And in a sense it can—but only as a reflection of the outlook, the traditions instilled over the years by owners, managers, and other employees. These qualities are real, and they are important. But that doesn't make the corporation human. If we look at it to go beyond its role, a role to carry on a business at a profit, we wander into quicksand.

"There are persons, respected colleagues of mine, who disagree. They believe that a corporation must serve social ends as well as making a profit.[10] At the emotional level, I may sympathize with that view; it sounds like the 'right' thing to do. But I can't see where it leads, where it ends. Who decides what the corporation should do? What is its obligation? I believe the corporation best serves society if it does what it is designed to do: to conduct its business—ethically, of course—for profit."

"That's what Larry meant," Blair Shanley broke in. "He believes, as I do, that the corporation should stick to its business. As I recall, it was Milton Friedman who said that, very well."

"I knew we'd get into Milton Friedman sooner or later; in fact I have his views in quotes here," said Iverson, smiling. "But I'd prefer, if you'll let me, to get into those details later. All I want to stress at this point is that a corporation, unlike a person, has only one, a limited, role—business. How far that role extends is another matter. And there we may get into some differences of opinion."

The Stakeholders of a Corporation

Continuing after a brief pause, Iverson said, "There's another aspect of corporate ethics I want you to bear in mind as we continue—or, perhaps, I should say two aspects. And these may affect

---

[9]For the leading discussion of this question, see Kenneth E. Goodpaster and John B. Matthews, Jr., "Can a Corporation Have a Conscience?" *Harvard Business Review* (January-February 1982), 132–141. Goodpaster and Matthews believe it can; however, they quote the influential philosopher John Ladd, with views quite similar to those expressed in this book.

[10]The matter of a corporation's social responsibility is looked at in more detail in Chapter 3.

the identification of stakeholders. One has the corporation itself as the decision maker; this occurs when the board or management, on behalf of the company, makes a major strategic decision—as, for example, your relocation decision we're going to discuss after dinner. It also applies when management or the board makes policy decisions, such as the modification of a pension plan, sick leave practices, and so on. These broad, corporate decisions are the types of matters we're thinking about tonight.

"The other aspect is the day-to-day decisions managers and other employees at all levels make in the company's operations—whom to promote, what vendor to select, when to extend credit, how to complete or approve an expense report. Those are usually individual decisions, at least at the outset, and the scope of the stakeholders involved is probably smaller. Among you at Hauser-Moore, only George now—and formerly Bentley—gets into that. But this aspect is the possible subject of a later discussion, not something for tonight.

"To sum up before we break for dinner, and I can see by my watch that it is about that time:

Many actions a person or a corporation takes have ethical implications.

To deal with ethical issues, we must have a sound conceptual basis, not just a vague sense of benevolence or goodwill toward the world.

We must also identify the stakeholders, those for whom we have responsibility and whose interests we should consider in our decisions.

The fact that a corporation is specifically created to conduct business for profit helps define its stakeholders.

Corporate decisions or actions fall into two broad categories, which may require different treatment. One involves strategic or policy decisions by the board or management; the other involves day-to-day decisions, mainly by individuals, in conducting the corporation's business. We are addressing only the former tonight, although I shall be glad to go into the other with you, or with others in the company, at some later date if that should appear desirable.

"Unless one of you has a comment or question for the whole group, I would suggest that we break now. I shall be glad to cover anything you might want while we eat dinner. Then, afterward, we can spend some time on a critique of the ethical implications of your relocation decision."

CHAPTER THREE

A Company's
Hard Decision—Revisited

"Do you want to move into a critique of our recent decision now?" Hauser asked as they rose from the dinner table.

"That is what I hoped to do," Iverson said. "But first I'd like to ask if there are any questions on what we discussed before dinner—although I may have covered some of those during dinner. And I suspect most of you want to see where this is leading before you venture a comment or question."

Ethical Relativism

"Carl, there's something bugging me," Hauser spoke up. "Maybe it shouldn't, perhaps something in the discussion before dinner slipped past me, but I do have a question. I've heard people say that ethics is an individual matter, that there are no absolutes, that a person can do what is right for him. Somehow or other, I can't agree with that, but how do we answer that? Or do we?"

"Now's a good time to address that, George. Let's call it 'ethical relativism.' If you hadn't raised it, someone else would have. And it has some ramifications I want to touch on."

Iverson continued, "It is true that there are no absolutes as far as personal standards are concerned. And, as we saw, there is more than one ethical model. But an individual must fit into society, not just adhering to its legal canons but also conforming to its ethical norms. Think what society would be like if everyone did his or her own thing. It would be chaos, a jungle. The 17th-century philosopher Thomas Hobbes put it so well, so succinctly, that I always remember his words; if individual relativism were the prevailing norm, life would be 'nasty, brutish, and short.'

"We may find differences around the margins, and these differences sometimes get blown clear out of proportion in strident debates over policy preferences. Most people in this country, however—and indeed throughout the world—would have little problem accepting Kant's imperative, or the utilitarian model, as a guide to resolving moral questions. Society is unwilling to accept selfish egoism.

"But it doesn't stop with the individual. Someone will say that you have to bribe customs officials in a particular country to get goods in, or that tax evasion is a way of life in some other country. Kickbacks, it is claimed, are essential if one is to get a contract in other parts of the world. It's the culture, we may be told—that we shouldn't try to impose American ethics on the rest of the world. This is a plea for acknowledging, accepting cultural relativism, an extension of individual relativism. When in Rome, the argument goes, do as the Romans do.

"Ethicist Norman Bowie has discussed this —just a minute, I have his article here and would like to quote from it:

> But in the world of 1989, any arguments that appeal to social stability will have to be applied universally. In the atomic age and in an age where terrorism is in some societies an acceptable form of political activity, the stability problems that afflict individual relativism equally afflict cultural relativism. If the necessity for social stability is a good argument for a cultural relativist to use against an individual relativist, it is an equally

good argument for a universalist to use against a cultural relativist.[1]

"But Carl," Albertson broke in, "isn't cultural relativism a fact? Isn't what you read from Bowie a plea for how the world should operate, not how it does?"

"A good point, Larry, and not easy to answer. The problem is that there are a lot of cultural differences among peoples, nations, that get involved with moral standards and suggest differences in ethics. And there are chaotic societies. Again quoting Bowie:

> Cultures differ in physical setting, in economic development, in the state of their science and technology, in their literacy rate, and in many other ways. Even if there were universal moral principles, they would have to be applied in these different cultural contexts. Given the different situations in which cultures exist, it would come as no surprise to find universal principles applied in different ways. Hence the differences in so-called ethical behavior among cultures would be superficial differences only. The cultures would agree on fundamental universal moral principles. One commonly held general principle appeals to the public good; it says that social institutions and individual behavior should be ordered so that they lead to the greatest good for the greatest number. Many different forms of social organization and individual behavior are consistent with this principle. The point of these two arguments is that superficial differences among cultures on so-called ethical behavior may not reflect genuine disagreement about ethics. Unless the relativist can establish basic differences about matters of ethics, the case for relativism cannot be made.[2]

"It is interesting to note that, despite the claim sometimes made that bribery is sanctioned in many parts of the world, it is

---

[1] Norman E. Bowie, "Business Ethics and Cultural Relativism," a previously unpublished article included in Peter Madsen and Jay M. Shafritz, *Essentials of Business Ethics* (New York: A Meridian Book, 1990), 373. This article provides the basis for parts of the discussion that follows, although the selection and interpretation are the author's.

[2] *Ibid.*, 369–370.

prohibited—at least as far as public officials are concerned—by the laws of practically every nation. When the Foreign Corrupt Practices Act became law some years back, there were cries that it was unrealistic, that it went against business practice in much of the world, and that it would make American business noncompetitive. Well, there is evidence today that American business may not always be competitive, but I have heard no serious claim that this stems from the Foreign Corrupt Practices Act. And interestingly, in some of the very countries where revelations of bribery by American companies led to that legislation, public officials there have been tried and convicted for accepting bribes."[3]

"This makes me uneasy," Albertson remarked, "smacks too much of unrealistic 'do-goodism.' Sure, bribes are wrong, here and I guess elsewhere. None of us want to get involved. But everything I've heard tells me that in the real world, companies doing business in some parts of the world may have to grease the palm of customs agents to get vital material through. We have to face that."

"Larry, you're absolutely right. We can't be rigid, and the Foreign Corrupt Practices Act recognizes that. It does not prohibit 'grease' payments to foreign government employees whose duties are primarily ministerial or clerical; such payments are often necessary to get the employees involved to perform their normal duties. This is different from offering bribes to get business, both in intent and in amount.

"I am not telling you that the same moral standards prevail throughout the world any more than I am telling you that everyone in this country observes the highest ethical standards. But I am saying that, in general, cultural relativism does not enjoy conceptual support within the framework of moral reasoning.

"Any other questions?"

---

[3] Some persons disagree with the wisdom, and indeed the ethical rightness, of the law. For a good discussion, see Mark Pastin and Michael Hooker, "Ethics and the Foreign Corrupt Practices Act" in Peter Madsen and Jay M. Shafritz, *op. cit.*, 382–390.

A Question of Relevance

Janice Freeland spoke up, "I do have a question—one that I hope won't take too much time, since I know you want to move on. But I think it's important. Obviously I believe the company needs to have some kind of a program. The Federal Sentencing Guidelines that I described earlier are persuasive on that score, to say nothing of the fact that having sound procedures and policing them make good business sense. But we can deal with legal compliance without all this philosophical background, can't we?

"Maybe this will all come out as we go along, but I'm wondering how relevant all this is going to be. I'm afraid that sounds rude, which I don't intend; but we can sit here, in a small group talking with a trained ethicist, and learn a lot that is interesting. And maybe we'll use some of it. I hope so. But everyone in Hauser-Moore won't have that advantage. Are we only gratifying ourselves, or is there a real value in this for the company?"

"That's a logical question, Janice—and it isn't at all rude. A lot of companies have or will design compliance-oriented programs, either as an end in themselves or as a response to the Federal Sentencing Guidelines. And there's nothing wrong with that. Many knowledgeable people, however, contend that narrow, compliance-based programs generally have not been successful in the past, especially if they focus on 'dos and don'ts' rather than giving the employee a framework in which to make decisions not covered by the law. As a result, a number of companies have broadened their perspective to recognize that ultimately a company's culture and values impact employee business behavior.

"Also, I recognize that I haven't told you how you can use the theoretical background we've been discussing." Iverson pondered how to explain, then continued, "Part of the problem is that it's hard to organize a discussion like this. I could start with an explanation of why ethics is relevant to a company, how an ethics program can be installed, tell you of companies that have done this, and then you could logically ask, 'What are we talking about? What do you mean by ethics? Is it a good idea to get into it?'

"We have to start somewhere. I've chosen to explain, to illustrate, what we're talking about first. Then we're on common ground . . . we can move into the practicality, the desirability. I would be wasting your time if I didn't think it could lead to something useful. But I haven't had a chance to get to that yet. Do you see what I'm saying?"

"Yes, I guess so," Freeland replied, "and I understand. But I won't throw my question away—I'll certainly hold on to it."

"Be sure to do that; it's important that we cover it," said Iverson. Hearing no further questions, he continued, "Now we'll get into the decision at your last meeting. Do you mind, Larry and Blair, if I discuss your position first? You half volunteered—at least Larry did—by your earlier comments, and I think the two of you have enough in common to make a joint critique feasible. I detect some possible shadings of difference in your views, but I can take those up as we go along."

A View That Shareholders Are the Only Stakeholders

"To summarize, as I understand, both of you take the basic position that the only stakeholders to be considered in this situation are the shareholders. Is that correct?"

Albertson nodded a vigorous assent, and Shanley, smiling a little uncomfortably, responded, "I guess that's right, although it makes us sound a little insensitive to hear it put in such blunt terms. We just can't be all things to all people, and it is the shareholders whose money is at stake. That's what business is about—as you, yourself, said a little earlier. Besides, it doesn't do anyone any good if the company goes bust, or operates marginally so it can't raise new money and expand. Maybe it's rationalization, but I think running an efficient operation is the best answer for all concerned even though someone may get hurt in the short term."

"That's certainly an understandable position, Blair," Iverson observed, "and one that has substantial support, academically and within the business community. Larry, I believe, and you both mentioned Milton Friedman, the well-known economist and Nobel Laureate, earlier, and I brought along a quotation of his that I had already intended to use:

> In [a free] economy, there is one and only one social respon-sibility of business—to use its resources and engage in activities designed to increase its profits, so long as it stays within the rules of the game, which is to say, engages in open and free competition, without deception or fraud.[4]

"That's my idea," Albertson broke in. "I get tired of these bleeding hearts who think that we have a license to use the inves-tors' money to solve all the problems of the world. I don't think I'm heartless, after all I headed up the United Way drive last year, but a business has to be run like a business. Don't you agree?"

"Sure," Iverson replied. "I agree that a business must be run like a business, but there can be differences in views of what that means. I quoted what Friedman wrote in 1962. Here's what he said six years later:

> In a free-enterprise, private-property system, a corporate ex-ecutive is an employee of the owners of the business. He has direct responsibility to his employers. That responsibility is to conduct the business in accordance with their desires, which generally will be to make as much money as possible while conforming to the basic rules of the society, both those em-bodied in law and those embodied in ethical custom.[5]

"You may think I'm reading too much into this, but I want you to note two changes that I consider important. First, he says 'gen-erally.' It seems to me he has become less dogmatic. Second, and this is the change I really want you to focus on, he refers to the rules of society 'embodied in ethical custom.' He seems to have

---

[4] Milton Friedman, *Capitalism and Freedom* (Chicago, University of Chicago Press, 1962), 133 as quoted in LaRue Tone Hosmer, *The Ethics of Management* (Homewood, IL: Irwin, 1987), 37.

[5] *New York Times Magazine*, September 13, 1970, reprinted in Thomas Donaldson and Patricia H. Werhane, eds., *Ethical Issues in Business* (Englewood Cliffs, NJ: Prentice-Hall, 1979), 192.

opened Pandora's box: Some might even say he's taken the lid clear off.

"Now this doesn't mean that he may not still think that shareholders are the only stakeholders. He may believe that they are the only ones whose interests are 'embodied in ethical custom.' And you, Larry, and you, Blair, may still feel that way. I'm merely pointing out that Friedman doesn't seem to have closed the door against other possible stakeholders. Let me ask you a question, either of you: Do you think the employees have any rights in this decision?"

"Yes," Shanley said, "they have rights—whatever may be called for in any contracts and law, matters that Janice and her people have looked into."

"I guess I didn't state my question well," Iverson came back. "What I had in mind is whether you think they have any rights beyond legal rights, what we might call moral rights."

"No. Oh sure, they have a right to be treated honestly—in other words to be given reasonable notice of Hauser-Moore's plans. I guess that goes with what you said before dinner—that they should be treated with the respect due them as human beings. Beyond that, though, I think we'd be getting into quicksand. We'd better stick to observing their legal rights and doing whatever else good business practice requires."

"OK, Blair, you're consistent. And you would have a lot of good company in your views. But I noted, Larry, that you said at the meeting that you would want to lean over backwards—if I recall your words correctly—to be generous to every one who will be hurt. You go on to say that this is because it is good business, not because the company owes them anything. Have I stated your position correctly?"

"That sounds right; that's how I feel. Why?" Albertson asked suspiciously. "Have I walked into some semantics trap?"

"No," Iverson grinned. "I just wanted to understand your rationale, especially your use of the word 'generous.' If you mean that your rationale is still business-related—that you think it would be bad business to look cheap—your position is consistent. If, on the other hand, this was an indirect way of saying that you would be buying off on an obligation, you would be contradicting yourself."

An Obligation Extending Beyond the Shareholders

Turning to Andretti, Iverson continued, "Stu, you seemed pretty firm on the notion that a company's obligations extend beyond the shareholders. Would you mind explaining your rationale?"

"Certainly. I'd be glad to. I don't want to be characterized as a do-gooder," Andretti responded, glancing at Albertson, "who believes the company owes everyone a living—everyone, that is, who knows about the company and many who don't. If businesses operated that way, they'd soon go broke. Everyone would lose. I believe, however, that the company has some kind of moral obligation to everyone it does business with. That, I guess, makes them what you call stakeholders. I'm a little fuzzy sometimes on what that obligation may be, but I believe that it exists, in varying degrees. It certainly goes beyond bare-bones legal obligations."

"Do you restrict that to those the company does business with, Stu?" Iverson asked. "And does that include the employees?"

"Especially the employees," Andretti answered. "We talk about the money the shareholders have invested in the company. And that, of course, is important, maybe primary. But the employees have invested time, sometimes much of their lives, in a company. The company has an obligation to them. There is such a thing as loyalty, mutual respect, that goes beyond pure dollars and cents but is not just softheaded sentimentality.

"Also, a company has an obligation, in my view, to vendors and customers . . . to do business with them the way we would want them to treat us. I guess that's Kant's categorical imperative, isn't it? A company owes something, too, to the community that has invested in it, along with other individual and corporate citizens, by making available a broad range of public services—water, fire and police protection, parks, cultural facilities, and many others. A company, in my opinion, cannot casually walk away from its responsibilities toward those who made these services available but cannot cut their cost off overnight. I'm all for efficiency and always ran a tight ship at my company, but I think I can do so and still help make the world the kind of a place we all want to live in.

"What I don't know, though, is how we value all these claims—the weightings and priorities. It's all very well to talk about obligations in general terms, but we have to price them out, don't we? Otherwise we're no further ahead."

"That's right," Iverson agreed, "and we have to get to that. All I hope to do for the moment, though, is to expose all of you, let's say sensitize one another, to the identification of stakeholders. Then, we can use that as a springboard for getting into how stakeholders should be evaluated and treated.

"I don't think, though, that you quite finished my question, maybe because I confused it with a second question. Would you restrict the stakeholder group to those the company does business with—including, of course, employees?"

Stakeholders Limited to Business Relationships

"Yes," Andretti answered, "if you include by that the indirect business relationships such as the community in which a company operates. I certainly don't think the stakeholder group includes any persons with whom the company has no relationship. Let me elaborate. Those of us in corporate management are continually barraged with requests for support of worthwhile causes, frequently in our communities but sometimes in places we've never seen. Often they are national organizations. Or a theater group, for example, in New York or Chicago. I don't regard these as stakeholders by any stretch of the imagination.

"I'll give you an example. The wife of one of our vice presidents used to be a dancer; she was good, and she's very interested in ballet—works hard at promoting it. Well, she got her husband to ask if the company would contribute $10,000 for some special ballet event scheduled to take place in several major cities—nowhere near us. In fact, the ballet company she's interested in never performs here. I had to say no, but I have a feeling she still can't understand why. I heard that she told someone that the company makes an annual contribution to our local museum and that she can't see the difference. I tried to explain that the museum is in the community, which makes it a stakeholder, perhaps, in your terminology, Carl, but I also thought there was a good business reason. She might have persuaded me as an individual to contribute to her ballet—not $10,000, of course—but I couldn't see that it had anything to do with the company. But perhaps I've rambled off the subject."

"No, Stu, you've answered my question. And quite clearly. Some of my colleagues don't agree; they believe that a corporation has social responsibilities that go further.[6] I believe, though, that that view is unrealistic, even dangerous. One chief operating officer said, and I have the quote here, 'Companies that truly care must be companies with staying power—and that means making money consistently.'[7] A writer, distinguishing between obligations and good deeds, had something else to say that I want to read:

> Much of the debate about "corporate social responsibility" focuses on doing good deeds such as contributing to charitable programs, providing extra funds to enhance architectural beauty or employee well-being, or donating executives' time and talent to community groups. These actions may be laudable and can certainly be understood as moral responsibilities rooted in respect for persons in the community. But they represent choices from among a multitude of possible good deeds, choices open to debate depending on the circumstances and on one's view of morality and the role of corporations. In contrast, there are fewer disputes that corporations should not

---

[6] For the more encompassing views of those who adopt the social contract theory of business, see Thomas Donaldson, *Corporations and Morality* (Englewood Cliffs, NJ: Prentice-Hall, 1982), especially Chapter 3.

[7] Lawrence Perlman, president and chief operating officer of Control Data, as quoted by Jagannath Dubashi, "The Do-Gooder," *Financial World* (June 27, 1989), 70.

knowingly market unsafe products (the definition of "unsafe," of course, occasions significant debate). Product safety is a moral obligation, not a good deed. In terms of the stakeholder notion . . . , avoiding injury . . . is a minimal moral obligation . . . , whereas reaching out to help within a stakeholder's wider circle might be good, but it is not necessarily an obligation.[8]

"Some of you may not agree with Stu or with that view, and if so I'd like to hear from you later. Right now, though, I'd like to go on with someone else's views that were expressed at the meeting."

Long View Required

Turning to Lerner, Iverson said, "Mike, as I looked over the summary of your recent meeting, it looked to me as if you were in somewhat the same position as Stu. You—"

"I don't think I'd quite say that, Carl," Lerner interrupted. "I said that there were others to consider, but I think I was taking a more global view, perhaps looking further down the road than Stu."

"Yes," Iverson came back, "but I'm not sure you aren't making a distinction without a difference, at least as far as stakeholder identification is concerned. I think you might apply different ethical models in dealing with stakeholders, a matter for later, but I question whether those you would consider stakeholders would differ much from Stu's. Who did he include that you wouldn't? And is there anyone you would include that he didn't? Think about it a minute."

"Possibly you're right, except maybe for the ballet—that's something I hadn't quite focused on," Lerner said thoughtfully. "At least I'll accept that for now and see where it takes us."

"OK," Iverson replied. "And the two of you, like Larry and Blair, have sound conceptual support for your views—support, I

---

[8] Michael Rion, *The Responsible Manager: Practical Strategies for Ethical Decision Making* (San Francisco: Harper & Row, Publishers, 1990), 59–60.

might say, that has been growing for some time. Back in the early 1950s, a prominent management theorist conceded a change in his long-held position that corporate powers were held in trust for the shareholders; he wrote that he had come around to the view that they were held in trust for the community.[9] I'm not asking you to go that far, but the trend over the years since suggests that an increasing number of people, and not just academics, believe that the definition of stakeholders in today's society extends beyond just shareholders.''

Pragmatism in One Response

"Now I'd like to turn to Janice. George, I hope you won't think I've forgotten you, but I'm saving you for last. Please don't read anything ominous into that; it just seems to fit better."

Glancing toward Freeland, Iverson said, "I couldn't tell what your thoughts about stakeholders were. It seemed to me—and correct me if I'm wrong—that you believed that it made business sense to relocate because of the results of the cost study and that you would want to do something for employees and the community, but I couldn't identify your rationale. Presumably you had the shareholders in mind, but why did you want to consider anyone else?"

"I don't know if I can tell you—maybe my feelings were, and still are, mixed," Freeland said. "I don't think I'd be willing to admit any obligation to anyone but the owners—that is, beyond legal requirements—but we'd feel like heels if we walked away and left a mess. Probably my main motivation is business; we'd have a real black eye in town if we did nothing, and we do have operations here. But deep down, I guess, I want us to be viewed as compassionate.

"Dick and I talked it over," she continued, "when we considered whether there were any legal angles to worry about, and

---

[9] Kenneth E. Goodpaster, "Business Ethics and Stakeholder Analysis," *Business Ethics Quarterly* (January 1991), 62.

I think we had generally the same outlook. The whole thing bothers me, but I think we're behaving responsibly, so I still can't quite grasp what the big deal is about our motives. People don't always agree, but in this case we came to something of a consensus—at least, no one said we were all wet. Doesn't that tell us something?"

"It certainly does," Iverson observed, "but perhaps only that the facts in this case were such that different people, by different routes, arrived at the same spot. Unfortunately, it doesn't always work out that way."

Importance of a Rationale

"Your answer was made relatively easy because of the size of the cost differential between the alternatives. What if the study had indicated a standoff cost-wise? I suspect that Stu might have pushed his view of obligations harder—and might have swayed some of the rest of you. You might have had a close decision in that event, and the motivations could have played a large part.

"Or," Iverson continued, "let us assume that this relocation decision involved a plant in a distant town where you had no other operations. Would you be as generous to the employees and the community as you intend to be here in Janesboro? There would be little business fallout, if any, if you behaved as ruthlessly as you could in that case—within the limits of the law, of course. Your answer to that perhaps smokes out whether your actions toward others than shareholders are influenced by a sense of obligation—a belief that those others have rights you should respect—or by business reasons. Those who are motivated solely by business considerations would never consider anyone other than shareholders if the others were not in a position to help or hurt them. So what motivates you can make a difference in that respect.

"Also," he went on, "motives show through. You might call it body language. People can often tell, in a variety of subtle ways, why a company is doing what it is. It may not make much difference at the time, but it can affect how employees and others regard a company. The employees who are continuing with a company may have a different attitude if they have deduced that management and the board felt an obligation to employees it had to terminate and behaved accordingly, as contrasted with doing the same thing, but grudgingly, because it was considered necessary for business purposes.

"That leads to another point," Iverson went on, "as to why the rationale makes a difference—consistency. If a company's board and its management have a guiding philosophy, an acknowledged agreement on who they consider their stakeholders to be, they are likely to act consistently under comparable circumstances. I've heard it said that the market doesn't like surprises; neither do employees or others associated with a company. There is an intangible but important benefit to a company in being viewed as an organization that can be counted on to act consistently, not one that wings decisions on an ad hoc basis."

Iverson paused, looked inquiringly toward George Hauser.

Problems Resulting from Personal Involvement

"Do I deduce, Carl, that it's now my turn?" Hauser asked.

"Yes, George, and in some ways yours may be the most interesting case—and," said Iverson, smiling, "the most difficult. It all comes from your personal identification with the company and its relations with the employees and the community. It's very hard for you to look at this matter objectively—to separate George Hauser from Hauser-Moore Manufacturing Company. Or Hauser-Moore from Janesboro."

"Is that so bad?" Andretti inquired. "That just shows that he is human." Albertson nodded agreement.

"No," Iverson said, "it isn't bad as long as he recognizes it and keeps it under control—as he did, at some cost to himself, I am sure, in the relocation decision. Before the company went public a few years back, George and his family had a greater right— but still not an absolute right, in my view—to treat the company as an extension of themselves. But now the company has outside shareholders, ones with no sentimental ties to the company or the community. They have a right to believe that the company is being run as a business, not as some adjunct of the founding family."

"It seems to me," Shanley broke in, "that you're supporting Larry's and my view that the shareholders are the only stakeholders. Isn't that true?"

"Not quite, Blair. The shareholders, both before and after the public offering, were and are stakeholders; their interests should certainly be considered. I had also said, though, if you remember, that George and his family may not have had an absolute right to regard the company as an extension of the family even before the company went public."

"Why?" someone asked.

"Because of the view some of you hold—Stu and Mike, for example—that employees and the community are stakeholders as well. If one accepts that view, those people were just as much stakeholders before the public offering as they are now.

"All I'm saying to George is that he has to be careful not to let his personal feelings confuse the issues. And the same is true for all of you. If one of you had a son or daughter, for example, who worked for the company and would be affected, for better or for worse, by the matter being considered, you should try to keep that out of your thoughts while reaching a decision."

The Meeting Summarized

"Let's recap," Iverson continued. I think all of you showed a good sense of responsibility in reaching your recent decision, even though most of you felt pushed into it. The only problem, as I see it, is that you weren't playing on a level playing field. And you got to your answer by various routes. If the facts had been different, you might not have reached the consensus that seems to give you—Janice, anyway—a degree of comfort. I think that you need to identify a stakeholder philosophy to apply when strategic or policy matters require decision. Although it might be too much to hope that all of you have the same notion what that philosophy should be, I think that you should hammer out an answer that all of you will then agree to observe, whatever your personal preferences might be.

"That pretty well buttons up my critique of your recent decision as far as stakeholders are concerned. As you will recall, Janice asked, in effect, what good all this is to you. In other words, is there anything you can get out of this that would be useful to Hauser-Moore if it wished to take ethics into consideration in reaching strategic and policy decisions? It looks as if we have some time now, so I'll try to take that on if you wish," Iverson said, turning to Hauser.

"Please do, Carl," Hauser said. "But first let's take ten to stretch our legs."

Matters to Consider in Addressing Dilemmas

"This should be pretty straightforward," Iverson said. "It's just a matter of putting together what we've already discussed this afternoon and evening. You have to decide what ethics theory to use. And you have to decide who the company's stakeholders are—in other words, to whom the theory should be applied.

"Let's turn to the theory. If we had lots of time, with ample opportunity to explore alternatives, I would probably have presented the utilitarian model and the rights and obligations model as neutrally and as objectively as possible. I would have enriched our discussion with material for you to read in advance, and we would have explored such ramifications as justice and fairness. Then I would have asked you to decide which theory or theories you would select under the company's circumstances—and why. Especially why.

"But we didn't have the time for that luxury so I pretty well made the selection for you—rights and obligations . . . because it seems to me that it best fits a company's decision making. And because, I think, it has intuitive appeal for most people; they fall into the thinking naturally. But at least I did expose you to another theory so the choice isn't entirely blind. Also, you can always change.

"I do have one plea, though," Iverson went on. "Don't commingle the two models—or casually bring in others you may learn about. You end up with something that is neither fish nor fowl, a form of what I believe some writer refers to as naive eclecticism.

"Now I know there are those who differ on that point. They say that ethical analysis should not be confined to just one theoretical model—that to do justice to an ethical dilemma, one should bring to bear as many moral perspectives as are applicable. Ethical dilemmas, they say, are so complex that treating them from only one perspective may give too narrow an answer, or the wrong answer.

"Conceptually, there is much to be said for that viewpoint, but is it practical for anyone other than a trained ethicist? Would a business executive, faced with a multiplicity of decisions, have the training or the time to go through multiple analyses for even relatively important decisions? I doubt it. It is better for that executive to have a comfortable understanding of at least one model for day-to-day use, possibly with some feel for one or more others to use as tests of conclusions reached in unusually troublesome situations.

"Also, a risk for the layperson using an eclectic approach is that it can support inverse reasoning. The worst thing is to select first the answer you want and then to shop around among the theories for support. Let me ask: Does using the rights and obligations approach make sense to you?"

"I guess so," Freeland said, "but probably because it comes, as you say, naturally . . . which raises the question—does all this put us any further ahead? Aren't you just telling us what we would have done anyway?"

"Fair enough, Janice," Iverson replied. "But would you have? In fact, did you? I didn't hear much mention of rights and obligations in our discussion of your recent board meeting. Maybe some of it was implicit in what some of you said and did, but you didn't identify stakeholders' rights as an important issue. The advantage to what we have done is to lay it out specifically—to begin to introduce a discipline into your decision making, at least as far as ethics is concerned. And that, I think, is vitally important."

"OK," said Freeland thoughtfully, "I can see that, but I'm still puzzled how I apply the model."

"I understand, and we'll get to that in another session that I understand George will mention later. Now, though, let's get to the matter of stakeholder identification, possibly a more troublesome matter for some of you."

Continuing, Iverson said, "Stakeholder identification is, as I said a few minutes ago, a subjective matter that each company has to decide on in the light of its own traditions, its own sense of values. I don't know if the discussion today has changed any views, but I have heard opinions regarding who should be considered stakeholders of Hauser-Moore that range from shareholders only to all those with whom the company has a direct business relationship—shareholders, employees, suppliers, customers, the community at large, and local government. There isn't a right answer that someone—Larry, say, or Stu—can *prove* is correct, either by logic or with empirical evidence.

"It's up to you, as the board, to make the identification. Be as specific as you can, recognizing, however, the need for flexibility if something new comes up. If you have your stakeholder concept spelled out, in writing, it is far less likely that you will flounder around when a troublesome question comes up.

"But my watch, George," Iverson said, "and the way I see some of you shifting about tells me that we've had enough for now. I realize I've thrown a lot at you. And that I haven't tied everything up with a nice ribbon and bow. During the break, George said that you'd like to have at least one more session, so I'll wait until then to get into structure, how you can organize your decision making to reflect these factors we've been discussing without having to reinvent the wheel each time. In the meanwhile, I'll pass out the paper on ethical theories that I mentioned at the start of our session. I'd suggest that you read this when you get a chance—it may help bring together what we've been discussing."

Hauser rose and shook Iverson's hand. "Thanks, Carl, for a stimulating evening. I don't know if I agree with, or even understand, everything you said tonight, but a lot of it struck home. And it started me thinking. Perhaps all of us will be better prepared for more give-and-take next time.

"I'll ask each of you to mark your calendar for the special morning meeting two weeks from today. This is to discuss certain interim changes and any developments in the search for Bentley's successor. I checked with each of you and found that everyone but Blair can make that date, the best attendance we could get anytime during the next month. And I didn't think we should defer meeting for too long in view of all the matters demanding our attention.

"I think we'll finish by noon, and I asked Carl if he could join us for lunch and afterward to button up this part of our ethics discussion. He could, so we'll look forward to the wind up he has promised us."

CHAPTER 4

How Does a Company Decide What Is Right?

Two weeks later Carl Iverson and the Hauser-Moore board had just finished lunch. Turning to Iverson, George Hauser said, "Well, Carl, I guess we're ready to learn some more about ethics. Perhaps we'd better get started, since I know that Janice has another meeting to attend later this afternoon. I've thought quite a bit about some of the things you told us last time, and I may have some questions about the earlier stuff as well as getting into the new material."

"Thanks, George, that's fine," Iverson began. "I hope no one is expecting me to pull a rabbit out of the hat—to tell you how, in a few simple steps, you can come up with easy, clear-cut answers to your ethical questions that will make everyone happy. If so, I'm afraid you'll be disappointed. Unfortunately, as we all know, life is seldom that simple. Or, perhaps, I should say fortunately, since existence would be pretty boring if every problem virtually solved itself." Pausing for a moment, Iverson grinned as he said, "Sometimes, though, all of us would probably like to give that a try."

A Review of What Ethics Is About

"Let me first lay a little groundwork for this discussion—mostly a repeat from a couple weeks ago, but I believe some repetition of basic concepts is desirable. The most troublesome ethical dilemmas result from conflicting rights. Two sets of stakeholders may have contrary and irreconcilable rights; both are valid, although they may not be entitled to the same weighting. Solving the ethical dilemma requires reaching a decision in which one or both parties may suffer some harm. An example, if you will recall, was the sheepherder/environmentalist confrontation I mentioned last time.

"Ordinarily, a decision maker eventually concludes that certain rights outweigh others: That is how one reaches a decision. Maybe he or she deems the loss of the rights of one set of stakeholders to be more harmful than the loss of competing rights to another. For example, someone might say that a threat to the health of one group is more important than the property of another. Now the decision will be subjective, and someone else might reach a contrary conclusion. But as long as the person making the decision has conscientiously identified and balanced the rights, the dilemma will have been addressed properly.

"Always remember that the ethical aspects of business decisions are intertwined with the other aspects," Iverson went on. "So-called business and ethics considerations cannot be separated and dealt with in isolation. The two are mixed, and you'll find yourself using a lot of soft input, subjectively weighted, and arriving at answers that will require testing with commonsense judgment. Still, though, we can and should be systematic in our approach so that we give consideration to all the appropriate factors and deal with these ethical issues on a reasoned, consistent basis.

"With that background but getting away from generalities, I want to demonstrate how the approach might be used in an actual situation; I find that that holds our attention better and makes the discussion more understandable. If it's all right with you, I'm going to use your relocation decision to illustrate the approach.

Possibly you're a bit tired of talking about it, but it offers the advantage of something to which you can relate. Also, we don't have to waste time describing some hypothetical case."

"I guess that's OK," Hauser interjected, "since you told me earlier that it won't impugn the decision we actually reached. I'm not an escapist, but you know how traumatic I found the relocation . . . my wife on my back . . . calls at home, occasionally abusive . . . friends at church and at the club who seemed as if they'd just as soon not talk to me. I got a feeling sometimes, I must admit, that maybe we'd gotten everything wrong. It would really be rubbing salt in the wounds if we were to go through some exercise and find that we had screwed everything up royally and come to the wrong answer."

"I understand, George, and I hope I would have been smart enough not to use this approach if I had thought it would exacerbate a problem. But it won't." After a pause to see if anyone else had a comment, Iverson continued, "Now I'll pass out a single

---

**Steps in Dealing
with Ethical Dilemmas**

Define the problem.

Identify the stakeholders.

Identify the practical alternatives.

Determine the measurable economic impact of each alternative.

Identify the immeasurable economic consequences of each alternative.

Arrive at a tentative decision.

Decide how to implement the decision.

---

[1] The step-approach notion came from Manuel Velasquez's lectures in the Arthur Andersen Business Ethics Program and, by coincidence, has the same number of steps; however, the steps are not identical.

sheet of paper and ask each of you to take a minute to read it. It's my seven-step approach to dealing with an ethical dilemma in business—nothing magical, or even particularly original, but useful, I think, in organizing one's thoughts."[1]

"Has everyone finished?" Iverson asked. "OK then, let's begin with the first step."

Define the Problem

"You may think that it is obvious, but surprisingly people too often start to attack a perceived problem before actually defining it. We have to understand the facts before we can consider a solution—or maybe even conclude that there is an ethical issue to be dealt with. In your case, we all know the problem, so I won't belabor it. But I will restate it to show you what I mean:

> Hauser-Moore has an aging product line that is losing money. The company has come up with a promising new product line that will replace the old one. It will require expanded facilities and extensive retooling. This can be done either here in Janesboro or at a different location although the costs to do so and the impact on various individuals and groups may differ.

"Any problems with that summary?" Noting no disagreement, Iverson went on to the second step.

Identify the Stakeholders

"Everyone, I know, will agree that the shareholders are stakeholders. Are there any others?"

"Larry will probably disagree," Janice Freeland said, glancing his way with a smile, "but I believe we have to include the employees who would lose their jobs."

"Any others?" Iverson asked.

"Sure," Stuart Andretti said, "local suppliers, some of whom have built their businesses around Hauser-Moore and have contributed to its success."

"I may be a voice crying in the wilderness," Larry Albertson interjected, "but I suspected we were headed this way, and I want to protest before we plunge further in this direction. The employees, I can see, although I may disagree that they are stakeholders. But any others—no. These suppliers are businesses; they've been well compensated for their transactions with Hauser-Moore, and we don't owe them anything. I'm sorry Blair Shanley isn't here, because I am sure he would support my viewpoint."

"I understand and half agree," said Janice Freeland, "but let's include them for the start, then we can take them out later if we agree they don't belong. Will that spoil your analysis, Carl?"

"No, Janice," Iverson replied, "in fact, I think that's how we should go. And, as we shall find later, there will be another chance to address Larry's concern. But are there any other stakeholders?"

"Yes," Andretti said, "the customers, certainly. And at the risk of giving Larry apoplexy, I would add the community at large. Hauser-Moore is very important to Janesboro; the city has added many services to accommodate the company, and many individuals and small businesses will suffer greatly from any significant reduction of Hauser-Moore's local operations. My only question, Carl, is whether we should consider these as a group or try to break them down into categories such as schools, the Community Fund, apartment owners, other parts of the housing market, various merchants, government, and so on? These are very important—some individually and certainly in the aggregate."

"If we were going through this in earnest and if the stakes were big, I think we should have some breakdown, but for purposes today we had just as well leave them all together. Any others?"

Hearing no suggestions, Iverson said that it was time to go to the next step.

Identify Practical Alternatives

"Now we'll consider what practical alternatives there might be. In a way, we may have jumped the gun on this by setting up two alternatives in defining the problem. There isn't a clear line of demarcation on handling this, and I don't believe that's important as long as we consider the alternatives somewhere. But this is the time to ask whether there are any other possible answers. Sometimes, surprisingly, we identify a choice at the outset, perhaps between two unappealing alternatives, without giving enough consideration to whether there is another option. I don't know what it would be here, but can anyone think of one? What about shutting down the old line without opening a new one?"

"Absolutely not," Hauser exclaimed vehemently. "Who would that help? That would be the path to decline, and I'm not presiding over the demise of the company. Dick Bentley may have made some mistakes, but he was on the right track in addressing this problem. We have a good new product, and we're going to make it somewhere. The only legitimate question is where."

"At least," Iverson said, laughing, "I got your attention. OK, so that isn't an acceptable alternative. Are there any others?"

"Well," said Hauser, "it didn't turn out to be an acceptable alternative in our situation, but this seems to be a good place to discuss something that's been bothering me. And, though it did not turn out to be an alternative this time, it might in some similar situation. You don't mind, do you, Carl, if we digress a bit."

"Not at all. What's bothering anyone is more important than sticking to an agenda. What is it?"

"When the cost study was made, as I am sure the other directors will remember, Bentley had them put in a possible savings from getting wage and tax concessions if we were to stay in Janesboro. The amount was $6 million. It wasn't enough to tip the scales, or even come close, so we didn't pursue the matter. I was ready to try for it if necessary, but I've since wondered if what we were contemplating was quite ethical—if it wasn't a bit like blackmail. Telling the employees and the city to give us what we want or we'll leave. But I know a lot of companies do it. What do some of you think?"

"No question," Albertson said, "it would be like any legitimate cost saving. What question could there be about it?"

"It will probably surprise you, Larry," Andretti joined in, "but I agree—as long as we are sincere and deal honestly with the other parties involved."

"But I can't get over the fact," Hauser said, "that it sounds like blackmail."

"It isn't that at all, George," Andretti responded. "It's telling it like it is. Is it blackmail to tell a supplier his price is too high and that you'll go elsewhere where you have a better offer—unless he can match it? You get the best deal you can when you negotiate your labor contract, don't you? I can't see the difference as long as you're honest about it."

"What do you mean by that—being honest in that situation?" Albertson asked.

"I mean that you don't lie, or bluff. I think it's more ethical to level with employees or the local government and tell them, 'Look, we've got a problem if we stay here—we need your co-operation,' than to pick up and move without giving them a chance to participate in a solution. What I don't think is right would be to threaten to move, to ask for special favors, if you have no intention of moving—perhaps nowhere else to go. That type of tactic would probably ultimately backfire anyway. You can only cry 'wolf' so often."

"That's what I'd focus on," Lerner said. "Getting concessions like that is often only a Band-Aid, not a real solution. I wouldn't say that it would be unethical under the right circumstances, but I think it might frequently be poor business. We've talked here at Hauser-Moore about the likelihood that much of Janesboro's heavy industry will probably leave in the next few years anyway. In a situation like that, it's questionable how desirable it is to contribute to a lingering death through concessions that don't really solve the basic problem."

"As you've been talking," Janice Freeland broke in, "I've been wondering about something. Everyone is talking about this as something to be done only in a crisis—maybe when a company might otherwise have to close or move a plant. I can't see the logic of any dividing line on the basis of the arguments I've heard.

Why couldn't we, or any company, do this anytime we thought we could reduce costs by doing so? I'm afraid I don't see the distinction."

"Because," Andretti said, "there probably isn't a distinction. Conceptually I think this is always an alternative. Practically it probably isn't; it would destroy a business if the employees or the community were approached for concessions on a more or less routine basis. The situation would become chaotic—and filled with mistrust and antagonism."

"I hear all you've been saying," Hauser interjected, "and probably agree from a business standpoint. One of the reasons I was glad not to have to consider it for the old engine line relocation was that I figured it would open up a lot of problems—friction with workers in our other operations, requests to open our books, arguments about the economics of relocation, a lot of unfavorable publicity, all that. Probably I agree with Larry and the rest of you, but are there any ethical limits? Stu says we can't lie, and I have a gut agreement with that, but what do we have to tell people when we're negotiating something like this?"

Is Bluffing Ethical?

"George, you've hit on one of the toughest issues in business ethics," Iverson said, "and I'll admit I can't give you any quick, easy answers. In fact, even though I would like to agree with what Stu said a bit ago, that we shouldn't bluff, I'm afraid things aren't that simple. We can't take time now to cover the matter in the depth it deserves. But I will try to offer some high-spot observations; then some time later, if the opportunity presents itself, we can discuss bluffing in more detail.

"Some years back—in the late 1960s, if I recall correctly—the *Harvard Business Review* carried an article entitled 'Is Business Bluffing Ethical?'[2] The author, Albert Z. Carr, held that it is—that

---

[2] Albert Z. Carr, "Is Business Bluffing Ethical?" *Harvard Business Review*, Vol. 46 (January/February 1968).

business is a game, that bluffing is a part of playing games, and that the rules of legality and the goal of profit are the sole ethical guidelines. Now most of us, if not all, wouldn't go quite that far today, but Carr has raised some points that are rather difficult to reject categorically. I—"

"Don't be so sure that most of us wouldn't go that far, Carl," Albertson interrupted. "He sounds pretty close to Friedman."

"But not quite, Larry," Iverson shot back. "Remember, if you will, that Friedman didn't say that staying within the law is enough; he added that we must stay within the bounds of ethical norms embodied, I believe he said, in custom. And that's what we're talking about—what are those norms? And what should they be? For those who regard employees, suppliers, customers, and others with whom a company is directly involved as stakeholders, regardless of the extent, winning from them by bluffing should be carefully considered.

"All bluffing, you might say, is a form of lying. To use Carr's game analogy, raising in poker when you have nothing in your hand is lying; you are deliberately fostering a false impression. Or in a baseball game, distracting the pitcher by pretending you're going to steal second when you have no thought of doing so. A fake pass play in football. There's nothing wrong with any of these, of course—they are part of the game, and the game is far richer, more interesting because of the bluffing. But should business be treated like a game?"

"That's a good question," Andretti broke in, "and I have some trouble with the analogy. But I'd like to go back to something else you just called attention to. Friedman said, in effect, that businesses should operate within the ethical norms embodied in custom—isn't that right?" Seeing Iverson nod, Andretti continued, "Isn't some bluffing built into business custom in such areas as labor negotiations, property purchases, attempts to outmaneuver competitors and so on? Am I stretching it to say that bluffing in such cases is embodied in custom?"

"No, Stu," Iverson said, "you're not stretching it. You're on the right track—but one with pitfalls. You have to be careful that the wish does not become father to the thought, that you not rationalize that whatever you wish to do to gain an advantage is sanctioned by custom. And remember, custom in this area is continually evolving. For example, in just the last 20 or 30 years, the old 'buyer beware' approach to home sales has changed to such an extent that sellers and realtors are now generally required to disclose major known defects. Indeed, some of the examples that I recall Carr citing in his article would probably be out of bounds today.

"We are in a very complex area of business and the whole gamut of human relations—just how far to go with full disclosure. I do not think custom or anything else justifies an overt misstatement of a material fact. Period. That much is easy, at least for me. But the definition of lying also includes the omission of relevant facts. Here the situation gets more murky. Full disclosure must have a limit. A salesperson, for example, is expected to emphasize the strong points of a product. Perhaps we should say that that practice is embodied in custom, taken for granted. No one, I am sure, would expect him or her to present a balanced, objective analysis of the product such as we might find in *Consumer Reports*. It would certainly be unrealistic to think that he or she should volunteer to customers that some competitor's product, let's say a type of pump, had a record of fewer repairs.

"You should not present half truths, anything designed to create a false impression, either by artful arrangement or by omission of facts. On the other hand, one need not bring out every fact that conceivably might influence the other party if it is not material to a fair understanding of what you have been discussing. Let's apply that to our pump salesperson. Obviously, he or she shouldn't lie about the repair experience with the company's pumps, whether voluntarily or in answer to a question. By artful wording, he or she shouldn't imply that the experience is any better than it is. But—"

"Excuse my interrupting," Freeland interjected, "but aren't you on a slippery slope there? You used the word 'material.' Material to whom? Isn't the repair experience material to the purchaser? I have trouble seeing where this leads us—or, I should say, leaves us."

"You're right, Janice, the slope is slippery. To avoid falling requires judgment—honest judgment, I hope—necessarily influenced by self-interest but not overly so. How's that for a vague answer? But I think it's realistic. Every product presumably has some features better than some others on the market, some worse. Buyers recognize this and should ask searching questions—questions about matters of concern to them. And answers to those questions should be honest. Sure, someone might argue that the fact that the company's pump repair experience is not as good as some other company's is material to the buyer; however, in my opinion, the salesperson need not volunteer that fact—unless, of course, it is so poor that he or she shouldn't even be trying to sell the product!

"Getting back to what started this discussion—the appropriateness of a company's approach in obtaining concessions from labor and the community—I think we can get pretty good guidance from Kant's categorical imperative—"

"I was wondering," Lerner interrupted, "when we might use some of the ethical concepts we discussed last time. They sounded pretty good, but I've been waiting to see how you'd apply them."

"Here goes for an example, Mike. If I, as the manager of a business in a community," Iverson resumed, "can say that the concessions I am thinking about requesting, and the means that I would use in seeking them, are ones that I would consider appropriate for every other business in the community that is similarly situated, there is probably no ethical problem in my trying for them. That's the universality aspect of the categorical imperative.

"Or put another way, if I would feel that the request and the way it is presented are reasonable if I were in the shoes of those being asked to make concessions—even if I didn't like the result, I believe there would be no ethical problem. That's reversibility. And it isn't an easy answer, since there can be differences of view concerning what the other side might consider reasonable. It is a sound approach, though, if honestly applied.

"To sum up, I agree with Stu's earlier observation—that this is a better answer than to pull out without giving those we would be leaving a chance to share in the solution. With that," Iverson concluded, "I think we'd better move on unless you, George, or anyone else wants to discuss this further." Hearing nothing, he said, "OK, we'll run to the fourth step."

Determine Measurable Economic Impact of Each Alternative

"This is an area," he observed, "you had pretty well nailed down from the outset. I won't go into the specific dollars here, but the study given you before your decision presented the alternative costs of staying here, along with an expansion and retooling, versus setting up in a new location. The only thing I'm not clear on is whether it included, as a cost of moving, the things you were going to do here—setting up some placement arrangements and possibly some retraining for terminated employees, making payments in lieu of taxes to the city, continuing the level of your Community Fund support, and so on."

"Yes, Carl, these costs were included in the study," Hauser responded. "Although I was unhappy that no specific plans had been formulated at the time we were asked to make a decision, Bentley had given the fellows who made the study a round figure for those costs, and it was included. It turns out, as the definitive plans have been developed, that the figure Dick gave them was clearly in the ballpark."

"Well, then," Iverson continued, "it looks as if we have the measurable economic factors pretty well identified. Any questions?"

"Yes," Freeland asked, "doesn't almost any action have a price tag? There are certainly intangible benefits and costs we haven't quantified, but that doesn't make them any less real. And even the stakeholder impact that we are considering—and I know,

Larry, you think we shouldn't, at least other than shareholders—needs to have some kind of quantification if this whole exercise is to mean anything. Shouldn't we try to hang a dollar sign on these, even if we know it can't be precise?"

"Your point is very well taken, Janice," Iverson responded, "although I don't believe we should address it as you suggest. True, everything has an economic effect, but sometimes it defies quantification. I don't believe that we benefit by trying to measure the immeasurable; we may only fool ourselves with a representation of certainty where none exists. It reminds me of my old statistics professor's definition of spurious accuracy: using data that are correct plus or minus 25 percent and then carrying calculations to the fourth decimal point!

"Under my approach, these soft factors may not be tied down tightly, and you may feel a bit frustrated with some of them. The important point, though, is that we aren't going to ignore them. Here, Janice, is where we'll address them."

Identify Immeasurable Economic Consequences of Each Alternative

"Can any of you mention one of these immeasurable factors that should be considered?"

"Yes," Michael Lerner spoke up. "As the directors will remember, I mentioned at the meeting when we decided to relocate that I believed the long-term future of Janesboro would be tied to high tech, not the kind of heavy industry in which Hauser-Moore is involved. I referred to this again a few minutes ago when we were discussing concessions. I even went on to say at the meeting that I suspected that, a few years hence, we might find that an expansion for the new product line here would turn out to be a costly mistake. I have since had the economics bureau of the university do more on this. Although I can't prove or quantify it, I am confident that that will be the case."

"Good, Mike," Iverson said. "I remembered this from the meeting notes I was given and hoped you would bring it up. The fact that something like this can't be tied down in dollars and cents doesn't make it any less important; indeed, sometimes these immeasurables can be the most important matters to consider.

"Does anyone have anything else?" he asked.

"Maybe you don't want to cover this here," Albertson said, "and remember that I'm not a stakeholder enthusiast. But just for discussion, as long as we're going down this primrose path, should we consider the intangible, but I am sure economic, impact of the loyalty that the community has toward Hauser-Moore? You certainly wouldn't find this elsewhere, at least not for a long, long time. I think that this is something to consider."

"I agree, Larry," Iverson came back, "and I don't believe that this violates your principles. I'd put this under a business benefit to the company rather than a stakeholder consideration. Now, if it's all right, we'll move to the next step."

Arrive at a Tentative Decision

Moving over to an easel that held a flip chart, Iverson reached to throw back the top sheet. As he did so, he said, "You'll see that I have set up a comparative summary of the factors to be considered in reaching a decision. Normally, of course, I couldn't do this in advance, and I'm afraid that doing it this way may create an impression that this analysis is more cut-and-dried than would be the situation in real life. Since we are all so familiar with the details of this case, though, I risked doing this to save time. If our discussion had proved me wrong, I'd have just skipped this sheet, but that is apparently not the case. To the extent there are any differences, we'll cover them as we go along." Saying that, he uncovered the summary.

"Now let's run through them quickly. First, take a look at measurable economic factors. As I understand, the cost study Bentley initiated and that you still consider reasonable shows a net present value of $3.5 million for the savings that would result from relocation. We could, of course, have shown the benefits broad, since the gross benefit of relocating, as I understand it, is

---

Comparative Advantages

In Favor of Staying	In Favor of Relocating
Measurable Economic Factors	
None	P.v. of savings—$3.5 million
Immeasurable Economic Factors	
Impact of employee loyalty	Long-term trend away from
Community support	heavy industry in
	Janesboro
Stakeholder Considerations	
Shareholders-	Shareholders-
Above economic factors	Above economic factors
Employees-	Employees-
Job retention	Retraining/placement
	efforts
Suppliers-	Suppliers-
Continuing business	None
Government-	Government-
Continuing taxes	Two-year payments in lieu
Other community-	Other community-
Community Fund support	Two-year Fund support
Benefit to local business	

---

more than $10 million. This is offset in part by the advantages to staying put—for example, $6 million of possible wage and tax concessions and lesser, but still important, savings from not having to incur the cost of retraining and placement efforts for terminated employees and the cost of demolition for the facilities to be abandoned. However, I saw no point in splitting these out.

"We then come to the immeasurable economics. For staying here, we have the employee loyalty and community support—factors that Larry mentioned. I know of no acceptable way to assign dollars to these factors, but any company would be foolish to ignore them. On the other hand, though, we have the benefit in moving of escaping Mike's projected decline in the viability of basic industry here. I am not an economist and do not have the sense of this community; but if what Mike says is true, this could well be more important in the long run than the measurable dollar savings attributed to the relocation.

"We now come to the stakeholder considerations—in other words, the place where we try to balance everything out. It includes the rights of the shareholders as expressed in the measurable and immeasurable economic consequences and the rights of employees, suppliers, and other community interests that may be identified as stakeholders. Please take a minute to look this over. Any questions?"

"Yes," Albertson said, "even if I accept for discussion all these stakeholders that have been mentioned, I can't see how you can just list them and act as if one is as important as another. It doesn't make sense to me."

"I would agree," Hauser joined in, "except that I doubt if that is what Carl intends to do. Am I right?"

"You certainly are." Iverson came back. "I'm reminded of what the pig said in George Orwell's *Animal Farm*, that all animals are equal but that some are more equal than others. Some stakeholders are more equal than others: Some are further removed from the impact of a decision, others may be close but are affected in only a minor way. Some have greater rights, that is, if you accept the concept of rights for any stakeholders other than the shareholders. For example, a work force of loyal, longtime employees has greater claims, in my view, than a young group of employees in a newly started business. We have to weight the various stakes in reaching a decision. I am not suggesting that we can do this on any mathematically precise basis—for instance 15 percent for this stakeholder, 40 percent for another. It's a judgment matter."

"But still, Carl, you have the shareholders in there just like any other stakeholder," Freeland broke in. "Surely they deserve more consideration than that. Maybe I'm getting closer to Larry in my thinking."

"Janice, they *are* just another stakeholder," Andretti joined in. "But I'm sure Carl will tell us that they have heavy weighting. Isn't that true, Carl?"

"Yes and no," Iverson responded, "and we'll never resolve this in any precise way. The weighting will vary with the circumstances. My approach would always be to look first at the shareholder impact and to make a tentative, preliminary judgment that this gives us the answer. Then I would appraise the other factors to see if they should modify the preliminary decision. If the answer were close from a shareholder perspective but I found some strong factor, one way or the other, affecting employees, it well might tip the balance. For example, I would be strongly influenced if one alternative enabled the company to save the jobs of employees where the other might result in significant terminations. This would have even more significance if long-term employees were involved.

"On the other hand, the shareholder considerations—which are the same as what many people, like Larry, would consider the company considerations—would be overriding if they went to the survival, or even the future growth, of the company. It does no good, obviously, to try to help the community at the expense of the shareholders if the result would be to harm, perhaps even destroy, the company and lose everything."

Pausing a moment to organize his thoughts, Iverson continued, "Another way of saying this is that, by definition, the rights of every stakeholder cannot be satisfied in a business dilemma. There are conflicts. That's what creates the dilemma. A large multilocation company might give heavy weight to its obligation to a community in deciding to continue operations of a marginal activity, whereas a small, single-operation company, under exactly the same circumstances, might find it necessary to relocate as a matter of survival. One would not be acting more ethically than the other; it would be a matter of operating within practical constraints.

"All this, of course, assumes as a minimum, a floor, if you will, that what is contemplated is legal and not morally outrageous. By that I mean that a company is limited by ethical constraints in what it can do to survive—it does not have a right to survive at any cost."

"I see what you're saying, and it makes sense to me if handled properly," Andretti observed, "but isn't this whole process subject to manipulation? Might not a cynic claim that we are paying lip service to stakeholders other than the owners by listing them but then dealing them out through our weighting?"

"Sure, Stu," Iverson responded, "but how can you avoid that? It happens even if you don't prepare a list. At least by identifying the stakeholders, decision makers are forced to consider their interests. More often than not, I am sure, they'll come out with a more ethically sensitive answer than they would if they didn't go through the exercise. What we're doing here is putting structure in the decision process and, I hope, increasing the sensitivity to ethical considerations."

"OK," Hauser nodded, "I can see that. And I like the general approach for something like the relocation decision we had to deal with. But you surely wouldn't expect everyone in the company to carry a pad of paper around and prepare an analysis like this every time he or she had to decide something. We'd never get any products out and sold."

"A very good point, George," Iverson acknowledged. "An effective manager deals with a multiplicity of problems, with a constant flow of interrelated information, and must often make fast decisions.[3] I would go through all this for major decisions. There aren't too many of those, and it's worth the effort. It also puts structure into your thinking—something you'd use, less formally, even in routine situations. Maybe you wouldn't put anything down on paper, but I'd like to think that a supervisor, for example,

---

[3] For a good discussion of the complexity and ambiguity present in managers' decision making, see Michael Rion, *The Responsible Manager: Practical Strategies for Ethical Decision Making* (San Francisco: Harper & Row, Publishers, 1990), 35–39.

might go through a similar, if less-structured, thought process in deciding what to do about a long-term employee whose performance has begun slipping.

"But I'd like to play around with this decision making a bit before we go to the last step. With the facts we were dealing with, the answer may seem to some of you to have come a little too easily. Given the large savings that would result from relocation, someone may think we've been using a cannon to shoot a mouse."

Stepping over to the flip chart and pointing, Iverson continued, "Let's try a hypothetical—let's cross out the $3.5 million present value of the indicated savings and write in $100,000 instead. And let's assume further that Mike had not had his Business Research Bureau study to spring on you—we'll cross it out. And one thing more, that Bentley hadn't put you under the gun with his option and that there hadn't been a leak. What would you have decided? Stu?"

"That's easy. In the first place, no matter how good the study might be, it could easily be off enough to eliminate the indicated $100,000 savings to relocate. Placing too much emphasis on that figure would be what I believe you called spurious accuracy.

"But even if I believed the $100,000 to be completely reliable," Andretti continued, "I'd have no hesitation opting for staying put. Although admittedly I can't assign a precise dollar value to such factors, I believe that Hauser-Moore's obligation to its stakeholders other than shareholders—and in those I include employees, suppliers, and the community generally—far exceeds $100,000."

"Surprisingly, I agree," Albertson chimed in, "but for different reasons—business reasons. I think the goodwill of the community and the loyalty of the work force are worth far more to the company than a lump-sum payment of $100,000. Put another way, the company could never buy those items for that amount, or probably for quite a bit more."

"I hear you both," Iverson said. "Now what if the present value of the savings to move were $500,000?"

"No question," Hauser broke in. "I'd never vote to move for that amount. My feelings are probably a mixture of a sense of obligation and a feeling that that answer would be good business. And, I might say, I would personally like that result—although, remembering what you said earlier, I'd try hard to keep my personal feelings from influencing my vote."

"I don't think we need carry this further," Iverson said, "because in real life we would be dealing with fixed amounts—estimates, undoubtedly, in many cases, but still not a range of hypothetical assumptions. What I wanted to show you was that the decision process I have given you would be much more useful in many situations you might face than in the relocation case, where the differential was so large. Obviously it wouldn't give you the answer, because there might still be significant differences in values various persons would attribute to immeasurable economic factors and to stakeholder obligations; the important point is that it would bring these issues into clear focus for the consideration they deserve.

"Now," Iverson went on, "let's go to the last step."

Implement the Decision

"I haven't really much to say here, and maybe this isn't even a step in the dilemma solving. Someone must have already found that the alternatives could be implemented; otherwise, we wouldn't have had the information to feed into our decision making, and we would have been wasting our time. I have put the step in, though, to show that we were engaged in serious business, that we meant to follow through on whatever our analysis pointed to.

"And there is another point to consider—let's not throw the game away just as we've won it. A company might go through the most careful study, give appropriate weight to various economic and ethical factors, and come to a sound decision. Much of the benefit of the effort might be lost, however, if the execution were not well handled. I am not suggesting that we regard this as a PR effort, but it is important that a company's actions not only be ethical but that they be perceived as sensitive and ethical. The way in which an action is carried out can be tremendously important. And that is a part of ethics, since it is an effort to see matters through the eyes of others, such as employees, who may be vitally affected.

"Unless one of you has a comment or question," Iverson continued, "that buttons up what I wanted to cover now about the ethical aspects of decision making. Is there anything else you want to touch on?"

"Yes, Carl," Janice said, "I do have a question, and I hope you won't think that I keep subjecting you to a cross-examination. But I can't help wondering how practical all this is. It looks fine on paper and works well on a hindsight basis for a situation we all understand. But how well can it work in practice? Don't these situations sneak up on us, frequently not giving us enough time— or information—to do a neat, tidy analysis such as the one we've just been through?"

"Janice, I can't deny the validity of your concern," Iverson said. "In some situations we might not be able to organize the data as well as we did here. And the last thing I would want to do would be to oversell the procedure, then have you try it and decide that it was fine for a textbook but wouldn't work in real life.

"I don't believe, though, that the problem is as great as your question might suggest. The toughest part, I think, would ordinarily be to determine the alternatives and to develop a reasonable cost analysis, matters that a company would have to go through in any event. Look at Hauser-Moore's relocation decision: Didn't you have, or at least couldn't you reasonably have had, all the data we have used today at the time you made your decision? What I have shown you is just a discipline, a way to organize the information that would ordinarily be available in any event when you make a decision. The most that I claim for the seven-step procedure I have recommended is structure, and a way of forcing you to look at the immeasurable ethical issues involved.

"Is it perfect? Of course not," Iverson continued. "Will it always lead to the right answer? No, but I believe that it will result in a better job. And I am convinced that it is practical. Does that answer, Janice?"

"What you say makes sense," she replied, "but I'll want to give it a little more thought. Possibly my problem is that it makes us analyze what we are doing instead of subconsciously sorting out the factors as most of us probably have been accustomed to doing. Let's put it this way—I can't fault your approach, and I'm willing to give it a try."

"I'd like to add one thing," Andretti interjected, "or maybe it's more an amplification of what you just said, Carl. One of the biggest advantages I see to the discipline of the approach is that it should help ensure not overlooking some factor, some stakeholder. And if the company has established in advance, as a general policy, who its stakeholders are, everyone is more likely to get a fair consideration."

"That's right," Iverson responded. Pausing a moment to look around, he continued. "George, I'd enjoy going on with this, but my watch and my voice tell me we'd better bring this to an end. It's been stimulating and fun, at least for me; however, I don't want to wear out my welcome."

"I don't think you need worry about that, Carl," Hauser replied. "This has been extremely helpful. As I told you earlier, though, I think we now have a pretty good grasp of what is involved, and I doubt if we should take any more of the board's time, at least during meetings, to discuss these issues in detail. We'll have to take a little time to consider where we'll go from here. One way or another, though, I'll get back to you as to what we might want to do. You'll be out at Trinity for a couple more weeks?"

"Yes," Iverson answered, "and I'll be glad to answer any questions that may come to your mind. Before we break, though,

I want to thank you and everyone. It's been a most challenging and interesting session for me."

As they left, all the directors gathered around Iverson to express their appreciation and the hope they could get together again.

PART TWO

Ethical Issues from an Individual Perspective

CHAPTER FIVE

The Individual's Role in Business Ethics

Michael Lerner and Carl Iverson had finished a review of how things were going in Trinity's executive training program. As Carl got up to leave, Mike asked, "Have you a few minutes to discuss something else, something that I've been thinking about ever since our discussion of ethics with the Hauser-Moore board, not last week but the time before?"

Dropping back into his chair, Iverson said, "Sure. Is it something I covered, or something I didn't?"

"A bit of both," Lerner responded. "You said that you were covering only corporate decisions, for example, Hauser-Moore's action in relocating . . . matters that involved corporate strategic or policy decisions. You went on to say that decisions by individuals within a company are a different matter, something you would cover at a later date if anyone wished.

"I can understand some differences, but I'm not sure I have the whole picture. Although you will undoubtedly be dealing with this with the committee that George is setting up, I doubt if the board will ever take up that particular aspect, and I am curious. Would it take too much of your time now to fill me in?"

"Not at all," Iverson replied. "In fact, I'm all set for my seminar tonight, so nothing is pressing me. And if we don't finish now, we can come back to it another time soon."

Pausing a moment to organize his thoughts, he continued, "At the outset, I should admit that I may have oversimplified the issue by stating, or at least implying, that there is a dichotomy between corporate ethical decisions and those of individuals within the corporation. I did this to emphasize that the balancing of rights and obligations in strategic and policy decisions is usually far more complex than what we ordinarily think of as individual decisions involving choices between right and wrong. That doesn't mean, though, that dealing with individual problems is necessarily easier. Sometimes, it can be more difficult."

"Why is that?"

"Because the person may have to do soul searching alone," Iverson replied. "Corporate policy and strategic dilemmas may be very complex, but often—probably most of the time—it's a group effort. There's likely to be input from a number of people. Everything is out on the table. There is an element of the comfort that comes from a form of anonymity; everyone participates, so the matter of individual responsibility is less. Some individual decisions, on the other hand, are very personal. There's no one to talk to. The person feels exposed, almost naked.

"But let's get away from generalities and be specific," he continued. "I don't want to oversimplify the picture. Actually, ethical decisions in business constitute something of a continuum. They may start with ones like we talked about for Hauser-Moore, running through somewhat similar ones—usually on a somewhat smaller scale—that key managers may have to make. Then we have the kinds of day-to-day decisions that supervisors handle in carrying out their responsibilities, finally ending up with individual actions of people in the corporation. There are at least two kinds of the latter. I know that probably sounds like so many words, so I'll try to be more specific."

A Matter of Honesty

"We'll start with basics," Iverson said, "and talk about personal integrity."

"Good, Carl. I was beginning to wonder when you'd mention that. I trust that I have not been so naive as to think that ethics involved only lying, cheating, or stealing—and you've certainly opened the board's eyes to the breadth, the complexity, of ethical behavior—but I certainly thought I would have heard the word honesty mentioned at least once by this time."

"With the possible exception of Richard Bentley's behavior, and I doubt even there, none of the situations we've discussed have involved moral lapses where people put their own self-interest ahead of what is best for the company. We have addressed dilemmas from the point of view of company decisions—a consideration of rights and obligations, benefits, and costs in conducting the business of the company. Perhaps it is time to look at ethical lapses in which people put, or are tempted to put, what they want ahead of what is right. And these, I might note, are the toughest to discuss."

"Why?" Lerner asked with surprise.

"The problem," Iverson replied, "is the interjection of self, pure and simple. People have wonderful powers of rationalization where their own interests are involved. The matter's small, they'll claim—it makes no difference. Or everyone's doing it. An employee can be very sarcastic about a vice president's business trip to Kentucky at the same time as the Derby. He fails to see the similarity to his extending a meeting with a customer in Tucson to Monday, one that he could have finished Friday afternoon, so that he can spend the weekend golfing with a college friend.

"I'm not being cynical, Mike, but realistically we must recognize that it is easier to be virtuous about big problems, especially those in which we are not personally involved, than it is to face ethical issues on our own doorstep. We've all seen someone like the woman who will drop everything to attend a rally for some global issue—saving the whales, for example—but never quite has time to visit the man around the corner who has lost his job and is despondent over his wife's worsening emphysema. This may not seem like a good example, since it does not involve business, but the human element is the same. All of us have at least a bit of that woman in us.

"And people somehow or other tend to apply different standards when dealing with companies, including their own, than they do when dealing with individuals. Haven't you heard someone respond, when asked what he would do if he noticed that he got ten dollars too much in change, 'I would say something if I thought the clerk would have to make up the shortage'—as if that should have any bearing on his answer? The person who takes an ashtray from a restaurant as a 'souvenir' would probably never think of pinching one from someone's home where he or she was visiting. And yet the moral issue is just the same.

"But here I am coming close to preaching—always an unproductive way to discuss ethics. I must, however, spell out some basics. To start with—and it may seem to be stating the obvious, but the obvious is sometimes overlooked—a person should observe the basic rule of ethical behavior: One should not knowingly do harm. A person shouldn't lie. Or cheat. He or she should keep promises, both those made specifically and those implicit in one's behavior or position. Of course, a person shouldn't steal. Violation of any of these precepts harms someone.

Bluffing Again

"Just a minute, Carl," Lerner said. "It seems to me you're contradicting yourself on the matter of lying. Remember the last meeting with the Hauser-Moore board when you sort of opened the door for some bluffing, which obviously constitutes a form of lying? Now you're telling me one shouldn't lie. I was bothered a bit then, and more so now when you seem to go back on what you said."

"You've caught me in an embarrassing oversimplification; I'm glad to have a chance to try to clarify. This whole matter of bluffing or lying is one of the most elusive issues to get a hold of. Let's put it this way: The various forms that lying can take cover a broad spectrum. A lie can be an overt misstatement of fact. It can consist of a presentation of facts, individually true, in a manner designed to mislead the listener or reader. Or it can be the knowing omission of something relevant. A lie can involve facts, or it can be concerned with opinions.

"As I said at the meeting, I do not believe we should condone a bald-faced misstatement of facts—an out-and-out lie. That was what I was thinking of when I generalized a minute ago. But even there, there may be exceptions—telling a dying mother, for example, that her son is all right when he was actually killed in the same accident that hospitalized her. These are what we often 'sugar-coat,' calling them stories, or white lies. We ordinarily sanction these."

"Aren't white lies more often involved in matters of opinion rather than fact?" Lerner asked. "We often do this to avoid hurting people's feelings—for example, telling your wife you like her new dress even if you don't."

"Yes," Iverson replied, "and this is all right if used sparingly—not where important questions are involved. For instance, if a man's boss asks how he likes the decor of her new office, one she has designed herself, he'd be foolish to tell her he doesn't like it if it is only a matter of taste—style preference. On the other hand, people are often asked their opinions on critical business issues; indeed, having informed opinions in such cases, and expressing them, may be the most important part of a person's job. It is not only ethically inexcusable to duck on these issues, it is also poor business. The person who cops out on tough decisions, plays the 'me too' game regularly, may ultimately find that no one asks for his or her opinion.

"The tough bluffing, or lying, questions fall in between—deciding what constitutes acceptable full disclosure. As I said at our meeting, it isn't reasonable to expect a person to volunteer everything he or she knows. An individual should not misstate facts or present them in a misleading way, but accepted custom, business practice, does not normally require a person to bring up information adverse to his or her position if it is not required, asked for, or commonly expected in the circumstances. Of course, the information not disclosed must not be of overriding importance—something, for example, that might affect human life or health or make the transaction involved, taken as a whole, an act of deception.

"I still think that attempting to apply Kant's categorical imperative gives the best guidance. Put pragmatically, I think a good test might be: Don't get involved in anything you might want to call bluffing if it would embarrass you, or not be considered reasonable by others whom you respect, if it were to come to light."

"What about stakeholders?" Lerner asked. "You haven't mentioned them."

"These basic matters of honesty, integrity, do not ordinarily require any identification of stakeholders. An employee need not ponder who the stakeholders may be in deciding whether to put a dinner she didn't buy on her expense report—it is an unambiguous matter of right and wrong. Or to take a specialized calculator home for her son to use in his school work and 'forget' to return it. The head of purchasing for a company doesn't need to think about who would be hurt when a supplier suggests that perhaps he would like a wide-screen video dropped off for his newly added game room. These are matters of unequivocal right and wrong— not ethical dilemmas."

"But aren't there stakeholders involved in all ethical issues, whether or not we choose to call them dilemmas?" Lerner asked.

"Certainly," Iverson replied. "In all these cases, the company, or specifically the shareholders, are stakeholders. The person's supervisor whose performance is affected by a subordinate's productivity or use of company resources is also a stakeholder. Fellow employees are stakeholders. I'll grant you that the impact may sometimes seem small, but that's part of the problem—the employee can say it doesn't amount to much. But the principle is the same, and the aggregate of all these relatively minor lapses has a huge cumulative impact on the American economy."

The Matter of a Careless Mistake

"But I'd like to touch on a more subtle aspect of personal integrity. What about the employee who discovers he mistakenly shipped a customer's order from a lot that was awaiting testing because of quality concerns? There's no excuse; it was plain carelessness. If he tells his supervisor, there may be hell to pay. Returning the shipment will be costly. Perhaps, he thinks, the customer may have already used the parts that were shipped. Possibly there's nothing wrong with them, and no one will ever know the difference. I'm not going to complicate the problem by throwing in an assumption that human life might be at risk if the part breaks, but you might think about that."

"He has a real dilemma," Lerner said.

"I disagree," Iverson replied. "At least it isn't an ethical dilemma. Certainly not one for him to handle. The stakeholders that come immediately to mind are his employer and the customer, and they do not have competing rights in his decision—and that's what makes an ethical dilemma. His obligation is clear and unequivocal: to tell his supervisor."

"But, Carl, let me be a devil's advocate. Isn't the employee a stakeholder? He stands to lose a lot if he tells his supervisor."

Iverson replied quickly, "That doesn't make him a stakeholder in any ethical sense. A person has no right to weigh the impact on her- or himself when confronted with the obligation to be honest. And a decision whether or not to speak up is a matter of honesty. If you were to say that the employee is a stakeholder in the ethical decision in this case, it is not much different from saying that the burglar is a stakeholder in the homeowner's decision about installing a burglar alarm. We have no rights that benefit us, or afford us protection, from our own misdeeds, whether deliberate or accidental.

"That's interesting," Lerner said. "I'd never thought of it in quite that way, but I can't argue that you're wrong."

A Troublesome Request from a Supervisor

"But," Lerner asked after a short pause while he thought about the last point, "what about the situation when someone is asked by a supervisor to do something he or she considers morally wrong—not just obvious situations like being asked to steal proprietary secrets from a competitor. Something much more subtle. I have a feeling that the source of many ethics problems in today's business is the excuse offered that one is only following orders. Or closing one's eyes to something wrong because it is claimed to be outside his or her responsibility. Someone has said that most of the major scandals we read about could never have been carried out by one person alone—or even a dishonest person in collusion with others similarly inclined. It takes, I suspect, a lot of supposedly honest people to cooperate, or at least to close their eyes, for some of these massive frauds to occur."

"Very true," Iverson replied. "Employees owe faithful, efficient performance to their supervisors, and they are entitled to assume, in the absence of evidence to the contrary, that company policies—the things they are asked to do—are ethically sound. And that instructions are proper. But there is a risk here, a possibility for a copout . . . the opportunity to say that one is not responsible for the morality of an action, that one is only following orders.

"A person must be sensitive to the ethical ramifications of what he or she is doing. There has to be a limit, a point at which individual responsibility must take over. Following orders is no excuse for breaking the law. It does not absolve one from knowingly doing another harm, not respecting others' rights, even if what is ordered is not illegal. One cannot put his or her ethical sensitivity in cold storage when going to work each morning."

"What, then, should the individual do," Lerner asked, "if he or she believes that a required action is ethically unacceptable? There's an obvious risk."

"There certainly is," Iverson responded. "The first step is to be sure—to be sure of the facts and to think the matter through. A person cannot be a walking boil, so sensitive as to question virtually everything he or she is asked to do. We have all seen persons like that, and they are virtually impossible to change or to work with. At the extreme, they are themselves unethical in riding roughshod over the rights of others while trying to impose their own standards.

"But there are situations," he continued, "in which an individual, after careful thought, concludes that he or she is being asked to do something improper—directed, for example, to pour hazardous used solvent down the drain at the end of the day's work rather than preparing it for what he knows is the safer but more costly disposal. Being told that everyone does it, that the law never contemplated making a big thing out of small amounts . . . rationale like that.

"The first recourse, of course, is to discuss the situation with one's supervisor—and I know you may say, and rightly, that the problem might be the supervisor. That, however, does not free the person from responsibility to speak to the supervisor. And speaking to the supervisor does not necessarily end the responsibility, either; if the answer is unsatisfactory, if the matter is clear to him or her, and serious, the only recourse may be to refuse to comply. One who does this must recognize that the action may jeopardize his or her future—but there may be no ethical alternative. I'm reading right now a book of essays, not one that I thought would have anything to do with ethics, and one writer had something to say that is very relevant—just a minute, and I'll dig it out of my junk here:

> When you are fighting your own little battles—as opposed to Dan Rather's Big Battle—you know exactly what you are fighting for, and exactly how right or wrong you are. In such cases, it is rational to be stubborn, to resist, even when people of big sense are telling you to "lighten up." In the face of injustice, and against overwhelming odds, a little muleheadedness is more than "understandable." It is essential. The biblical character Job knew this. Whistleblowers who reveal the sins of powerful corporate executives know this. Rosa Parks on her

bus in Montgomery, Alabama, knew this. So did Martin Luther King, Jr., and Gandhi and Bonhoeffer.[1]

"Now, Mike, I want to make clear, as I am sure you know, that it would be an impossible world if everyone wore a hairshirt, taking offense at every little thing that might differ from his or her personal moral code. The writer I just quoted said that you should season your principles with doses of good humor. We have to show respect for others—a little tolerance—and observe a reasonable perspective and sense of what is important. But the bottom line is this: People should do what they believe is right on matters of consequence—and be willing to take whatever the consequences may be."

Knowing That Something Wrong Is Going On

"Carl, let me move over to something a bit more subtle. Difficult though it may be, I cannot argue with its being an individual's responsibility to stand up for what's right if he or she is asked to do something clearly out-of-bounds. Doing the right thing may be costly, but that's the only right answer.

"Let's shift a bit, though, and assume that someone not directly involved—let's call the person a nonparticipant—sees or hears about something that a fellow employee or the company is doing that is morally unacceptable. What is the person's responsibility?"

"Much the same," Iverson replied, "although possibly shaded a bit. I believe that many of our more flagrant ethics breakdowns in recent years could have been nipped in the bud if someone had felt a responsibility to speak up. Of course, as the record now shows, there were others who played the game with Boesky, say, or Milken. Some hoped to profit themselves. Others did what they were asked without any direct gain, probably to protect their jobs.

---

[1] Gary Comstock, "Grandma's Backbone, Dougie's Ankles," included in *A Place of Sense: Essays in Search of the Midwest*, edited by Michael Martone (Iowa City: University of Iowa Press, 1988), 120.

But I suspect that there were many more who knew—or could have known, if they had not deliberately closed their eyes to what was going on."

"You think, then, Carl, that someone in a company who thinks something wrong is going on, even if it isn't anything in which he or she is involved, should blow the whistle?

"Yes, Mike, I do—with some qualifications. First, perhaps, the matter involved should be more significant. One needn't set himself or herself up as the prickly conscience of a department or a company; that might be self-defeating. Even if asked to do so, for example, I wouldn't approve an improper expense report. On the other hand, even if I knew someone else had put a dinner on his report that he didn't buy, I probably wouldn't report him to the supervisor—at least for one lapse. Similarly I wouldn't run to the boss if I saw him stick some computer disks in his briefcase as he cleaned his desk off to go home. But I probably would think less of him, and might watch him more carefully in matters where I was involved.

"On the other hand, I shouldn't remain silent if I learned that he was accepting kickbacks on some orders. And I would certainly feel a responsibility to take some kind of action if I knew he was signing off on some quality inspections that he wasn't making. It all comes down to what is really important."

"In all these cases, Carl, I gather that you know something is wrong. What if you only have a suspicion?"

"How strong a suspicion?" Iverson shot back. "One shouldn't try to play detective without strong evidence unless something very important is involved. Don't try to seek out ethical lapses if you have nothing more than a vague suspicion that something is wrong. Don't act on idle gossip. But don't let what I've just said be an invitation to avoid seeing or hearing things that are going on. Maybe the guidance I've heard that they give auditors—don't be suspicious, but keep your eyes open and maintain a healthy skepticism—is a pretty good policy.

"To sum up, Mike, the role of a whistleblower isn't easy. It can be distasteful, sometimes costly and even dangerous. But a person has to live with himself or herself. Don't close your eyes to avoid seeing what you know, or are almost sure, is there. Remaining silent when one knows that something wrong is going on is almost as bad as participation."

"I guess that's it," Lerner said thoughtfully. "We all like a happy ending, but there are some tough calls we can't duck, no matter what the cost. People can hope they don't come their way. And, I guess, work for the right company."

The Shipping Department Supervisor's Problem

"Now, Mike," Iverson said, "let's turn to those situations where managers or supervisors have to deal with real ethical dilemmas, ones where there are conflicting rights. We'll start with a rather routine one that a man in the course handed in yesterday. I had asked the members to prepare simple ethics vignettes, written as if they were to be published as a short story. He didn't say, but it may be one that he had seen, or he may have heard about a situation like this in his company. And it's a good example of what supervisors may run into."

Iverson handed him a paper. "It might be easier for you to read this—it'll only take a minute," he said. "I'm not violating any confidence; the writer's name isn't on this sheet. Besides, I told the class I would read some of the papers aloud as a basis for discussion at a later session, without identifying whose they are."

Handing the paper back, Lerner observed, "Not a bad writer, is he? I wish all of our students organized their thoughts that well. But regarding the problem, all of us, I guess, have to handle situations like that from time to time. What can you tell me that makes the resolution of them any easier?"

"Here, for a company as well as the individual supervisor," Iverson said, "policy is all-important as a starting point. A supervisor shouldn't have to undergo the stress, or waste the time, to start from scratch on each of these problems. And the company shouldn't run the risk of having comparable situations handled inconsistently. Also, the further you go down the chain of com-

The Case of the Irregular Employee

The head of the shipping department sat in his office, looking over the attendance record of an employee who had been with the company for 32 years and was now within two years of normal retirement. The employee's husband had died a year ago after a long illness, and she seemed to have lost much of her interest in work, and life itself. Although she had previously been regular in her attendance, during the last year she had missed a number of days because of claimed illness—illness that he suspected was largely in her mind and would not have kept her away in the past. Several times recently he had talked to her about her attendance, but the result had not been satisfactory.

His choice lay between recommending that she take early retirement or living with the situation for two more years. On the one hand, he understood that she had adequate financial means to maintain her standard of living even with a reduced pension. Some of the other employees, he knew, resented the problems her frequent absences caused and the additional burden this threw on them. A failure to act might impair his effectiveness as a supervisor. And he was well aware that the money the company was paying her could buy a lot more productivity out of a more motivated employee. He was also afraid that letting the matter drag on might create a bad precedent if similar situations should arise in the future.

He couldn't forget, however, the contribution she had made during the many years before her husband's illness and death. He was well aware that letting an older employee go could expose the company to charges of heartlessness, even age discrimination. Also, despite her recent lapses in attendance, he knew that she valued her association with the company, and he feared the effect on her of being put out to pasture. Didn't the company owe her something, he wondered? And he thought how he would wish someone to treat his wife under similar circumstances.

mand in these situations, as you may have sensed, Mike, the more the personal angle enters in. It is relatively easy to be objective about a situation when those involved are nameless and faceless; it is much more difficult when someone you see every day, someone whom you have perhaps worked with for years, is involved. That is why having a policy is so important.

"It goes without saying that the policy should be well crafted—should carefully balance the strictly business and the ethical concerns. The likelihood of a sound, moral answer is far greater with a good policy, thought through in advance, than it is with ad hoc decisions made by individual supervisors. Heartless as it may seem to manage from written rules, decisions flowing out of a good, clearly stated policy are likely to be better, more ethical, than ones decided by individuals. The personal factor is eliminated. It won't depend on whether the supervisor happened to like the employee. Or whether the supervisor has a jaundiced outlook because of the treatment he feels that he has received from a superior.

"On the other hand, though, no supervisor should disengage his or her own ethical sensibilities, relying solely on policies. No policy, I would again stress, can foresee all circumstances. It must be flexible and allow for modification through appropriate up-the-line discussions. The supervisor has a personal responsibility to be alert, to question whether the results appear ethical in applying policies to day-to-day decisions."

The Dilemma of the Shopping Center Manager

"Let's turn now to a situation where a manager in a responsible, sensitive position has to handle problems similar in nature to ones addressed by the board or top management. Just a minute, I have a short example I'd like you to read—one that a participant in the course a couple years ago gave me and that I plan to use in class tonight." Iverson pulled a sheet of paper out of his pocket and handed it to Lerner.

A Supervisor's Dilemma

A company owns a number of shopping centers in several states. Karen supervises the company's operations in the northwest quarter of one state; she has overall responsibility for eight centers of various sizes. One of the older centers in her area has several vacancies, and some of the tenants have said that they will probably move when their leases expire unless the owner does something to upgrade the center and improve traffic.

Shortly after Karen renewed the lease of a longtime tenant, a major company in a closely related line of business, which had expressed a tentative interest earlier, told her that they were seriously interested in leasing vacant space a few doors away. This would offer serious, possibly devastating, competition to the tenant that has just renewed its lease.

"Excuse me, Carl," Lerner asked as he finished reading, "before you go on, I have a question. Don't lessees in shopping centers usually protect themselves against such competition by seeing that appropriate restrictions against competing businesses are included in the lease terms? It seems to me that I've heard that somewhere."

"The very question I asked, Mike, when Karen gave me this case. She told me that that is common today. And larger, more sophisticated tenants have probably done so for some time. In this case, the longtime tenant probably hadn't thought of it."

After pausing a moment, Iverson resumed, "You can see what was bugging Karen. This development confronted her with both business and ethical problems—and see how often these are mixed together. Who had valid rights that she should consider in reaching a decision? Certainly her company had, since leasing the vacant space would not only bring in new rents but would probably help traffic in the center—that, in turn, would increase the likelihood of her leasing other vacant space, maybe even retaining some of the tenants who have been dissatisfied about traffic in the center. On the other hand, if the longtime tenant were to fail because of the competition, it would give her company a black eye in the rather closely knit community and would result in another vacancy. So it was clear that the shareholders and top management of her company were stakeholders.

"But Karen's biggest uncertainty was whether her company had any obligation to the present tenant other than what was spelled out in the lease? Did the fact that she had had an indication that something might develop while she was conducting negotiations have any bearing? Did she have any obligation to say anything to the tenant at that time?

"And what about the other tenants?" Iverson went on. "If it was likely that the prospective tenant, with its name recognition and advertising clout, would increase traffic, did the other tenants in the center deserve any consideration in whatever decision Karen makes? Did the city itself have a legitimate stake, since Karen knew that it, like many other communities, was vitally concerned about revitalizing the downtown area where the shopping center was located . . . and, of course, receiving sales tax revenues?

"A point that Karen, to her credit, told me she recognized was that she must not confuse sentiment with ethics. Part of what was worrying her was that she had known and liked the present tenant for a number of years; she dreaded taking an action that would destroy that relationship. At the same time, she knew that she could not let her personal feelings muddy up a decision of what was economically sound and morally justifiable."

"I don't envy her the task of deciding," Lerner said thoughtfully. "But did she have to handle this alone? Hadn't anyone given her any guidelines?"

"A good question . . . and one I asked Karen. She said the company had a rather general philosophy in this area, but not in writing and not specific enough to give her much guidance. Fortunately, though, top management, while very profit-oriented, tried to run an ethical operation and was open to discussions of difficult problems. She said she planned to talk with her regional vice president as soon as she got back to see what his views might be."

The Purchasing Agent's Difficult Decision

"Now, if you don't mind, Mike, I'd like to go through another example before I attempt to draw any general conclusions," Iverson continued. "Here's a situation the purchasing agent of a medium-sized manufacturing company faced. The company had experienced a slowdown, the result of an extended recession, with no end in sight. Inventory, both raw materials and finished products, was too high, and strict orders had gone out to curtail purchases and production. For one key part, the company had five suppliers, with 20 percent of the orders going to a small local fabricator. The company had used this supplier for a number of years for several reasons—demonstrated reliability, ready assistance over the years when emergencies arose, fair (but not always the lowest) prices and a desire to support local business. Besides, the purchasing agent had developed a good, if not close, relationship, with the owner.

"The agent—I'll call him Jim—had to reduce purchases by about one-fourth and had proposed cutting back all suppliers proportionately. The local supplier had immediately pleaded for special consideration, pointing out that his business was heavily tied to the company's and that he could not make out on such a reduction for any length of time. In support of his plea, he reminded Jim of his ready availability and willingness to help in numerous past crises.

"At the same time, an out-of-town supplier, a subsidiary of a major company, called and offered a special price reduction if it could retain or increase its level of orders."[2]

"What a dilemma!" Lerner observed.

"Yes, a real problem," Iverson agreed. "On the business side, times were tough, and the company could save a bundle by taking the big supplier up on its offer. And how dependable can it be

---

[2] In *The Responsible Manager: Practical Strategies for Ethical Decision Making* (San Francisco: Harper and Row Publishers, 1990), 3–5 and thereafter, author Michael Rion explores the issues involved in a similar purchasing dilemma—one that, supplemented by the price-reduction offer of a competing supplier, was the genesis of the one presented here.

to stay with a small vendor that is so vulnerable that the company's proposed 25-percent curtailment would jeopardize its viability?

"On the other hand, it's good to have several suppliers available; Jim wouldn't want to get in a spot where he would be too tied to a big supplier, especially if it had squeezed the smaller ones out. Besides, it certainly had been invaluable over the years to have ready access to a local supplier that really wanted the company's business, in good times as well as bad.

"Jim also thought about the ethics of the situation, although he might not have put it in those terms. Certainly, as a starting point, he owed the shareholders—or, as he would probably have put it, the company—the best deal he could legitimately get. But did that go beyond immediate money? Did the company have some obligation to a local supplier who had always bent over backward to help with problems? If so, what kind of a price might you put on that obligation?"

"What did he decide?" Lerner asked.

"I don't really know—I've often wondered myself. But the answer to that specific dilemma is not the reason I brought it up; my purpose is to show you the types of situations individual supervisors face . . . problems where written policies can help, but ones where ultimately the supervisor should apply ethical analysis techniques.

"Karen and Jim could both use something like the seven-step approach I went through with you and the other Hauser-Moore directors. You and I haven't time to do that now, and we don't even have all the facts we need, such as costs, in these cases—but I will identify some common threads that run through situations like this . . . cases in which a responsible manager, but not a member of top management, faces complex dilemmas that have many of the same earmarks as major strategic or policy decisions that managements or boards must handle.

"First, there should be some policy guidance available. This, in my opinion, is a key to handling situations like this. As I told your board the other evening, it should have established guidelines that identify the stakeholders it believes should be considered in strategic and policy decisions. It is no less important, probably even more so, to cover tough decisions that managers in a company are likely to face. It helps to reduce their stress and frustration. And it ensures consistent treatment by different managers in comparable situations."

"You're not suggesting, Carl, that these decisions can be routinized, are you?" Lerner asked. "It seems to me that no two dilemmas are identical. Don't we pay managers to make these tough decisions? Isn't it risky to chance forcing square pegs into round holes?"

"No, Mike, these decisions cannot be routinized," Carl replied. "As I mentioned, or at least intended to, policies should be written in general terms that allow flexibility. They should enunciate a company's philosophy but without tying a manager's hands or providing him or her with an alibi if the decision goes sour. And any manager worth his or her salt knows when to question a policy and discuss a problem with superiors; that is a sign of strength, not weakness.

"That's my second point: There should be a management structure that gives managers like Karen and Jim someone to go to with their problems without their being made to feel that they aren't handling their own jobs. Karen felt she had it; I don't know about Jim. Let's call it an ethically sensitive environment in which people can feel comfortable in sorting out problems such as these.

"But I see," Iverson noted, "that you have some telephone messages piling up. And I really don't have a whole lot to add on this, although it interests me so much that I'd probably ramble on and on if nothing stopped me."

"I wish we had more time," Lerner said rising and joining Iverson on the way to the door, "and we probably will along the way. You know, I find myself getting wrapped up in some of this. And I'm beginning to see how much good ethics is tied up with good business in some of these cases—it's certainly not the either/or situation many people assume.

"I can't help thinking it may turn out that the relocation problem was a blessing in disguise. It certainly has focused the

Hauser-Moore board's attention on the ethical implications of its actions. Not that it was ever knowingly unethical—George Hauser would never have put up with that. And much of his sense of integrity permeates Hauser-Moore, I am convinced. But his personal influence was already waning with his reduced day-to-day participation. And we can see that Dick Bentley didn't have the same outlook—although I do not believe he was dishonest, at least in the conventional sense. It was just that he was more opportunistic, not as interested in things other than the near-term bottom line.

"As I told George when all this broke and I got him to invite you for the first session with the board, a company cannot take its ethics for granted; it is something that requires nurture. Part of the answer, I guess, is increased sensitivity. The rest is to have a well-designed program."

They parted, agreeing to have lunch together soon.

CHAPTER SIX

Some Tough Soul Searching

A lot happens at a company like Hauser-Moore below the board level—sometimes things that the board never learns about, or learns about too late. Let's spend a little time with one of the Hauser-Moore employees, a person you met briefly in Chapter 1 but whose name may have slipped your mind—Tim Saunders.

As he is finding, behaving ethically is not always easy. Ethical dilemmas have a way of sneaking up on a person. Sometimes they are hard to recognize at the time; if recognized, there may not seem to be a clear-cut answer between right and wrong. A person's self-interest often gets in the way and confuses the issues. And occasionally a person may have to pay a price for making an ethical decision.

Spelling Out His Problem

Saunders and an old friend, John Stratton, had just met and were catching up on recent news over a drink. After a while John observed that Tim seemed distracted, even a bit on edge, and asked if anything was bothering him. Tim shifted uneasily in his chair, absently toying with the empty ashtray; then after a brief pause admitted, "You're right, John, I am a bit worried—about something at the office. That's why I asked you to meet me—so I could bounce something off someone I trust, someone who has no axe to grind.

"Maybe I'm making a mountain out of a molehill, but the problem I want to talk about is really bugging me. I haven't said anything to Joan, since she's getting ready for next Thursday's move to our new house. Besides, she probably couldn't be objective."

"Sure, Tim," John responded, "I'll be glad to listen and give you any thoughts I have, which will probably be worth about what you pay for them. After all, I know next to nothing about your work. If the matter is as difficult as you seem to think, I may not even understand."

"That's no problem. What I'm bothered about isn't technical; in fact, you'll probably grasp my concern better if you don't get bogged down in the details. I'll start at the beginning."

Tim leaned back and began, "Last spring my boss—you've heard me speak of Harry Burns, a real nice guy who's done a lot for me—called me in and said that the company was going to expand one of its product lines. The top management was trying to decide whether to keep production here, which would require a major expansion and retooling, or to move it out of state near some of our major customers. He gave me a lot of background information and asked me to make a comparative cost study of the two alternatives. He stressed the importance of the study—said he thought it would be a good opportunity for me to broaden my exposure within the company."

"Isn't that when you called last spring, saying that you were too busy to join our annual fraternity golf outing?

"That's right, John; you've got a good memory. Well, Harry called several people while I was there, generally outlining what was going on, warning them that it was confidential and asking them to give me any cost data and analyses I might ask for. He told me to get back to him if I ran into any roadblocks or needed to talk over assumptions.

"I got right at it, since I knew they wanted to make a decision within a month. Of course, I had to make a number of assumptions, but that didn't bother me because most of them seemed pretty clear; besides, I discussed the work with Harry every day or so as I went along, and he agreed with the approach I was taking.

"The only thing that really bothered me in a big way," Tim continued, "was some of the costs of closing down the line here—removal costs, environmental studies for site cleanup, employee termination payments—all that kind of stuff, you know. Quite a bit of detail and a major factor in any cost to relocate. Joe Hendricks, the manufacturing manager, gave these to me, but he wasn't particularly helpful in supplying details or support. I was a little surprised that the total wasn't bigger, but Joe got impatient when I tried to press him—told me in so many words that he knew his business better than I did. Perhaps the chemistry between us isn't the greatest; he obviously resented it when I caught an embarrassing mistake of his last year.

"Well, the upshot was that I decided to accept his figures and not create a fuss. After all, Joe has a lot of experience and was pretty close to the CEO—the one who just left, you may have seen that in the paper. Besides, I'd been told where to get figures, but no one told me to go behind what I was given and check them out."

"Sounds reasonable to me," John interjected, smiling encouragingly.

"Yeah," Tim said. "It probably is."

Reservations about Some of the Figures

But he still looked uneasy. He remained silent, unable to shake the thought that he had really had serious misgivings about Joe's figures at the time; they hadn't rung true. And, a matter he didn't mention to John, Tim couldn't forget what he had told his boss. When Harry asked him point blank whether he felt comfortable with all the underlying detail, he had said yes. In fact he recalled

Harry's specifically mentioning that sometimes Joe was a little careless with figures —didn't like to be questioned—and was glad to know that Tim felt good about the ones he had provided. Now, Tim couldn't help asking himself why he hadn't pressed harder with Joe . . . or at least indicated his uneasiness to Harry. In retrospect, it seemed foolish, unnecessary.

Could it have been that he didn't want to antagonize the CEO's friend, he wondered? Or could he have been influenced by the rumor that the CEO hoped the study results would support relocation? Or was he just too anxious to get done? He sat, drumming on the table, as he continued to agonize over his problem.

Finally, seeing that Tim was lost in thought, John volunteered, "But there must be something more to it. How did the job end?"

Tim brightened for a moment as he recalled, "The study showed that it would be much better—cost-wise, that is—to relocate than it would be to keep the new line here. Harry was so much impressed with the organization and flow of my final report that he asked me to accompany him and make the presentation to the board of directors. It went smoother than I could have believed and, after complimenting Harry and me on our presentation and excusing us, the board authorized the relocation to Hendersonville. It was announced a few days later, and many steps required to get things going are under way. A date has been announced for closing the product line here and opening it there. Employees here have been told about termination arrangements, and plans have been made for hiring and training at the new plant. The company has bought a plant site there; I understand a building initially intended for someone else was already started. And negotiations are almost complete for contracts involved in cleaning up facilities here and completing the building we bought.

"The other night, though, I woke up thinking that those figures Joe had given me just couldn't be right. My subconscious must have been nagging me. I got up early the next morning, Saturday, and went through them; in fact, I spent the whole weekend looking at them from every angle. I still don't have proof positive—that would require more information from Joe—but I am 99 percent sure that he left out certain removal costs and underestimated termination payments, intentionally or otherwise. And, if my estimate is anywhere near correct, it means that we may have come to the wrong answer; it might be more economical to retool and expand here—possibly by a fair amount."

What to Do, If Anything

"Have you told Harry?" John asked.

"No. I was about to, but I wanted to think it through before putting him in the middle. After all, he stuck his neck out by selecting me to make the study, then went out of his way to see that I got credit for the work. In fact, that's probably why I got a big raise a couple months ago. He'd probably be in the soup with me if anything goes wrong."

"Yeah, Tim, I see what you mean about talking to Harry, at least for the moment. But let's look at it another way. Surely all the figures that went into the study aren't that firm. You mentioned assumptions; besides, it will be at least a year or so, won't it, before the actual move? And then it'll be a while before operations settle down. Maybe the advantage to staying put is not as clear-cut as you now suspect. Besides, there'll be a lot of other changes in the meanwhile—there always are—and perhaps no one will ever be able to pinpoint any mistake, if there even was one. After all, you don't absolutely *know* that Joe's figures were wrong; you just suspect it."

"That's true," Tim responded slowly. "I don't know for sure. But can I cop out on that? I've told myself the same thing, more than once, but I haven't been able to get it out of my mind that I have an obligation to find out. After all—"

"Just a minute," John interrupted. "Let me play devil's advocate. The move has been announced. Didn't you tell me most of the contracts have already been negotiated? Maybe even signed by now? What use is there in locking the barn after the horse has bolted? What would happen now if you told people about this? Could they reverse field even if they wanted to? You'd probably do serious damage to Harry's future in the company, to say nothing of yours. For what good?

"And another thing, what if you're wrong?" he continued. "You'll never know if you don't get information from Joe. If you ask for it, you won't get it without creating a big ruckus, if I understand Joe from what you've told me. If you do get it and find that you were wrong, you'll look like a damn fool. Even if you were to find that Joe had been wrong, he could always say that he gave you whatever you asked for and that if you hadn't been satisfied, you should have spoken up then. As far as I can see, you are in a no-win situation if you open up this can of worms."

"Perhaps, John, you're right. I may be too close to the problem to see things clearly. I just don't know. At least it's been helpful getting the matter off my chest. I'll give it some more thought because I've got to put the matter to bed soon, one way or the other. And thanks for your help—as always—and tell Peggy I appreciate her giving me part of your evening. I'll let you know what happens."

Tim paid the bill; they walked out and parted with a handshake at the corner. Then Tim walked slowly to his car. The decision that John's questions and comments seemed to be pushing him toward—to let sleeping dogs lie—might be the best under the circumstances. And he could always tell himself—or anyone else, if the mistake ever came out—that it had been an honest error.

But he couldn't get out of his mind the fact that the company was likely to lose money because of what he had done, a loss that might still be avoided or at least reduced if the decision could be reversed. In addition, he was haunted, as he had been the last couple nights, by the faces of the terminated workers, long-term employees with stunned looks, he had seen a couple months ago coming out of the meeting when management announced the relocation . . . a relocation, he knew, that was resulting because of what he now feared was his flawed study.

What should he do, he still wondered? He knew he would probably spend a few more nights tossing and turning as he mulled over his problem.

Resolution of Saunders's Problem

Several weeks later, George Hauser and Stuart Andretti were having lunch together. They were old friends, as their families had been for years, and they got together whenever either was in the other's hometown. Because these meetings gave Hauser a chance to discuss company matters informally with a fellow director, in depth and on a relaxed basis, he always looked forward to these opportunities. With all the stress still remaining from Bentley's resignation, the search for a successor, and continuing strains resulting from the plant relocation, the chance to talk now was particularly welcome.

"Well, George," Andretti said, "I gather that the other directors agreed that the move should go forward despite learning that the study we had been given earlier had a serious error. I assume you were able to reach all of them. What did you tell them?"

"The straight facts," Hauser replied. "I didn't have any choice. I didn't go into any details except to answer any questions, but I basically told each of them that an error had been uncovered and that, instead of a $3.5-million benefit in moving, the revised figure was only a little over $1.6 million. I said it was something that dropped through the crack between a couple people—nothing deliberate.

"I went on to say that I still recommended sticking to the decision to relocate that we had made earlier. I based this, I told them, on several factors. First, the $1.6 million is still a pretty good savings. Second, we have announced the move, notified the employees who are being terminated, let some contracts for work to begin in Hendersonville and demolition to start here—a lot of stuff like that. Although I'd reverse everything if we had been seriously wrong, it would have been costly and would have created a very serious credibility problem for the company."

"Did all the directors agree?" Andretti asked.

"Yes, although Janice Freeland pressed me whether I was completely satisfied now that the figures are reliable. I told her that we had checked and double-checked—as we should have in the first place—and that I was personally willing to vouch for the care and reasonableness."

"I'd be surprised," Andretti said, "if no one asked what your initial position would have been if you had had the $1.6-million figure instead of $3.5 million earlier."

"Mike Lerner did," Hauser responded, "and the question was implicit in the discussion with Larry. I covered it with both of them as accurately as I could. It was hard, of course, to put myself in the position of several months ago so, try as I would, I couldn't really say what I would have done.

"I told them, though, that I would probably have supported the move even with the lesser indicated savings. After all, $1.6 million is a lot of money. And I would have been strongly influenced by Lerner's comments about the economic long-term climate for heavy industry here—although I would probably have insisted on a lot more discussion of that. Still, it would have been a lot harder for me. As you may recall, I answered Carl Iverson by saying that I would have opted for staying if the indicated savings had been $500,000. I don't know where I would have fallen off between there and $1.6 million. Maybe it's just as well I didn't have to face that."

"Did anyone get into personalities—ask who'd screwed up?" Andretti asked. "It would be a natural question; in fact, I wonder myself."

"In a way," Hauser came back. "I gave them some general answers, covered any specific questions, but I didn't see any point in making it seem as if we were looking for scapegoats. Indeed, responsibility for this runs fairly high, and I certainly don't exclude myself. We may have gotten sloppy. That and some of the ethical implications are things I'd like to discuss with you—now, if you have time.

"Sure," Andretti replied.

"Fine, but I think it would be better to go back to my office to do that," Hauser said. After a few more minutes on other matters, they got up and left, stopping for a few words with some friends as they went out.

Developments Leading to Disclosure of Mistake

Back in the office, Hauser asked, "Do you want me to start at the beginning?" Seeing Andretti's nod, Hauser began, "A couple weeks ago, Harry Burns called and said that he, Joe Hendricks, manager of manufacturing operations, and Tim Saunders needed to meet with me—that it was rather urgent. As they walked in here a few minutes later, I gathered we had a problem. All three, but particularly Burns and Saunders, looked quite nervous.

"Burns opened the discussion. Three days before, Saunders had told him that he had been turning the Series F cost study over in his mind the last week or so and was convinced that the indicated savings from relocation were overstated. As he had thought about it, he had concluded that the costs to close down here were understated, probably significantly. He didn't have anything specific but had concluded that the results just didn't make sense.

"According to Burns, he had initially tried to reassure Saunders, who was quite upset by the whole thing; then, after sitting down and going over the figures, he began to understand what was bothering Tim. At that point, he decided there was nothing to do but go to Hendricks, who had given them the figures, and settle the matter, one way or the other, for once and for all."

"What did Hendricks say? I've met him several times, and from what I've heard he doesn't take kindly to being challenged."

"You're right, Stu," Hauser said. "It didn't come out directly at this meeting, but from what I learned later I gather that he initially told Burns to go to hell—not to come bothering him when he was busy with some cock-and-bull story about something that was done and settled. But Harry, to his credit, stuck to his guns and told Hendricks they were going to get to the bottom of this—if they had to get my backing first, he'd go for it.

"Apparently Hendricks simmered down and offered to let them see the support for everything he'd given Saunders if they'd get at it promptly and close the file for good. Well, Saunders and Burns together went over everything with a fine-toothed comb the next two days. The upshot was that they didn't find anything wrong with Joe's figures—other, of course, than the usual nits and differences that are bound to be found in such detailed figures.

"What they did find, though," Hauser continued, "was that the costs of some important things that they expected, things that they assumed Hendricks had included, were nowhere to be found. When they hit Joe with these, he replied that of course they weren't in his figures—part of those, he said, should come from engineering, the rest from human resources. You aren't interested, I know, Stu, in the details, but they involved environmental studies, some of the termination payments, and a bunch of miscellaneous details."

"But shouldn't someone have found this?" Andretti asked. "Overlooking $1.9 million of costs when the indicated savings is only $3.5 million is incredible. What did you say?"

"I guess I blew up," Hauser replied. "I let them know in no uncertain terms that this was inexcusably sloppy work—something that might cost the company millions of dollars, to say nothing of the impact on its credibility. I hadn't yet, you see, assimilated the results enough to know whether we might have to revamp all our plans.

"After that, we spent the next couple hours going through all the details. I wanted to satisfy myself that what we now had was something that we could rely on, that we wouldn't find in a few weeks or months that there were some other holes in the study big enough to drive a Mack truck through. Burns and Saunders, of course, assured me that that was no problem, but I'd pretty well lost confidence in any assurance they might give me.

While they were there I gave explicit instructions for someone completely independent to check out the whole study over the next week and report directly to me on what he found. As it turned out, to jump ahead in my story, the study did turn out to be essentially reliable except for this one big error."

"But what about the people involved—Burns, Hendricks, and Saunders? What are you doing about them?"

"That, Stu, is something I want to go over. And to discuss the ethical implications, something I might not have focused on if we hadn't been having these sessions with Carl Iverson."

"The ethical issues? I guess I hadn't thought of ethics being involved in this—but, of course, it has to be. Have you talked to Iverson about them?"

"No," Hauser replied. "It may sound silly, but I am sensitive about all this. I don't want to start asking someone outside the company how we ought to look at everything, no matter how much we may like him and how much I am sure he respects our confidence. Besides, I've been doing a lot of reading of the material he passed out and other stuff he recommended and feel confident of being able to pass on some of this myself.

"That doesn't mean, Stu," he continued, "that I wouldn't look for advice if we had a problem that required it . . . or that I may not want to discuss my thoughts with Carl later. He will be coming in soon to work with our committee on the ethics program the board has authorized. For the moment, though, I'm a bit touchy on this whole study and relocation mess and don't care to discuss it any more, unless it is necessary, with anyone else."

"I sure understand, George. Shall we get into some of the details now?"

The Role of Tim Saunders

Hauser said that he had decided while going over the study with Hendricks, Burns, and Saunders that he would talk later with each of them individually. He was still upset and thought it might not be the best time until he could cool off a bit. Further, he knew any discussion would probably be frank and critical, maybe painfully so, and he realized that discussions of that type should be private. He decided to start with Saunders and asked him to come in at ten the next morning.

Saunders had looked very nervous as he entered, Hauser said, and he had tried to put him at ease. He stressed the good features of the study and then asked Saunders for his explanation of how the error occurred.

"I'm interested in what he said," Andretti commented, "and how he said it. That's a tough mistake to explain."

"I must say," Hauser replied, "that he handled himself very well—seemed to be open and candid and didn't try to pass the buck. He admitted that Joe Hendricks had probably intimidated him—Joe can be rather formidable and there was something I didn't quite catch that had created a bit of a strain between them last year. He had asked for backup but then didn't press for it when Hendricks stonewalled him. He said that he knew Hendricks had a good reputation around the company and decided he could accept the material from him without seeing all the support."

"Why didn't he discuss this with Burns? That would seem to be natural."

"Yes, and I never got a really satisfactory answer. I can guess, though. By the time Saunders got back to Burns, he felt committed and had pretty well rationalized away any problem. He probably thought that he would look silly now if he and Burns went back for something he had backed down on earlier. I suspect he didn't think there was a big risk and that he'd rather take that than to appear weak and indecisive. That's just my guess, but I think I'm right."

"Then whatever made him start having second thoughts? And strong enough ones to make him raise the question with Burns?" Andretti asked.

"That's the real question," Hauser said, "and I suspect Saunders doesn't even really know. I think he always knew, subconsciously, that he hadn't really done what he should have. It began to grow on him. He admitted to me that he was concerned about the people who were losing their jobs; he didn't want it on his conscience that it had happened because of a mistake of his. He kept rehashing the figures in his mind and finally concluded they didn't quite make sense. After studying them and agonizing a few days, he decided he had to talk to Burns."

"Did he talk to anyone else first?"

"Yes, but the wrong person," Hauser said. "He said he discussed the problem with an old college friend—no one in the company. It didn't even seem to occur to him that this was wrong until I told him—that he was dealing with confidential company information, information that he had no right to disclose to unauthorized persons. I pointed out how devastating such information could be in the wrong hands—if it should become public. He'd never even thought of that angle, but then he said that his friend was someone who would never talk out of turn. I made clear, though, that that was beside the point, that he had no right to take it on himself to decide such matters. I think he understands now."

"Did his friend counsel him to disclose his concern?"

"Interestingly, Stu, I don't think so. The friend, I believe, tried to convince him that it wasn't a problem—a problem, anyway, that he could do anything about at this stage. But Saunders finally couldn't buy in on that.

"And that brings up what I consider another interesting ethical point. I think the friend, with the best of intentions, tried to help Saunders avoid the problem. But it turns out that he wasn't really doing him a favor; Tim really knew he had a problem, and he wanted someone to level with him. This is a case that really demonstrates to me that honesty, telling it like it is, is the best answer. Saunders wanted sound help, and he didn't get it—and I think his friend should have recognized it."

"Did Burns give him a hard time when he went to him?"

"Not really, which is both Harry's strength and his weakness. He initially thought Saunders was overreacting—that he was dreaming up problems—but he heard him out. Finally he dug into the figures and saw the problem. Then he agreed that they had to pursue the matter.''

"I wonder," mused Andretti, "what Saunders would have done if Burns had told him to forget it."

"I came out and asked him. I could see that he had thought about this. He said that if Burns had really convinced him he was wrong, he would, of course, have dropped the matter. Otherwise, he told me, he had already decided he'd have to bring the matter to my attention. But now, if you have time, let's look at it from Burns's perspective. I had him in to talk the next afternoon.''

The Part Burns Played

"Harry Burns has always been an enigma to me. Loyal, smart as a whip, and very personable. Grasps concepts almost immediately. He's considerate to those who work for him. But he just doesn't get into details—avoids them, I'd say. The thing that's always saved him is his ability to select people, and to take care of them.

"Saunders never said it, but reading between the lines I could see that Harry hadn't given him much supervision—and hadn't really dug into the results when Saunders finished. Talked to him, asked some questions, but wasn't very probing.''

"Maybe," Andretti said, "he was distancing himself to avoid responsibility."

"That's something that would come to one's mind. But in Harry Burns's case, I don't think it's true. If it had been, he wouldn't have been so willing to step up and accept responsibility when the mistake came out. He would have tried to talk Saunders out of pursuing the matter; if that hadn't worked, he'd have tried to wash his hands of it. He would have made a big point of the fact—one that Tim mentioned—that he had even asked specifically if Saunders was satisfied with Hendricks's figures.

"There's no question," Hauser continued, "that there were some ethical lapses as well as poor business judgment on Harry's part. He put a young man, at a critical stage in his career, in a difficult situation and did not give him the support he deserved. He didn't help lay out the job and he didn't see that the results had the necessary critique. He didn't follow through on his obligation to either the company or Saunders."

"But he didn't try to pass the buck," Andretti observed.

"That's right, and that's a plus. Also, I am sure that, misguided as his actions may have been, he honestly wanted to give Saunders a chance to shine. One thing I've always noticed about Harry, he's not selfish."

"What are you going to do about him—and, of course, Saunders?" Andretti asked.

"I had a blunt talk with Harry—he deserves that. I told him that he had let everyone down on this—that he couldn't look for any promotion this year, or maybe ever unless he gets more tough-minded and gets into the details of whatever he is responsible for. I doubt if he's really going to change—he's probably at a dead end. At his age and with 31 years under his belt with Hauser-Moore, I certainly am not going to crucify him. And he does have good qualities. We'll find a place to use those but not risk his inattention to details, as we should have before."

"How did he take it?"

"I'm not sure how much our conversation surprised him—or will even upset him after he's had a chance to think about it. He may have recognized that he lacks something to move into any higher management ranks. People frequently do, as you know, and are almost relieved when the uncertainty is put to rest.

"And to his credit," Hauser went on, "he expressed concern about Tim Saunders. He was afraid he'd let Saunders down and had wrecked his career. I reassured him on that, telling him that Saunders is young and, in my view, has quite a bit of potential. He may even come out better after this fiasco. I think that made Burns feel better."

The Stonewalling by Hendricks

"How did your talk with Joe Hendricks go?" Andretti asked.

"I've regarded him as one of the most promising managers in the company, and I was terribly disappointed to find him involved in this mess. And I sure told him so."

"What was his excuse?"

"He didn't really have one," Hauser answered. "He was embarrassed and admitted that he'd given Saunders a hard time. It wasn't that he was holding anything out, certainly not that he meant to do anything that would hurt the study. He thought that the information he gave Saunders was all he needed, and he just hadn't wanted to waste time explaining. He didn't give a thought to the whole picture.

"I pointed out how serious the consequences could have been. Also, that in a company everyone has to work together—that no one has a right to guard his own territory and keep others out. I went on to tell him that he has good prospects in the company but that, to realize them, he must learn to have more respect for the feelings, the rights, of others. He tends to be so goal-oriented that he rides roughshod over anyone who gets in his way, and I told him this would hurt his progress in the company unless he can learn to cooperate better with others."

"How did he take it?"

"Quite well, I think," Hauser replied, "although we have to recognize that he wasn't in a good position to argue. He looked rather chastened—and he should've been. But it won't hurt; he has enough self-confidence and self-esteem to recover."

"Anything else?" Andretti asked.

Hauser's Confession

"Yes—and you're the only one I'll tell this to. I recognize that I bear a heavy responsibility in this whole situation—not anything I did, but what I didn't do. I let myself get too detached—turned everything over to Dick Bentley too fast. Probably I wasn't even fair to him by throwing him into an unfamiliar situation without enough thought to the transition. He undoubtedly welcomed having a rather free rein, and I may have even rationalized I was doing him a favor. But I let the company down. I lost sight of Hauser-Moore's traditions and let it become just another company, entirely too focused on the bottom line, too easily.

"Bentley was at fault in not keeping me posted on the study, but I knew it was going on and didn't ask any questions. I'd heard that Harry Burns was responsible for the study, and I knew Harry and his weaknesses well enough that I should have at least told Bentley that the work would require some checking.

"Perhaps, Stu, that is one reason I'm letting Burns down a little easier than I would have otherwise; I should never have let him get in that position. Harry's father was a good friend of Dad's, and I may have focused too much over the years on his good qualities and overlooked his weaknesses.

"Aside from that, though, when the results came in, I should have asked for more details and have insisted that the work be thoroughly checked. I blame myself greatly for letting the study go out without more checking and for letting the board act on it so fast.

"All in all," Hauser concluded sadly, "I think the whole mess discloses a little dry rot that set in at Hauser-Moore, probably even before I stepped down as CEO, and it is something I intend to address before we get a successor to Bentley. I want to restore whatever we may have lost of our tradition, our firm culture."

"Well, George," Andretti observed, "I don't know whether you need to blame yourself that much, but I hear what you're saying. And I don't want you to accuse me of being like Tim Saunders's friend—telling you what I think you'd like to hear rather than the truth. Sometimes we all get too detached. But if you can put Hauser-Moore back on the course set by your father and yourself, this soul searching will have been worthwhile."

And with that, Stuart Andretti got up, shook Hauser's hand, and agreed to join him, with their wives, for dinner a week from Saturday.

PART THREE

Aspects of a Corporate Ethics Program

CHAPTER SEVEN

Ethics Can Be Taught

It is now two months since Carl Iverson last met with the board of Hauser-Moore Manufacturing Company. A couple weeks ago, the board had authorized George Hauser to retain Iverson to advise the company on the development of an ethics program. Iverson had agreed and had advised Hauser that he should appoint a steering committee composed of several executives, not primarily officers, who would have a sincere interest and would bring a practical perspective to bear on any proposals. He went on to say that there should be a clear indication that the program had support from the top; to Iverson's delight, Hauser said he would chair the committee.

After consultation with Iverson, Hauser had selected his committee, giving consideration to a number of factors. Aside from the critical qualities of independent thinking—even outspokenness—and leadership, he had looked for diversity—age, sex, and field of expertise. He had wanted people who would be receptive to new ideas but, at the same time, would challenge anything that did not make sense. He had sought people who not only would bring different perspectives to bear on issues but also would have the respect of employees throughout the organization, an essential factor in the later implementation of any program that would be developed. In addition to himself, the committee consisted of:

- Andrew O'Malley, director of human relations. A contemplative but firm man, O'Malley (age 45) looked out for the company's interests in establishing and administering personnel policies but, at the same time, was regarded as a warm, sympathetic executive.
- Sarah Stevenson, assistant director of engineering. Under a no-nonsense, almost brusque exterior, 37-year-old Stevenson was known as a fair and thoughtful administrator as well as a skilled professional.
- Joseph Hendricks, manager of manufacturing operations. Hendricks, 41 years old, had a reputation as an achiever, a bit hard-boiled. Sometimes careless of others in his impatience to get a job done, he was losing some of his abrasiveness with experience and was generally regarded as a "comer" at Hauser-Moore.
- Cynthia Downs, director of internal auditing. Downs, 33, had been hired from Hauser-Moore's auditing firm six years ago and had been named to her present job last year. Although relatively quiet, she was known to be tenacious and goal-oriented, but with an ability to work well with people.

Other than George Hauser, the only committee member previously encountered—or, rather, heard of—in our story is Joe Hendricks, the manager who had created the problem for Tim Saunders. His inclusion may come as something of a surprise, but Hauser had concluded that the difficulty had resulted from Hendricks's manner and, possibly, insensitivity, not from an intent to mislead Saunders. Hauser valued him as a promising, incisive executive and hoped that his service on the committee would not only add a useful viewpoint but would also help to make Hendricks aware of obligations that leaders in the company have toward others, particularly those junior to themselves.

Background of Ethics Program Explained

The committee, along with Carl Iverson, had begun its initial meeting at 8:30 a.m. in the small conference room next to Hauser's office. Hauser had told the members to block out the entire day for the meeting, not making or accepting any telephone calls except for emergencies. He began with a brief explanation of the background for the proposed ethics program, pointing out that he had been thinking about one for some time but that certain recent developments had convinced him and other members of the board that now was the time to get started.

The recent decision to locate the new small engine plant in Hendersonville, Hauser told the committee, had triggered the creation of the committee. Without going into names or details, he said that the board had been forced to make a fast decision without the consideration it would have wished about the impact on affected employees, suppliers, and the community at large. Iverson, who was leading a section of Trinity's executive training program, had met twice with the board to discuss the role of ethics in business decisions.

Subsequently, Hauser continued, some questions had arisen regarding the reliability of the cost study on which the relocation decision had largely been based. Although management and the board had satisfied themselves that, despite some errors in the study, the right decision had been reached, matters that came out in a review of the study reinforced the conclusion that this was an appropriate time to put an ethics program in place at Hauser-Moore. As a result, the board had authorized such a program, and he had appointed this committee to advise him on its implementation.

With those opening remarks and a brief introduction, Hauser turned the meeting over to Iverson. "I'm delighted to be with you today," Iverson began, "and I look forward to working with you in the development of the Hauser-Moore ethics program. George has told me a bit about your backgrounds, and I think we have an excellent mixture of experience and talent to accomplish what we have in mind. And I want each of you to realize that we must work as a team, informally and candidly. If I say anything that is unclear or that you disagree with, speak up—and I'll do the same with you. This has to be a joint effort. But first, I want to describe the ethical background—the guidelines and constraints—that will influence what we do."

For the next hour and a half, Iverson outlined ethical concepts, his view of a company's role in ethics, and how the individual fits into this picture. The discussion was lively, with occasional differences in views emerging as the various members interrupted with questions and comments, particularly when the matter of rights came up.

A Concern about Rights Gridlock

"Carl," Sarah Stevenson spoke up, "conceptually I have no problem with the rights and obligations approach you suggest, although I'm afraid people today place more emphasis on the rights than they do on the obligations. But I am bothered about the practicalities in the real world. I not only read the material you sent out, I also read a recent article—or rather a couple articles—in *The Wilson Quarterly* [1] that I brought with me. If you don't mind, I'd like to read a few sentences:

> Scarcely a question now comes before the American public without some fundamental issue of rights being invoked. There is said to be a right to life and a right to die, and a right governing virtually everything that might occur between the exercise of these two prerogatives. There are said to be women's rights, gay rights, and handicapped rights, a right to work and a right to smoke, to name only a few. To a degree that must astonish even Western Europeans, concern about rights animates many contemporary American public debates—over

---

[1] "What Are the Rights of the People": James H. Hutson, "A Nauseous Project," and Gary L. McDowell, "Rights without Roots," *The Wilson Quarterly* (Winter 1991), 56–82.

judicial nominations, congressional legislation, federal grants to "artists," even performances by pop music stars.

and then further on:

The very idea of rights has been cheapened by the widespread use of rights rhetoric to morally inflate what are, in reality, only policy preferences—over everything from abortion to affirmative action. And the transformation of ordinary political questions into non-negotiable questions of right has diminished our public life, turning the give-and-take of normal debate into all-or-nothing clashes.

In the process, we have become increasingly confused about what rights are and how they are best preserved . . .

Stevenson continued, "Now I'm not climbing on a soapbox, but I am concerned that we may get all tied up in knots resolving company problems by paying too much attention to whatever someone may assert are his or her rights."

"Right on, Sarah," Joseph Hendricks broke in. "Just the other day I read about a French company that proposed installing public pay toilets in New York, at no cost to the city . . . apparently very attractive, and badly needed, facilities. There was an immediate outcry about handicapped access, so the company offered to make some of them accessible to the handicapped. That, it turns out, was completely unacceptable to the handicapped advocates, even when it was pointed out that public space limitations would make it physically impossible to enlarge all the toilets to accommodate the handicapped. At that point, as I recall, the president of the French company said, in effect, 'You Americans may have rights, but in Paris we have toilets—and you haven't!'

"That, Carl," Hendricks continued, "is the sort of thing that worries me about this rights business. Don't think I'm not sympathetic to the plight of the handicapped—what I've cited is only an example, not the focus of my concern. It's broader. Where's the trade-off when rights or benefits for some, but not all, can be honored? Is it all or nothing? Are we going to get ourselves into a gridlock where we can do nothing in the company because, every time an issue comes up, we start worrying about all these competing rights and become immobilized?"

"A very legitimate concern," Iverson responded, "and one for which I don't have a pat answer. I could say that we are a part of American society and can't escape its problems as well as its advantages, but that is no real answer. What I would rather have us focus on are specifics.

"Everyone would agree," he went on, "that there *are* rights a company should observe; for example, shareholders obviously have rights. Many people, as we have discussed, believe others have rights—employees, suppliers, customers, segments of the community in which a company operates. Unlike the broad societal concerns expressed in the article from which Sarah read, however, the company can, and should, limit those to whom it has responsibility."

"How is that?" Cynthia Downs asked.

"Because, as I said a while ago when reviewing the limits on corporate ethical responsibilities, the corporation is, by its very nature, restricted to the conduct of business for profit.[2] That means that it has ethical responsibilities only to those directly affected by its business operations. Everyone, I grant you, will not put the outer limits at the same spot—that is, identify the same stakeholders; but at least it means that each company can and should have a defined sphere of stakeholder responsibilities.

"Different people," Iverson continued, "will have different views of just how far the rights of those agreed-upon stakeholders extend. That is a further point on which a company's board and management should reach broad agreement. Once that is done, a company is operating within an agreed-upon area of acknowledged rights. That doesn't mean, of course, that someone outside—or maybe even inside—might not challenge the definition, but that would be the case even if the company didn't define its responsibility in the first place—didn't even think about rights.

---

[2] See Chapter 2, page 64, for reference to a differing viewpoint, one that holds that a corporation has broader social responsibilities.

"What I'm trying to say is that your concern about rights gridlock, in society or even in a company, is legitimate. But I would argue that we cannot ignore rights just because of what we might consider abuses. A company can define the stakeholders to whom it believes it has an obligation and the general nature of that obligation. This should enable it to avoid getting tied up in a lot of claimed rights that it does not consider relevant to its business, to its ethical responsibilities."

After several minutes of general discussion, Iverson suggested a 10-minute break, following which he would get into the main topics he hoped to cover in this initial session.

Returning from Hauser's office to the conference room, Iverson observed, "I think, George, you've got the right mix on the committee. They certainly are outspoken, particularly Joe Hendricks and Sarah Stevenson, but not in a negative way. The chemistry seems right—at least at this stage."

They reentered the room, and Iverson said, "Now it's time to get down to the nitty-gritty. There are three matters, or rather questions, that I hope we can cover today:

- Can ethics be taught?
- What should go into a company ethics program?
- Is business ethics worthwhile?

"It's really hard to say which should come first because they are closely intertwined. For example, some—not everyone, I know, but some—might say that everything else is irrelevant and need not be addressed if ethics isn't good business. Someone else might say that there's no use proceeding if we can't change people; that is, if we can't teach them ethics. I understand all of these arguments but am confronted with the need to start somewhere, and I prefer to examine first the question of whether ethics can be taught, at least to adults."

Appropriateness of Ethics Training

"Excuse me, Carl," Sarah Stevenson interrupted, "but aren't we putting the cart before the horse? Isn't ethics a personal matter? Before addressing whether ethics can be taught, I'd have questions as to whether ethics should be taught."

"A very good question," Iverson responded. "At the risk of voicing a cliché, I'm glad you asked it. It is something that I skipped over that we should cover now. To do so, I am going to make an important distinction, one that I want to be sure all of us keep clearly in mind throughout our discussion.[3]

"In my opinion, we should not, and perhaps could not even if we wished, teach moral standards of behavior, as such—the goals, norms, beliefs, and values held by a person. These are personal and reflect the teachings and experiences of a lifetime. I think this is what some people have in mind when they say, as I'm sure you've heard, that you can't teach people ethics. They tell you that a person's ethics is something learned at home, in church, and in school, pretty well established in a person's early years. Trying to inculcate these by lecture would be a waste of time—and wrong, since it would amount to little more than indoctrination.

"We can appropriately, however," Iverson continued, "teach ethical analysis. That is what we discussed—very briefly, I'll admit—in our earlier discussion this morning when we considered ethical models and then went briefly through the seven-step approach I said might be used to deal with ethical dilemmas. Note that nowhere in that discussion did I endorse any particular moral standards; instead I focused on a consideration of rights and obligations. And even there I didn't tell you—in fact, I couldn't have told you—how to identify and value the various rights and obligations involved in solving a dilemma. So, you see, teaching ethical

---

[3] Much of the discussion that follows immediately reflects ideas gleaned from LaRue Tone Hosmer, "Adding Ethics to the Business Curriculum," *Business Horizons* (July–August 1988), 9–15, although the author assumes responsibility for any condensations and interpretations.

analysis does not result in a teacher's imposing his or her set of values on those being instructed."

"If that is the case," Stevenson came back, "what's the use of the instruction? If there is no common denominator so far as moral standards are concerned, where does all this lead us—out of the woods or deeper into them? Aren't we going to be all over the lot?"

"It may look that way," Iverson admitted, "but I believe the picture will come together more clearly in a bit. I'll ask your indulgence, Sarah, and perhaps some of the rest of you, to put a couple building blocks in place before we get to the important question you just posed.

"First, I want to emphasize that the training we will be talking about this morning is for managers, not for the rank and file within the company. We shall—"

"Just a minute, please," Andrew O'Malley said. "I'm no flaming liberal, but I think that has a bad sound, rather elitist."

"You can't be serious, Andy," Joe Hendricks broke in. "We're not talking about different drinking fountains for managers and the rest of the organization. Managers may have different needs in ethics training just as they have other requirements that are different. In fact, and I'm saying this partly to prove to Carl and everyone that I read the advance material, treating managers differently in this respect may be ethically sanctioned. Somewhere I read, maybe in relation to Immanuel Kant and it made a lot of sense to me, that people should be treated differently only if there are differences in circumstances that make this appropriate. And I'll bet that you are going to tell us that managers have different ethical problems that make this appropriate. Isn't that right, Carl?"

"Maybe, Joe, I'd better have you conduct the meeting," Iverson said with a smile. "You are absolutely right. Realistically we can't expect the person on the assembly line, the computer operator, the payroll clerk to deal with ethical dilemmas that involve complex competing rights in the company. It's fine if they understand the concepts, but they won't have occasion to use them in their work. The management is responsible for establishing policies for these people to follow—policies that reflect ethical concepts. Some kind of training for these people may be appropriate, but it is not the same type that we have been and will be discussing.

"Managers, on the other hand, should understand ethical analysis. Even though many of their actions, perhaps, will be governed by established policies, they should be able to understand, to explain the rationale of those policies . . . and to challenge them, if appropriate. Some of them, too, will advance to top management roles where they will need to analyze issues from an ethical perspective."

"I hear what you say," O'Malley responded, "and agree with much of it. But I do have a nagging concern. One of the criticisms of U.S. business today is the lack of worker participation in decisions, the fact that work is routine and boring. I realize we can't handle strategic and policy decisions in a town hall atmosphere, but I want us to keep in mind the need to make all employees feel that they are important. That is my plea. And I believe it is ethically based."

"And well stated," Iverson replied. "It is a reason that some kind of ethics training for the entire organization should be considered a ways down the road—and not too far down. But for the moment, I believe we have to concentrate on managerial training.

Stages of Moral Development

"Now I want to discuss very briefly, and I'm afraid even simplistically, some of the ideas of Lawrence Kohlberg, a psychologist well known in his field but probably a stranger to most laypeople.[4] Something on him was included in the reading material I sent out—remember?" Seeing several nods, Iverson continued, "Now, all of Kohlberg's ideas are not universally accepted, and especially

---

[4] For a technical but quite interesting and useful discussion of Kohlberg's ideas and their implications, see David E. Cooper, "Cognitive Development and Teaching Business Ethics," *Journal of Business Ethics* 4 (1985), 313–329.

some of the conclusions drawn from his research, but he describes the stages of moral development in a way that my experience relates to and that I hope you will find useful.

"Kohlberg identified six stages of moral development, but these fall into three broader classifications that will suffice for our purposes. We shall call them:

Preconventional
Conventional
Postconventional

For convenience, I'll list them on this blackboard so that you can keep better track of what we're discussing.

"A person in the preconventional stage," Iverson continued, "is almost exclusively self-focused, reacting to everything in terms of how it affects himself or herself. Such a person responds to clear authority and to punishment. A young child is typical of this stage. He or she says that something is wrong 'because Mommy said so'—or 'because Daddy will spank me if I do it.'

"With growth in years and experience," he went on, "most people move into the second, the conventional, stage—at least most of the time. They look at things from the perspective of their peer group and respond to group norms. Their rationale to why something is right is likely to be: 'Everyone does it.' Anyone who has had or been around adolescents recognizes this stage; it is encountered with teenagers in its most virulent form—group conformity. But, according to Kohlberg and his followers, most adults never really move beyond this stage—although the manifestations are more subtle, possibly because people are involved with more diverse, more sophisticated groups.

"Finally we move to the postconventional stage—the stage at which people look at matters from a broader, more universal perspective. For justification of their actions, they now look to moral principles—not just to whether they'll get caught or what others are doing. In terms of the ethical models we discussed earlier, they look outside themselves and their immediate surroundings to evaluate issues as to what provides the greatest utility to society or as to how Kant's categorical imperative would apply."

Pausing a moment and looking around, Iverson asked, "Does this make sense?"

"Yes," Andrew O'Malley said, "it gives academic respectability and categorization to what I guess I knew to be the case all along, except that I would have suspected more people would be in the postconventional stage. Maybe we just don't like to see ourselves as others see us. But I can't see where this gets us."

"I can't either," Stevenson chimed in. "What does it mean to ethics training?"

"Just this," Iverson replied. "We want to move people who must deal with complex ethical dilemmas—managers, in the case of Hauser-Moore—into the postconventional stage. It is only there that they go beyond group conformity, that they reach decisions on the basis of broad moral principles. That should be the goal of much of any ethics training a company might initiate for its management group."

"Is that a realistic goal?" Cynthia Downs asked. "If most people never get beyond the conventional stage, isn't it naive to assume that, with a little training, we can move enough people into the postconventional stage at the company to make much difference? Or am I missing something?"

"If you're missing something, Cindy, I'm right along with you," Hendricks said, shaking his head. "Do you really think you can accomplish that, Carl?"

"Yes, with a couple caveats," Iverson replied. "Remember, we'll be teaching ethical analysis, not trying to change people's moral standards, at least not directly. If we expose people to an ethical model and then lead them through something like the seven-step approach we discussed earlier this morning, this forces them into postconventional stage thinking. Do you see how this works?"

"While they're focusing on it, yes," Downs said thoughtfully, "but will it stick?"

"That's the $64 question," Iverson said. "What you're asking is whether, a few months later, people will remember to apply moral reasoning in solving, even identifying, an ethical dilemma or whether they'll slip back into their old conventional mode. To be honest, I doubt that any company training program can move a person permanently, for all problems, into the postconventional mode. I do believe, however, that it is feasible for most of their business dilemmas, if properly reinforced—a matter I want us to discuss a little later. Can we at least accept such an assumption for now?"

Concern about Results of Ethical Analysis

"OK," said Stevenson, "I can see that using the approach you described could bring people's ethics reasoning to the postconventional level, at least for most managers, but I'm back to my earlier problem. Without any commonality as to moral standards, where does this get us? Wouldn't people end up spread out over the landscape? I don't mean to be flippant about this, Carl, and you, too, George, but aren't we just as well off being all over the lot operating the way we always have as we will be with all this fancy training?"

"Sarah," Iverson came back, "I'd be the first to admit we wouldn't have unanimity. That's too much to expect when you realize that, despite at least 2,500 years of effort, philosophers have never been able to reach any agreement on ethical models. But the situation is not as bleak as you seem to envision. Ethical analysis will, I am convinced, bring order out of the chaos that otherwise surrounds many moral dilemmas. It leads to structured thinking—and, as a result, to identification of differences in views within a company, or any group—which should lead to some kind of agreement on important problems. Quotations don't prove anything; however, knowing that this issue would probably come up—it usually does in meetings of this type—I brought an article written by a well-known professor of corporate strategy and managerial ethics. In it, he wrote:

Why teach ethical analysis in a program on business administration if it provides no single solution to ethical dilemmas? There are two valid reasons.

Ethical analysis may not lead to a single right or just or fair answer to a managerial dilemma, but it does lead to some answers that can be clearly seen to be more right or more just or more fair than other answers . . .

Ethical analysis also can lead to an evaluation of subjective moral standards and an examination of their supporting personal criteria. . . . Ethical analysis, if it accomplishes little else, does result in an examination of value priorities among the person's goals, norms, and beliefs, and does reinforce that person's confidence in his or her moral standards of behavior.[5]

"And this, I would argue, although I cannot prove it, is likely to result in far greater consistency than unstructured decision making based largely on hunch and experience."

Evidence That Training Changes People

"What you have just said makes sense," Hendricks admitted, "but is there any evidence that it works? I'll admit I have an innate suspicion of logically developed notions that no one can demonstrate will work. Maybe that's why I'm an engineer."

"Fair enough, Joe," Iverson responded. "I don't think your attitude is at all unreasonable. As my old grandfather from Missouri used to say, you don't want to buy a pig in a poke—something you can't see. I have some soft and some hard evidence.

"The soft evidence is in my own experience. As George mentioned when he introduced me, I've been teaching ethics at universities, leading ethics seminars, and working with companies on their ethics programs for quite a few years. Admittedly, this is not objective data that you can touch, taste, and feel, but I know that much of the training catches hold. I've gone back over the years to several companies and have a feel from their experience that there is a real result.

---

[5] Hosmer, *op. cit.*, 14.

"The hard evidence, though, that may have greater credibility comes from some studies that have been made. I have one here in the form of an article by James R. Rest, a University of Minnesota psychology professor and the research director at its Center for the Study of Ethical Development. The following are among important findings based on his surveys of recent psychological research:

■ "Dramatic and extensive changes occur in young adulthood (the 20s and 30s) in the basic problem-solving strategies used by the person in dealing with ethical issues."

■ "Deliberate educational attempts (formal curriculum) to influence awareness of moral problems and to influence the reasoning/judgment process can be demonstrated to be effective."

■ "Studies link moral perception and moral judgment with actual, real-life behavior."[6]

"But doesn't that suggest," O'Malley inquired, "that his research is directed toward education in an academic environment? Would this necessarily apply to company training?"

"I can't speak, of course, for Rest," Iverson answered, "but I would think that comparability of results would depend on three factors: the education levels of those involved, the quality of instruction, and the depth of instruction.

"The population involved in the studies Rest used were presumably college students, probably both graduate and undergraduate. I believe that managers at Hauser-Moore would constitute a similar group; most of them would have gone to college, and others, I believe, would have backgrounds and experience that would be reasonably comparable.

"Quality and depth of instruction are obviously important factors. Certainly an informal training program conducted by persons without adequate exposure to ethical concepts and analysis

---

[6] James R. Rest, "Can Ethics Be Taught in Professional Schools? The Psychological Research," *Ethics: Easier Said Than Done* (Winter 1988), 22–26.

techniques would not achieve the same results as the structured teaching that underlies Rest's conclusions. It may be that even the best of company training programs would never have the content, time, or overall level of instructor competence that the better ethics training in university courses has. On the other hand, as a professor who has worked in this field for years, I must confess that some of the university courses that purport to address ethical issues may not meet the highest standards of competence. To sum up on this point, I think that Rest's findings would apply, although possibly to a lesser degree, to a well-organized company training program."

The Effect That Can Be Hoped for—and Expected

"I am sure the findings of this researcher you've been referring to," Sarah Stevenson said, "represent averages—they'd almost have to. What I'd like to know, and maybe no one can answer this, is whether the improved sensitivity to ethical issues he finds involves mainly people who were not a major problem anyway. Maybe those who weren't going to do much wrong anyway showed the greatest increase in moral sensitivity. Does training have any impact on Dennis Levine or those involved in WedTech—people like that—who have been involved in the big scandals that are costing all of us so much?"

"Sarah," Iverson replied, "I doubt if ethical training would have had any effect on what those men did. I may be wrong, and I hope I am, but the value systems of those people made success— amassing money, achieving power—so important that they would never have gone through any ethical analysis, or, if they had, they would have ignored the results. But I hope that you are not inferring from this that ethics training is not really effective, which I am convinced would be a wrong conclusion."

"Why?" Stevenson persisted.

"Because these major scandals did not involve just the few people you mentioned, or even just them and the associates mentioned in the newspapers. Almost any irregularity of any size requires the passive acceptance, the looking the other way, if not the active of participation, of other people—people you and I would regard as honest—even people like us. As the professor wrote in an article I referred to earlier:

> A course on ethical analysis would probably not have changed the value rankings or the moral standards of Ivan Boesky, Dennis Levine, or Timothy Tabor (though ethicists are always filled with hope), but it would have reinforced the value rankings and moral standards of their associates and peers. Those people would have felt more confidence in their own norms, beliefs, and standards, and would have been more willing to take action based upon those norms, beliefs, and standards.[7]

"But that isn't all," Iverson continued. "We lose perspective if we focus just on major scandals—or even on dishonest acts, major or minor. Obviously I have no figures, but I would feel comfortable hazarding a guess that the myriad of less-important irregularities—ones that take little space in, or never reach, *The Wall Street Journal*—cost companies and the public every bit as much as, probably more than, the more spectacular cases that titillate readers.

"Even more important," he went on, "remember that ethics deals with far broader issues than just patently dishonest acts. It involves the treatment of employees—and suppliers. It also is involved in plant relocation decisions . . . and many everyday actions—everything that involves how people, or companies, treat one another. It involves solving ethical dilemmas with competing rights, matters that must be dealt with by ordinary people trying to decide what is right. This is where moral sensitivity and ethics training are so important."

The Need for Reinforcement

"Carl," Hauser asked, "how long does training last? We surely aren't talking about a one-shot program."

---

[7] Hosmer, *op. cit.*, 14.

"No, we're not, George," Iverson responded. "I wouldn't say that a one-time program is worse than nothing, but it might not be much better. For one thing, you have a continuously changing group that needs the training—new people from outside, promotions, retirements, all those factors that result in personnel changes at the managerial level. But that isn't the most important reason, not by a long ways. The principal reason is the need for reinforcement."

"What do you mean?" Cynthia Downs asked. "I suspect I know, but I'd like to have you explain it."

"Of course, Cindy—and I intended to, because it's very important. It is such a truism, maybe so obvious, that I haven't bothered to bring any support, but education in any field, not just ethics, requires use and reinforcement. People forget, they get busy. They lose the enthusiasm that immediately follows a good educational experience. They don't get exposed to new ideas.

"This may be particularly true with ethics," Iverson continued. "Significant ethical dilemmas don't arise every day for everyone. People lose some of their sensitivity; they may fail to recognize moral issues when they do come up. They may be under some peer pressure to conform, to go along. They need the reinforcement, the new ideas, and the renewed interest that come from continuing training.

"This happens even in school. Cynicism takes over unless something is done to counter it. I was rather depressed to read the experience of one professor who attempted to introduce ethical concepts into his courses, only to find that his efforts were being undermined. A teacher of some advanced classes once told him—and let me read this:

> Some of my students come in talking about ethics and social responsibility. I can tell they took your classes. It takes me three or four weeks to convince them that none of that stuff matters.[8]

---

[8] Herbert Rotfeld, "Ethics Training or Not, Business Will Still Be Business," *Chicago Tribune* (February 29, 1988), Section 1, page 11.

"Of course, that's in school, not in business, but you and I well know that the same pressure exists, but more so, in many business environments. We need reinforcement, continual training to counter it."

"Do you mean repeating the program periodically, say annually?" O'Malley asked.

"No," Iverson replied. "That would be rather ineffective. People would say, 'Here we go again.' It would become old hat, you know. I don't want to get into details today—indeed I couldn't if I wished—but the timing and content for a company would depend on a number of factors—number of people involved, turnover, experiences within the company. A program should be tailor-made to fit the situation. The follow-up training, the reinforcement, should consider the makeup of the participants and should build on what has gone before."

"Carl," Hauser said, "I can see that it is time for lunch. Is this a good stopping point?"

"It's perfect," Iverson replied. "I've covered all that my notes suggest in the area of training—not the details of how it should be conducted but whether it is worthwhile, accomplishes anything. During lunch I can answer any questions you or others may have on that or anything else we talked about this morning. Then, if we have addressed all that satisfactorily, we can get into the elements of a company ethics program right after lunch."

CHAPTER EIGHT

Components of a Program

The committee members had enjoyed a lively discussion over lunch, exploring some of the nuances of matters discussed during the morning. Iverson was particularly interested in noting the increasingly active role that Joe Hendricks was playing in the give-and-take, since Hauser had regarded Hendricks's participation and support as one of the keys to a successful program implementation.

Now had come the time to get into the elements of an effective corporate program. But first, Iverson wanted to lay some groundwork.

Individual Ethics within the Corporate Environment

"There are knowledgeable critics," he said, "who believe that addressing ethics as an individual matter is an exercise in futility. People, they claim, have little choice but to operate within the constraints of their environment. As a respected management professor has put it—sorry, give me a second to find the quotation I want in these papers—OK, here it is:

> The problem is that ethics in management represents a conflict
> between the economic and the social performance of an or-

ganization, and if that conflict is not specifically addressed and resolved by the senior executives within the firm, the natural tendency of the middle-level and operating-level managers will be to favor the economic side of the balance. Why? Because under current managerial systems, their performance is measured by economic criteria and their future is dependent upon economic results.[1]

"Do you agree with that analysis?"

"I have no question on that score," answered Cynthia Downs. "It is only a matter of degree. Some people, of course, will rationalize the subordination of their ethical concerns without much of a struggle, while others, I'm sure, will hold out. As a general proposition, I agree with what he says."

Andrew O'Malley broke in, "I agree—and possibly more strongly. This is something I was going to bring up. In reading the material that you sent us, I was struck, and disturbed, by the article, 'Ethical Business and the Ethical Person.' You know the one I mean?" Looking around and seeing several nods, he continued, "The authors of that article put it much stronger, Carl, than the quotation you just read. It seems to me that they are saying that ethics has to start at the corporate level, possibly even at the societal level. It almost suggests that we can't have business ethics unless we change the basic way in which business is conducted. Although I know all of you saw that article, I want to read a paragraph or two that I highlighted:

> Studies have consistently shown that individuals with strong moral and ethical values are not predictors of their ethical and moral behavior in an organizational environment. Rather, the ethical level of behavior is more determined by:
>
> ■ The climate (environment) of the organization;
> ■ The role of "significant others," such as executives, superiors, and peers;

---

[1] LaRue Tone Hosmer, *The Ethics of Management* (Homewood, IL: Irwin, 1987), 169.

■ The existence of slack (or the lack of it) in productive resources;

■ The culture of the firm relative to its "social" linkages; and

■ The intellectual underpinnings of the business system.

The overwhelming weight of empirical literature discounts the individual as the determining element of a positive corporate ethical environment. The elements of business principles and executive behavior are far more critical than the "moral context" of the individual conscience. Therefore, ethical direction is in effect provided by the corporation—since the script is written in policies, directions, codes, decisions, and structures, and the players are guided by the script. Their behavior will use the script as a substitute for their conscience.[2]

"Andy, that's nothing but a copout," Hendricks exclaimed with some heat. "It's the same wooly thinking that leads some people to say that criminals aren't responsible for their own acts, that they are unfortunate individuals who were abused as children, suffered from poverty, and so on. I'll admit that it may be hard sometimes, but people have to take responsibility for what they do, not pass the buck to someone else. Don't you agree, Sarah?"

"Yes, Joe, but only up to a point. I read that same article with considerable interest and got a bit sore, wanting to argue with the authors in a few places. And I think they may have overdrawn their conclusions. But there is no question that a lot of people tend to park their consciences in the coatroom when they arrive at work. That's wrong—and I agree with you there, Joe, that they shouldn't—but it's the real world."

"It sure is," Cynthia Downs spoke up. "I was reminded while reading the article of an experience when I worked in public accounting. The controller of this client was almost painfully upright in many respects—someone told us he spent many of his evenings working on church or charitable organizations, and I

² Bernard J. Reilly and Myroslaw J. Kyl, "Ethical Business and the Ethical Person," *Business Horizons* (November-December 1990), 25.

would have had no hesitancy in trusting him to handle any money I might have.

"But when it came to company matters, I have never met anyone who could scramble so hard to produce the earnings that the CEO wanted. He would come up with convoluted rationalizations and even withhold documents. We used to wonder how he could reconcile his business behavior with his personal values. He may be an extreme, but I have seen enough examples to know that some people are able to build up a wall between their personal ethics and what they think is required of them in business—and not seem to suffer from any twinges of conscience.

"Apparently," she continued, "some companies expect this of their employees, an unquestioning willingness to work for any company objective as long as it isn't illegal, and sometimes without that limitation. In other cases, I suspect it is just a matter of insensitivity, that the company has never thought to tell the employees that no one expects them to go against their consciences, and the employees feel that they are expected to achieve results, with no questions asked."

"That's a pretty good summary, Cindy," Iverson said. "All of you, in different ways, are bringing out just what we need at this stage. Obviously we may have some differences of emphasis, but I believe all of us would agree on two points—that individual character, ethical awareness, is essential, but that corporations must be ethically sensitive and provide an environment in which the individual is comfortable following his or her conscience. That is what I wanted to have everyone recognize before getting into what should go into a company ethics program—that ethics is a corporate as well as an individual problem and that a responsible management must face up to its responsibility for the workplace environment.

"You recognize, I'm sure, that we're not going to design an ethics program for Hauser-Moore this afternoon. There is no such thing as a standard program; each of the components must be tailored to fit a company's operations, and its philosophy and traditions. Some parts take a lot of time and effort to develop;

the whole program probably can't be implemented all at once. What we are going to do now is to consider the nature of the items that go into a program—the components. After that, George and the rest of you will have to assign responsibilities for developing the various parts and establish a timetable."

With that, Iverson stepped over to the flip chart at the end of the room and turned over the top page, showing the following listing:

Elements of Program

Creating the Environment

Statement of values
Corporate tradition/culture
Tone at the top

Implementing the Program
Code of conduct
Established procedures
Training
Hot line
Ongoing oversight

"Here," he pointed, "are the areas I hope we can cover this afternoon. You will note that I have split these into two main parts, one the creation of the ethical environment and the other the implementation of the program. This split is somewhat arbitrary. As I am sure you have already recognized, there is some overlap. But I think that looking at the program in this way is useful; the first three elements, which we might consider a foundation, should underlie the design of an ongoing program."

Statement of Values

Referring to the flip chart, Iverson said they would now talk about a corporate statement of values. He inquired whether this meant anything to anyone. The committee members looked uncertainly at one another, so Iverson continued, "None of you has asked why Hauser-Moore wants to have an ethics program. In your case, this is, perhaps, not surprising. Probably before, but certainly since being appointed to this committee and having had a chance to go through the advance reading material, you had a good idea what ethics is about. And George's introductory comments helped bring this into sharper focus so far as Hauser-Moore is concerned.

"Everyone, though, doesn't have that perspective. And if the people in an organization have little or no idea what the goal of an ethics program is, they are likely to look at it from a mechanical viewpoint. They need to be told, and to be reminded again and again, why ethics is important to their company.

"A good statement of values," Iverson continued, "which is sometimes referred to as a mission statement or a credo, should be the cornerstone of a company's ethics program. It tells the organization, and the world, what the company stands for. It is positive, dealing with goals—obligations to employees, to customers, to suppliers, to the community. You might call it a compass."

"Maybe I'm alone in this," Cynthia Downs spoke up, "but I have a little difficulty visualizing what a credo or whatever you call it really looks like . . . and what a company does with it once one is prepared."

"Fair enough, Cindy; I'll try to be more specific. A company can, probably usually does, have diverse reasons for wanting to be regarded as ethical. One reason could be strictly altruistic, a belief that being ethical is the right thing to do—a desire to be a good corporate citizen. Another reason may be a belief that good ethics is good business, that a company with a reputation for being ethical is perceived as a better employer and a more dependable supplier of goods or services. For some companies, a persuasive argument is that a good ethics program will help them avoid those problems that have plunged too many companies into serious legal problems and damaging publicity. All of these reasons, and probably some others I haven't thought to mention, are valid and legitimate. In my view, though, a company's statement of values should focus on the first reason I mentioned—that being ethical is the right way to behave. Period."

"Why?" O'Malley asked. "Shouldn't we try to 'sell' the program?"

"Yes, Andy," Iverson responded, "but not here or in that way. Remember that this is a statement to the employees, to suppliers, to customers, and to the public generally. I believe that it should take the high road, and that is certainly appropriate for Hauser-Moore. If the statement is drafted to suggest self-interest, that the company is being ethical to gain an advantage, it is less likely to serve its purpose with those who read it. It could even make the effort appear somewhat cynical."

"But, Carl, you still haven't quite told me what the statement should look like," Downs persisted.

"You won't let me get away with generalities," Iverson laughed. "I believe that a good statement should be brief, focusing attention on what is really important—the organization's shared values. It should not be detailed or defensive; for that reason, I don't believe it should be written by the legal department. Certainly not by public relations people. To be sincere, credible, it should have support at the top, of course, but should represent the accepted views, endorsed by practice, of the rank and file. George, from our discussions, I think you could give everyone a good idea what Hauser-Moore's credo should say, maybe not in a polished form but in substance. Would you mind giving us your thoughts?"

"I'd like to," Hauser answered. "This is something I have given quite a bit of thought to recently, and I'll try to put it concisely. In my view, Hauser-Moore's statement of values should say that it recognizes that its business is inextricably tied to the public interest and that its business decisions should never be made solely in the financial interest of the company. It could enlarge on this by saying that all decisions should give due weight to the interests of all its constituents—its shareholders, its employees, its suppliers, its customers, the community in which it operates, and the public at large."

"That, I think, is a good, strong start," Iverson observed. "Any questions?"

"Yes," Downs said, "I have one. The statement sounds fine, but how and where will it be used?"

"It should be discussed periodically in meetings at all levels of the company," Iverson replied. "It should be a key part of the company's training program. Above all, it isn't something to be put in a drawer, or just to pin up on the wall. It sort of caps the role of company culture and management tone—matters we're about to discuss. It summarizes these and reminds people of where they should be headed.

"I suspect Hauser-Moore's wrestling with the relocation problem would have been easier if the board had had a statement of values. The members might have focused sooner on whatever obligations it believes it has to employees, suppliers, and the community. Not that I have any reason to believe the answer would have been different, but it would have been handled less traumatically. And the various stakeholders might have been happier."

Role of Tradition

"But now," Iverson continued, "it's time to turn to the next element, corporate tradition—a more formal way, perhaps, of characterizing a company's personality. Because a company does have a personality to be recognized, dealt with, perhaps nurtured—"

"Excuse me, Carl," Sarah Stevenson broke in, "perhaps I ought to wait—maybe you'll clarify this—but didn't you say this morning that, while a corporation is legally a person, it is not a human being? Can it have a personality?"

"A good question, Sarah, and I'll try to answer it. A company doesn't think; it doesn't have emotions. It is created by human beings for a specific function, to conduct a business. Anything it does, for good or bad, reflects decisions and actions of those people who own and manage it.

"But that doesn't mean," Iverson continued, "that it doesn't have a personality as we normally think of that term—a set of values, responses, ways of identifying itself that are distinctive, that set it apart from other business entities. You surely have noted that with companies or institutions you deal with—a subconscious, perhaps, but clearly recognizable way of conducting themselves. To go outside business, for illustration, think of the Marine Corps . . . its esprit de corps. For better or for worse, every entity has this—let's call it 'tradition' or 'culture'—that begins developing from the first day of its existence."

"OK, but what does tradition have to do with the installation of an ethics program? I guess I sense a relationship, but you can't create a tradition overnight," observed Andrew O'Malley.

"You're absolutely right, Andy," Iverson responded, "about creating an instant tradition—you can't. But you must recognize the tradition a company has. It is that on which the ethics program must be built—the foundation, if you will. The foundation may be weak, may need some shoring up, but it is what underlies whatever you create.

"I'm glad you brought up the point that a tradition cannot be created overnight. We've all seen the absurd, sometimes pathetic attempt of some people to manufacture a family history, maybe using a coat of arms bought from some company that sells them through magazine advertisements. Or buying an old house and covering the walls with paintings of persons that the owner hopes visitors will assume to be distinguished ancestors.

"You can't buy a tradition," Iverson continued. "You can't retain a consultant to create one. A man who has written lucidly and eloquently on the subject—I'd like to give each of you a copy of his book because there's a lot else in it, but it's out of print— has likened the constructing of a corporate tradition to the gradual building, over many years, of a coral reef. Because I think this is so important, I'd like to read you something that he has said:

> [W]e forget both the density and duration of the activity underlying the surface facts with which we deal. We forget that, like an iceberg, nine tenths of their mass lies hidden, well below the normal waterline of vision. And we forget that the

part we can see is not just "there" but is very much something built, something constructed or pieced together over time.

Corporations, the institutions of modern commerce, are such constructed things, and the work that managers do takes place in such "built" environments. Phrased so baldly, the point seems obvious. But in the normal course of events—and, especially, in terms of how we regularly talk and think about the work of management—the point disappears from view. As a practical matter, we do not commonly treat a corporation as the cumulative result of an historical process of development, nor do we think of it in the present as an edifice held together by the bricks and mortar of tradition. Yet it is, and we should.[3]

Elsewhere he says:

[I]nstitutions do remember all the time. The style of a business presentation, the kinds of evidence that tend to sway decisions, the shared sense of what constitutes relevant information about a new market or product, the deep-seated visceral preference for certain lines of business—all these characteristics, and a thousand others like them are the subtle products of memory. In no two organizations are they exactly the same, nor in any two parts of the same organization . . .[4]

"Doesn't that tell us something important—obvious, once focused on, but often overlooked?" Iverson asked. "We never write on a completely clean slate; everything we do, everything we think, builds on our experience—on our persona, which reflects our history. It is the same with a corporation. We have to recognize this when we undertake something new.

"And," he continued, "besides the fact that whatever program you develop for Hauser-Moore must be built on its tradition, there is another aspect to bear in mind—that this program, like everything else that goes on at the company each day, is a part of the ongoing building of Hauser-Moore's tradition. We are not

---

[3] Alan M. Kantrow, *The Constraints of Corporate Tradition*, first Perennial Library edition (New York: Harper & Row, Publishers, 1988), 2.
[4] *Ibid.*, x.

just bound by a static tradition; we are participants in the creation of an ongoing culture."

"But, Carl, you seem to assume that Hauser-Moore not only has a tradition but that it is a good one on which to build," Stevenson said. "Fortunately, I believe that is true. Are you telling us, though, that a company with a lousy tradition, and there certainly are such, can't initiate an ethics program?"

"No, Sarah," Iverson replied, "but they'll have a lot tougher time. They can only build on what is there, but without a good foundation they'll have to start rebuilding one, trying to save what is good, getting rid of the bad, and bonding the whole thing together. With the inertia that is built into any tradition, good or bad, changing it is a tough job. And the people involved will need to pay a lot more attention to reinforcements, some of the other features we'll be talking about.

"Looking at Hauser-Moore, I can't claim to have a real sense of its tradition, certainly not in any depth. But I do sense that it exists and is positive. I would only suggest that you take concrete steps to nurture it. It may even be, George, that it mainly reflects your father's and your attitudes. Nothing wrong with that, but it means that you have to broaden the base. You must be as concerned with the ethical qualities of your management as you are with their technical competence. Tradition is fragile: It takes years to build, but it can be destroyed overnight. Protect it.

"Don't, though, make of it more than it is," Iverson went on. "Don't put it up on a pedestal. Most of all don't get 'preachy' about it and risk making it the butt of jokes among the employees. But, in every way you can, including some matters we'll discuss later, reinforce it and make it implicit in everything Hauser-Moore does, a part of the company's accepted culture."

Importance of Tone at the Top

Turning back to the flip chart, Iverson said, "Now let's talk about tone at the top. Does everyone understand what I mean by that?"

"Isn't it pretty much the same as tradition?" Hendricks asked.

"Let me try," Downs broke in. "Isn't tone at the top just a part of tradition—not the whole thing but just the attitude of top management?"

"Right, Cindy," Iverson responded. "Tradition is the buildup of company culture over the years, admittedly mainly from the top. What I refer to as tone at the top means the attitude of, the flavor imparted by, the current top management. This tone will ultimately affect the company's tradition, one way or the other, but at any given time it may even run counter to tradition. We have all heard of companies with fine traditions that slip, operationally and ethically.

"As much as, maybe even more than, tradition, the tone of top management influences a company's ethical behavior. Let me be specific. If the officers begin abusing their position, treating company property like their own, this attitude trickles down throughout the organization. Employees ask themselves why they shouldn't fiddle a little with their expense accounts when they see excesses higher up."

"Surely you don't mean, Carl, that rank doesn't have its privileges, to use an old military saying," Hendricks asked. "Surely George is entitled to charge things that a new employee can't—first-class travel, for example. Let's not carry this egalitarian attitude too far."

"That's not what I meant, but it's good that you brought it into focus, Joe. Different levels of expense reimbursement are certainly appropriate at different levels within a company as long as they relate to company business. What sends the wrong signals is a perception that top executives take advantage of the situation—manufacturing reasons for using the company airplane for personal trips, having the use of company-owned apartments in resort areas, decorating their homes with company property, and so forth. Accepting expensive gifts from those the company does business with is another example. Sure, what they do offers no legitimate excuse for corner-cutting by employees; human nature being what it is, though, lax attitudes at the top encourage chiseling at the bottom."

"Isn't there more to tone at the top than management's not taking personal advantage of the situation?" Hauser asked.

"Yes, George, there is, and I may have started at the wrong end," Iverson replied. "It's a matter of management's showing by its actions what it really thinks is important—the type of action it takes when the morally right course of action seems to be contrary to the company's economic interests, at least in the short term.

"A company has, say, a top salesperson. There have been lots of rumors in the company about his or her behavior—even a suspicion of his or her paying off some purchasing agents. His or her expense reports would choke a cow, but no one speaks up to him or her. Several people have even talked to the sales vice president, but they've received nothing but a vague brush-off. It doesn't take much savvy for the organization to get the message: Ethics is fine if it doesn't cost anything, but profits come first.

"Or, you have a tough lady in charge of the public relations department. She humiliates employees in front of others. Several have quit, and there have been numerous complaints. But she's good at her job—manages to keep the company's name out of some sticky situations, no one is quite sure how. When the administrative vice president, reportedly, asked her to show a little more respect for her employees, she laughingly, but publicly, told friends over drinks that she had let him know where he could put the job if he didn't like the way she handled it. In a situation like that, what are employees to think about the employer's commitment to its employees—to its respect for them as people?

"I could go on and on," said Iverson, "but you get the point. Management has to support its ethics program, not just give it lip service. It's like body language. The way people behave or react shows what is important to them—the old saying that actions speak louder than words. Management can initiate sound procedures. It can promulgate well-written codes of conduct. It can do everything right—on paper. And yet, if it is slack itself or lets others get away with things, somehow or other the organization can see that the matter of ethics is not a real concern of management."

Glancing toward Hauser, Iverson continued, "And here we have another good example, somewhat different, of management commitment—and I mean a good example—right in front of us. I don't want to embarrass you, George, but it's your initiating and then chairing this committee." Hauser said deprecatingly that it was nothing, that he was interested and had the time. "Sure, George, you *made* the time," Iverson shot back. "A story I read the other day will make what I'm driving at clear. A group of CEOs had met to discuss ethics, and this is the story of a real meeting involving top people. One of them related this experience; I brought it along because I thought it might be useful:

> I'd like to tell you a story about a large, for-profit health insurance company that wanted an ethics program. The chief executive told us that he was trying to send this message out, but that his people were not getting the message down the line. We did a "memo audit," to see if he was sending it down the line. Sure enough, buried in the memos were little messages that, unless people read their memos differently than I do, were unclear as to what was actually going on. We told him that he, personally, should tell his people about his ethics program. I suggested he make a video. He looked me square in the eye, and said, "You mean sit in plastic chairs and drink coffee out of styrofoam cups with all those people?" [Laughter] This is an extreme case, but it illustrates part of the problem.[5]

"It sure does," Hauser said. "But you needn't worry about me with the styrofoam cup."

"I know, George. But what about the plastic chair?" Iverson responded amid chuckles around the table. "But that's what I wanted to get across. You started this program. You're chairing it. It has your active, visible support, and that is essential. When the training is developed, I'm sure you'll attend—and you should.

---

[5]CE Roundtable, "What to Do about Ethics," *Chief Executive* (July/August 1988), 66.

It's hard to convince an organization that something the boss doesn't have time for is really important. If he or she doesn't take part, it sends a message to the people in the next level, and they may decide they're too busy . . . and on and on, throughout the organization.

"Still another way for top management to set the right tone is by establishing realistic goals. You want to challenge your people, but be reasonable. I've seen situations, as I'm sure you have, or at least read about, where management set such high production quotas that the organization couldn't meet them without cutting corners. And when the chickens came home to roost, management claimed it couldn't understand what went wrong. Or setting extremely high earnings goals, and possibly releasing these to the public, is an invitation to creative accounting. Management shouldn't force, or even tempt, people to be dishonest.

"To sum up in a few simple words, a company ethics program is only as good as the visible commitment from the top."

"Carl," Joe asked, starting to rise from his chair, "can we have a 10-minute break? I'm sure I'll focus better on what's coming if I can stretch my legs—and maybe get a styrofoam cup of coffee."

Everyone laughed, and made for the door.

Code of Conduct

Fifteen minutes later (no one has ever seen a real 10-minute break), all the members were back in their chairs. "Now," Iverson said, "let's turn to what's involved in a company code of conduct. During the break, Joe noted that this was the next topic on the flip chart and asked me if this is the set of Boy Scout rules some companies pin up over the water cooler." Hearing some chuckles, Iverson smiled, "I can see that that amuses you, as it did me, and I must admit that his characterization fits for some companies. Too often, they are rather detailed lists of things to be done—or things not to be done. And it is sometimes a mixed bag; for example, it may include such things as a dress code . . . not very stirring, I'm afraid.

"Also, many of the codes tend to be too self-focused. A widely quoted 1983 study of 119 codes seemed, as the authors put it, 'to reflect a more abiding concern for conduct that is directly inimical to a firm's internal operations [for example, a heavy emphasis on conflicts of interest] than for relations in keeping with [its responsibility to the society of which the corporation is a part].'[6]

"Sometimes a code emerges as a response to legal or ethical problems that a company or an industry has found itself in. There is nothing wrong with this, but as a result cynics tend to dismiss the effort as PR. It may be written, or at least heavily edited, by house counsel, which is likely to make it rather sterile."

"I gather," said Stevenson, "that you are not an enthusiastic proponent of codes of conduct."

"I don't want you to jump to that conclusion, Sarah. I've given you the downside first, partly to show how a code can go wrong. If used in the right way, it can, and in many companies does, serve a very useful purpose. It reinforces the statement of values with specifics. It can, indeed should, be incorporated into ethics training. It can remind people of pitfalls. A code can provide a road map for designing compliance reviews, a matter I intend to address shortly.

"The important thing is that the code must be used. It must be a vital, living document. The company's employees must be aware of its existence and its significance. Although one survey found that half of the respondents' companies had written codes of ethics, about four out of ten said that the subject of ethical behavior was never discussed in the context of their work[7]—certainly a disturbing commentary, both on the companies' real interest in the subject and in the emphasis they place on their codes.

---

[6] Donald R. Cressey and Charles A. Moore, "Managerial Values and Corporate Codes of Ethics," *California Management Review* (Summer 1983), 59.

[7] Trends & Analysis, "Forget Ethics—and Succeed?" *Industry Week* (October 19, 1987), 17.

Some companies, I know, require employees, at least above a certain level, to sign that they have read the codes—each year, say—which is good if it is not handled in too casual or too perfunctory a way."

Iverson continued, "As someone remarked in a recent discussion, a sure indication of the effectiveness of a code is how often it is revised. Procedures change. So does the business environment. New problems emerge. If a code is to have an impact, it must be kept up-to-date."

Established Procedures

"But let's move a step down," Iverson went on. "Important as codes of conduct may be, they are of limited value if left at that point. They are too general. A company must get specific, with established, written procedures that make clear what is expected. You'd be surprised how useful well-documented policies and procedures are in facilitating ethical behavior. They provide guidelines for behavior—for example, to help a supervisor know how to handle an employee who seems to be taking advantage of the company's sick leave benefits. Or how to select suppliers.

"Another point—good procedures, and what you accountants, Cindy, call internal control, remove temptation. They help keep people honest. We've focused our whole discussion thus far on the assumption that people are inherently honest, that they want to do the right thing, that all that may be hindering them is a lack of understanding or pressure from someone else—usually someone above them. But there are dishonest individuals, amoral people, in this world, and a company would be foolhardy not to take reasonable precautions against them. Some years back, George Santayana, the noted American philosopher, wrote:

> Undoubtedly, there is little integration or integrity in most men's character; there is only habit and a plodding limitation in life and mind; and if social pressure were not added to lack

of opportunity disorderly lives would be more common than they are.[8]

"I hope that he's overly cynical," O'Malley interjected, "but I can't help relating it to something I read in the paper the other day. In a British public opinion survey, more than half of those questioned, as I recall, said they would cheat the government out of $80,000 of taxes if they could be sure of not being caught. And 11 percent of men and 3 percent of women even said they would commit murder to become millionaires if they were assured of getting away with it."[9]

"That's horrible. What a depressing view of human nature!" Downs exclaimed.

"Isn't it, though? I want to believe," Iverson said, "that fewer would do these things if facing an actual situation. But it is illustrative of the point I'm trying to make—that a company should have carefully designed procedures and controls to keep temptation at bay. As someone once said, we lock desk drawers to keep honest people out.

"But equally important, good procedures, strictly enforced, carry a message of what is expected. They set an important tone. An example involves the policies of what expenses can be charged to the company, how they should be supported, and who approves expense reports. We're dealing here with people's money, and it is very important to be sure that everyone is treated fairly and consistently, from top to bottom. I read somewhere that you can judge the strength of a company's commitment to sound internal controls by looking at its expense reimbursement policies. That may be a bit of an exaggeration, but there's a message there. You should try to sell the organization on ethics, train them well, but then you should establish fair, clear policies that don't invite, that even prevent, shortcuts.

---

[8] George Santayana, as quoted in *The International Dictionary of Thought* (Chicago: J.G. Ferguson Publishing Company, 1969), 402.

[9] "Survey: Britons Would Lie, Cheat, Kill—If They Could Get Away with It," *Chicago Tribune* (July 1, 1991), section 1, 12.

"And let's not forget procedures directly addressing ethics. Certainly you don't want to start preaching, but good reinforcement is important. The most important element, one we'll turn to next, is continuing training. Some companies have managers, at least, sign an annual statement that they have reread and are familiar with the company's code of conduct and have abided by its provisions during the last year. And that they do not have any conflicts of interest. I know that some people think that such signed statements become routine, boilerplate, and that people sign them without much thought. Some of that may be true, but a lot depends on whether the requirement is presented properly— and whether there is prompt follow-up in case signed statements are not returned. It's a matter of doing your best."

A few minutes of questions and some observations followed; then Iverson said they would turn quite briefly to training.

Training in Ethical Reasoning

"Having spent a good part of the morning on whether ethics can be taught, I do not plan to take much of your time now to describe the role of training in an ethics program. We would all agree, I imagine, that training can be effective and that it is important; the only questions concern how much and when. These are matters that we shall have to deal with in far more detail at another time, but I'd like to cover a few high spots now.

"You'll have to decide who should be trained—what levels of management to include. The general nature of the training. How often it will take place. Who will develop the material, and who will conduct the training. All very important issues."

"Generally, how often should training sessions be held?" Downs asked.

"Not too often, I hope," Hendricks broke in. "Seriously, I am more taken with this whole idea about ethics than I would have expected, so I don't want to sound negative. On the other hand, this is a business; remember, we have other training around here, and we have to be careful that we're not running an educational institution rather than working."

"You're right, Joe," Iverson said. "You mustn't overdo it. But I doubt if that will be a problem; you'll probably find that there's more you want to cover than you can get prepared and scheduled. Let's just leave it in generalities at this stage. It does no good to make a big splash at the outset and then drift off into nothing. Memories are short. People come and go. People need to be sensitized frequently. And learning needs reinforcement. Shorter, but more frequent sessions are the answer."

"What do you include in training?" O'Malley asked. "How do you keep people interested? We've enjoyed the informal discussion with you in a small group, but wouldn't an ethics lecture get boring?"

"Absolutely," Iverson replied. "Another reason to keep sessions short . . . not to lecture. To have good leaders, and for them to be well prepared. I would rely heavily on case studies, sometimes written and sometimes in the form of video vignettes; there are quite a few available. And there should be a lot of student participation.

"But now, let's take a short break—I see Joe looking at his watch—and try to get back promptly for the rest of the program discussion. We're behind, which is OK—I certainly don't want to run through this too fast—but I know all of you have tight schedules."

Inquiries and Whistle Blowing

"What's this hot line business that's next on the chart, Carl?" Stevenson asked when all the members had resumed their seats. "I know you'll get into it, but I've been puzzled each time I looked at your flip chart."

"I'm sorry, Sarah. I hadn't meant for it to be distracting. It may not be the best caption, but I wanted to be sure we wouldn't skip over an important concept. Let me ask you—anyone—what you'd do if you saw someone in the company—a fellow worker, say, or even a boss—doing something unethical? Maybe not monumental but clearly wrong. Harmful to the company, let's assume."

"I'd tell my boss," Downs said.

"But Cindy, maybe it isn't even in your department," Stevenson said, shaking her head.

"That's not the issue," Hendricks interjected. "Give your boss the problem to handle. Don't go sticking your nose into other departments."

"I don't think I agree," Stevenson said, "but let's change the scenario a bit. What if the one who is doing something you think is wrong is your boss? Maybe he or she has even asked you to do something that you consider unethical?"

"I'd still start with the person I report to," Hendricks said firmly. "Even more so. I owe it to my boss to discuss the matter face to face, not to go around his or her back."

"But," O'Malley asked, "what if you do and the boss says forget it?"

"Good question, but let's stop here," Iverson said with a smile. "You've done a very good job of identifying the problem—a common problem. And one there is no good universal answer for. One of the toughest things in any company is setting up a procedure for employees to follow when they have an ethics question, or see something they think is an ethics problem. It's tempting to take a pass on it, to say that it's the individual's problem to work out, but that's a nonanswer. You can't solve the problem, perhaps, but you owe it to the organization to give it a try. For lack of a better name on the chart, I referred to the process as a 'hot line.' "

"What about a place or number people can write or call anonymously?" Downs asked. "Doesn't that get the question out in the open but still protect the person raising the question?"

"You can't be serious, Cindy," Stevenson said with a grimace. "You'd be inviting poison pen letters. How distasteful!"

"That is a problem," Iverson agreed. "Many companies would not want to open up something like this—too much like 'big brother.' There'd be calls like 'Did you know Joe Doaks had his secretary out to dinner last night? Didn't get home until 3:00 a.m.' I think it opens up a lot of possibilities for an atmosphere of suspicion and distrust. Besides, there's no way to follow up if more information is needed on whatever the allegations may be.''

"Carl," O'Malley inquired, "don't some companies have an ombudsman for matters like this? Wouldn't that be a good solution?"

"What is that?" Hendricks asked. "It seems to me I've heard the expression, but I can't quite put my finger on it.''

"Someone in a company," Iverson said, "who fields difficult questions or complaints that the person originating them doesn't feel like taking up with a boss or someone else in responsibility. In theory, the ombudsman—a Swedish term, incidentally—is a neutral person who can respond to or take action on a complaint without compromising the person who made it. The ideal ombudsman is a senior person, perhaps nearing retirement, who has the respect of everyone in the company—sound judgment and access to anyone in the company that he or she needs to talk to. Someone who respects confidences. Someone who has no direct interest in the outcome. And someone who would take the job seriously.

"It's not quite that simple, though, in practice. First, finding the right person could be difficult. But that may not be the biggest problem. How does one protect the source? Often the issue being raised is something that only one person could possibly know anything about . . . or, perhaps, just a few people. Unless the problem is clear on its face, how can the ombudsman follow through without identifying the source? Isn't the accused entitled to face his or her accuser? See what I mean?"

"Even if the ombudsman couldn't avoid identification of the source, couldn't he or she see that the person who raised the issue is not penalized?" Stevenson asked.

Hendricks broke in, "That's fine in theory, Sarah, and it might work to a degree, but retaliation can be subtle—ostracizing the informer, finding little things wrong, shading a performance rating down. I don't think there is a perfect answer; the person who brings up an issue has to be willing to live with the consequences. All the system can do is to protect that person against overt punishment."

"But there ought to be a good answer somewhere," O'Malley said. "Surely with all the companies and consultants that have addressed this issue, someone has come up with something."

"If there is a good, generally applicable answer," Iverson responded, "whoever found it has certainly kept it secret. Much of how a company handles this problem, Andy, depends on its tradition, its structure, a whole lot of intangibles. What works in one place may not in another. Each of you should think about this quite a bit before the next meeting, think about what would work for Hauser-Moore.

"I won't duck the question, though. Although it's no panacea, I believe that the ombudsman approach probably has the most to offer. Quite a few companies have adopted it. It is certainly better than leaving the employees on their own. If you're going to tell your people that ethics is important, that you want and expect them to behave ethically, you owe it to them to open a channel for dealing with their problems. Joe is probably right in saying that they should go to their bosses—and some will. If that is their only alternative, though, I'm afraid many employees will probably swallow hard and try to ignore, or rationalize their way out of, all but the most egregious ethical dilemmas."

"I think we see the problem clearly enough," said Hauser, looking at his watch, "and I'll admit it finds me without a ready answer. But Carl is right—we can't solve it today. We should all give it careful thought and try to come back with some suggestions at our next meeting.

"You have one more point to cover on this, haven't you, Carl?"

Importance of Ongoing Oversight

"Yes, I have—and a very important one. All we've talked about today," Iverson said, "would be a waste of time if no provision is made for ongoing oversight—monitoring and updating. A program developed and put in place and then left unattended, like an abandoned baby on a doorstep, is likely to die. Whatever program you start requires continuing attention, and nourishment."

Stepping over to the flip chart and turning to a new sheet, Iverson said, "Here are three aspects of ongoing oversight to be considered:

- It must be clearly evident that the program has the continuing attention and commitment of the board of directors and top management.
- The program must be kept up-to-date.
- There should be an effective system for reviewing compliance.

"Take a minute to think about these. Do you have any questions about them?"

"Yes," Hendricks said, "I have. In concept I agree with all three, and I can buy the first two in practice. But I don't see how you can conduct a review for morality, which is what I would think a compliance review is. You may come across an example of unethical behavior, more or less by accident, but how can you monitor compliance with a company's ethical standards?"

"As we have discussed, Joe," Iverson said, turning to Hendricks, "a company should have a written code of conduct. And underlying that code, it should have detailed procedures, most of which would require some form of documentation as to compliance. This is true in dollars-and-cents matters; for example, obtaining three bids, say, for certain purchases, or the approval of expense reports. It is equally true in research and development, where possible new products must be subjected to tests. Records must be kept of quality control tests of products presently being manufactured. Procedures should require documentation of performance reviews for employees—the basis on which they are promoted or terminated. A well-run company leaves a more complete paper trail behind its decisions and actions than most of us realize. And these sweep in, or should sweep in, most of the areas where potential ethics violations might occur. What is needed is a program to review compliance with these procedures on a periodic basis, much along the lines of what the internal auditors do in the financial area."

"Who would conduct such reviews?" Hauser asked.

"The program can be administered in a number of ways, George," Iverson replied. "One logical place to put it is in the internal audit department since it has the structure, and the discipline to manage such a program."

"You don't mean, Carl, that we would have a bunch of auditors running around trying to check up in areas outside their competence, do you?" Hendricks asked. "Don't take me wrong, Cindy—your people are good in their own field, but I don't want a bunch of bean counters checking up on our manufacturing processes any more than you'd want engineers second-guessing the way the books are kept. They wouldn't even know what they were looking at."

"Don't get worried on that score," Iverson said. "I'm talking about the coordination and administration, and it doesn't have to be in the internal audit department—that's just one suggestion. The actual reviews would be conducted by persons knowledgeable in the areas being reviewed, but not persons reporting to the managers responsible for the areas. A good example, come to think of it, is the peer review process followed increasingly in a number of professions. Reviewers follow a structured process in evaluating the compliance of those being reviewed with the established standards of their profession and, where applicable, their firms.

"And let us by no means overlook the importance of doing something, promptly and firmly, about any violations that are discovered. Nothing sends a bad signal to people faster than unenforced policies and codes. Action should be fair and even-handed—but timely.

"I don't think, though, that we should take time on more details at this point. It's the concept I want to get across now; the particulars can be worked out as the program is developed. We must never forget, though, that ongoing oversight is an essential ingredient in any effective ethics program.

"The way in which the various steps, not just compliance reviews but all of oversight, can be accomplished," Iverson continued, "may vary from company to company. Familiar as I am becoming with many aspects of Hauser-Moore, I certainly haven't a sufficient sense of the company's dynamics to make specific suggestions—although I shall be glad to counsel with you and act as a sounding board. Just to get the ball rolling, I shall touch on the important features of the approach adopted by one company that I have worked closely with over several years.

- The audit committee of the board of directors has the oversight role.
- A committee of management people, headed by a senior officer, meets regularly to review developments and recommend changes in the program or in the company's policies and procedures where ethical issues are involved.
- A formal compliance review program is under the supervision of the internal audit department, with the reviews conducted by senior persons who are knowledgeable about the operations of the department being reviewed.
- Any violation is reported by the internal audit department to the supervisor of the individual involved, with a request that the supervisor notify the internal audit department within a specified period of the action taken. The results are included in periodic reports to the audit committee of the board of directors.

"This, obviously is the barest outline but provides you with some idea about how continuing oversight can be maintained."

After a short discussion, Iverson turned to Hauser, "I don't know, George, what you want to do now. I've taken more time on this part than I had expected, but I think it's all been worthwhile. It's 5:15 now, and I don't think we'll get through the next part, which I call 'Is Business Ethics Worthwhile?' before dinner. Besides I think everyone is 'sat out' for now. I have two suggestions—either cover the 'good business' aspects another time, or discuss them over dinner. Dinner, I know, was to be a social occasion, but that part of the discussion is not particularly heavy and doesn't require charts or reading material. It's up to you."

Hauser discussed the matter briefly with the committee members and then concluded that it would be best to continue over dinner if that was really all right with him. Strike while the iron was hot, he said—also, it might be hard to get the group together soon, especially for just an hour's discussion. With that, they broke, to reconvene at 6:30 at Hauser's downtown club where he had a private room reserved for dinner.

CHAPTER NINE

Is Business Ethics Worthwhile?

Before and during dinner, there was considerable discussion of the day's sessions, including a number of questions of Carl Iverson. In some cases, he was able to clarify or expand on issues by referring, without disclosing names, to situations that had come up in his teaching and consulting. As the table was being cleared after the main course, George Hauser announced that he wanted to take a few minutes, while everyone was together, to outline how he could see the program going after tonight.

"As I see it, we're committed to having an ethics program at Hauser-Moore, and, after today, I have a general idea what it will include. It might—"

"Excuse my interrupting, George," Joe Hendricks spoke up, "and I may sound a bit presumptuous. Please don't take this as negative—I think we'll probably end up there, and should—but aren't we putting the cart before the horse? Don't we have to decide tonight whether business ethics is worthwhile? Or are we to take that for granted, with Carl's comments tonight more or less a benediction on the effort?"

"You're right, Joe, and never hesitate to catch me up. I guess I have taken the answer for granted. Like the rest of you, I very much want to hear what Carl says tonight, and I'll admit that it could change things. I just didn't want to finish tonight and have everyone leave with a good feeling but without knowing where we'd go from here. I know Andy and his wife have to visit her mother at the hospital tonight, and I didn't want to tie people up after Carl finishes.

"Let's do it this way. Assuming we all feel, after the next hour, that we should go forward, I'll discuss details with Carl and then get to each of you with a piece of the program that I want you to handle or oversee during the next six weeks. Then I'll set a date six weeks or a couple months from now for another all-day meeting at which we'll review together what has been done and make decisions as to implementation. OK?"

Seeing indications of general agreement and noting that coffee and dessert were now on the table, Hauser turned to Iverson and suggested they turn to the subject of whether business ethics is worthwhile.

"Thanks, George," Iverson replied. "This will be relatively short but should be one of the most interesting parts of the discussion. Unless," he said smiling, "everyone is so crammed full of ethics for the day as to have lost their appetites. I won't risk asking that question. But there are two questions I'll pose at the outset—questions for us to consider during the next hour:

- What do we mean by "worthwhile"?
- And worthwhile for whom?

Meaning of "Worthwhile"

Turning to Cynthia Downs, Iverson asked, "Cindy, what do you think we should mean by 'worthwhile' in relation to business ethics?"

"I guess, does it pay?"

"I was hoping you'd say that," said Iverson with a smile. "Not because I agree, but to get the issue out on the table. I read somewhere, I can't remember where, that someone said what we need are some studies to tell us whether business ethics pays. I disagree, and strongly, on at least two grounds.

"First, I question whether such a study is possible, and how credible the results would be if one were made. I'm certainly not denying that ethics can affect profitability, one way or the other, but I don't know how you'd measure this. Profitability is the result of myriad factors, possibly the most important of which is competence. All the good ethics in the world won't make a poorly conceived and managed company profitable. A person who might have insisted on continuing the manufacture of buggy whips after the automobile came in could have been the most ethical person in the world, but that wouldn't have kept the company from going broke.

"Conversely, much as I hate to admit it," Iverson continued, "unethical people, people with the morals of alley cats, sometimes do seem to hit paydirt. We've all seen that—to our irritation and frustration. We hope their sins will overtake them, but sometimes they seem to continue prospering. Then, perhaps, we say to ourselves, 'Probably they aren't enjoying themselves.' But as we watch them smilingly sail out on their yachts with handsome men and beautiful women all over the decks, we aren't sure. Our final resort is to hope that they'll at least get their comeuppance in the next world, but that may seem uncertain and is quite some time away.

"No, Cindy, I'm afraid we can't—shouldn't—sell ethics on the basis that it will pay off. And, speaking personally, I don't like the idea anyway. It smacks of hucksterism. With the spotlight on ethics today, we see quite a few people trying to get in on the act, and one of their approaches is to sell ethics for what it will do for you, like a cure for baldness."

"But, Carl," Sarah Stevenson broke in, "I can see what you mean for individuals, but we're talking about business. The function of business is to make money. I wouldn't go so far as to advocate being unethical in order to make money, but it seems that it is only being responsible if businesspeople are concerned with whether an ethics program will pay off . . . and in the only way business results are measured—financially."

"But is that the only way business results are measured?" Andrew O'Malley asked Stevenson. "Profits are important, but if that is the only thing, all that we've discussed all day is meaningless. For example, if we were to agree that employees are stakeholders and should be considered, say, in a relocation decision, we aren't just looking at the bottom line. As I recall Carl's summarizing this morning, we might use dollars-and-cents considerations as a reason for taking the interests of employees into account if we had other operations in a community and didn't want to foul our nest there, but the stakeholder concept says we should consider them even if the plant to be closed is the only thing the company has in a town. That may be an unusual situation, and I don't know if everyone agrees completely with that answer, but we could list a lot of places where the company does what it thinks is right without identifying any monetary payoff."

"I happen to agree," Iverson said. "looking just at a money payoff is the wrong focus in deciding whether it is worthwhile for businesses to be ethical. It appeals to the egoistic view of people's actions—that they act only in their self-interest. That, I believe, is a mistake. If people acted only out of their own self-interest, we'd never have soldiers risking, sometimes giving up, their lives by rescuing a wounded comrade under enemy fire. We'd never see parents giving up a better home, a new car, vacations, to pay for their children's education. At a far more mundane level, we'd never have people leaving tips at the end of a meal if they knew they'd never be in that restaurant again."

"Carl, I don't intend to be rude, but you seem to keep slipping off into individual situations when what we're talking about is business," Joe Hendricks burst out, almost impatiently. "And what's more, I think you're contradicting yourself. You told us this morning that a company is created to conduct a business for profit. You went on to say that it isn't like a person, that it doesn't have emotions, and that it shouldn't be responsible for social concerns outside its sphere of operations. How do you reconcile this with an argument that we shouldn't be concerned with whether there is a payoff in business ethics?"

"A good question, Joe," Iverson answered. "All this gets rather involved, and it's easy to generate misunderstanding when we discuss it. I'm glad to have a chance to put it in focus—at least I hope to.

"I don't believe that it is a company's responsibility to reform the world. Shareholders don't invest, I'm sure, so that directors and managements will feel free to use their money for all kinds of good deeds, even acknowledged good, worthwhile ones like saving baby seals. Companies should stick to their business. In doing that, though, they should behave ethically. They should consider stakeholders—employees, suppliers, customers, government, the community at large, and, yes, the environment. And to build on the example I just stated, yes, they must consider the baby seals and be willing to spend money to protect them if their operations impact the seals' survival. At the fringes, Joe, the dividing line may be murky, but a company should consider the rights of those it identifies as stakeholders in the conduct of its business, whether or not there is a dollars-and-cents payoff. OK?"

"That helps," Joe replied slowly. "I see what you mean, although I'll want to give it a little more thought."

Worthwhile to Whom?

After a brief pause, Iverson continued, "We've talked so far in quite general terms, and I think this may lead to some uncertainty. It's time to look at the second question, worthwhile to whom? That will be the test of whether what we've been talking about makes any sense. I think we have to look at four groups or persons:

- Society
- Persons acting in their individual capacities
- Persons acting as agents for their companies
- Companies

"This enables us to bring our consideration into sharper focus.

"First let's take society—and we can probably cover it rather quickly. For society, there can be no question. Ethics concerns how people behave toward one another—respect for others as human beings, respect for their rights. Indeed, society would collapse if most people did not behave ethically. What if everyone felt free to lie? To cheat? To steal? If everyone were concerned only with Number One? There would be chaos.

"Trust is essential to human activities. People have to believe in one another. Government, business, all our institutions can operate only on the assumption that most people are moral most of the time. It is only rogue operators, pirates if you will, who can succeed by being unethical—and only because most people aren't! They are able to freeload on an essentially moral world."

"That makes sense, Carl," Sarah Stevenson commented thoughtfully, "but knowing that, why shouldn't I, or any person, take advantage of the situation by behaving unscrupulously? What's to stop me from being a freeloader?"

People in Their Personal Capacity

"That's a good question, Sarah, but you're moving away from whether ethics is good for society to the next area, the impact on people acting as individuals. And that is fine with me if you're all satisfied that ethics is not only worthwhile, that it is essential, at the societal level." Pausing to look around, Iverson continued, "You seem satisfied, so let's address Sarah's question—what's to stop her, or anyone else, from freeloading and taking advantage of the mores of society generally? Any takers?"

"I guess her conscience," O'Malley offered. "Most of us have a conscience that keeps us in line, at least most of the time."

"Yes," Iverson replied, "and fear. Fear of being caught. Being punished. Being scorned by family and friends. There are the notorious freeloaders, few in number but large in visibility, who seem to know how to walk close to the edge, who don't give a damn what others think. Most of us, though, aren't made that way.

"And," he continued, "I can't prove this, but intuitively most of us, I believe, think that bad behavior doesn't pay off for most people in the long run. Sure, someone may get a one-time windfall from some unscrupulous act. A few may succeed for longer periods, possibly even permanently. They may have the skill, the cool nerve, to manipulate the system to their own ends. But most people who are generally unethical lose out. They do something illegal and get caught. Or they get a bad reputation. People don't want to do business with them. Other people look for ways to do them in. They overreach.

"But we've been concentrating on persons acting in their capacities as individuals. Perhaps someone in business for himself or herself. A Boesky type, let's say. Or a dominant figure in a company—someone who runs things pretty much as he or she wishes. Legally such persons may be agents, but they feel few constraints; they operate as though the activity, whatever it may be, is their private preserve.

People as Agents of a Company

"Let's turn to the person—an officer or employee—who is acting as an agent for a company. People who think they are constrained by corporate policies and procedures, who regard themselves as acting on behalf of others. They are probably the most torn, under the most moral stress, because they may suffer from ethical schizophrenia—persons who, rightly or wrongly, may feel it necessary to leave their personal ethics at home when they head for work . . . the situation described in the article I read earlier—that it's pretty hard to expect the individual to behave ethically unless the system provides the right environment.

"This is the area that gives me the greatest problem. It is easy for me, who has nothing at stake, to take the high ground, to say that people must follow the dictates of their conscience. And part of this lies in the fact that it is probably the right answer. If everyone did that, it would be a pretty wonderful world, wouldn't it?

"But I'd like to read something that J. Irwin Miller, a well-known business leader and former president of the National Council of Churches, told a group of future ministers in relating the quandary of a manager who could not get a shipment across the Indonesian border without giving the customs clerk a $100-bribe. Caricaturing the response of well-intentioned critics, he said:

> [You can] tell him that corporate America is a cruel system indeed, that it must be changed in the interest of equity and justice not only for exploited workers, but as well for trapped middle managers like himself. You can even add that . . . you are going to dedicate your own ministry to working for political, economic and social change. That may hearten him, but what if he goes on to say, "That's great, but what do I tell our employee in Jakarta this afternoon?"[1]

"Most of us would like to give a morally impeccable answer—or to duck the issue. And I might not hesitate to tell a rising young star, confronted with a tough ethical problem, to do the right thing. He could probably survive, might even benefit from showing his independence and integrity. But what about a 58-year-old manager, someone who hopes that the declining company that he has been with for 30 years will survive until he is ready to retire—a man, perhaps, with a daughter in college and a sick wife?"

"Are you trying to tell us, Carl, that ethics is relative?" O'Malley asked. "Doesn't that open the door to all kinds of rationalizations?"

"Are you trying to make me squirm?" Iverson asked, with a somewhat rueful smile. "If so, you're succeeding. But no, Andy, I wouldn't say ethics is relative. I would, though, say that ethics is sometimes ambiguous. I would never want it on my conscience that I encouraged someone to do something clearly immoral, possibly illegal—something that would violate most people's sense of propriety. Something that a person would never want his or her family to know about—a pretty good test, incidentally.

"We all know, though, that there are gray areas. Or minor violations. I wouldn't, for example, want to see someone make a

---

[1] J. Irwin Miller, "How Religious Commitments Shape Corporate Decisions," *Harvard Divinity Bulletin* (February-March 1984), 4, as reported in Michael Rion, *The Responsible Manager: Practical Strategies for Ethical Decision Making* (San Francisco: Harper & Row, Publishers, 1990), 52–53.

federal case of it and report a fellow employee whom he or she saw, just once under time pressure, pour a pint of noninflammable solvent down the drain. Or report someone whom you heard make a personal long-distance call on the company telephone. There is a place for whistle blowing, but save it for something important, or pervasive.

"Let's leave this subject here," Iverson said after a pause. "It's the area that doesn't have a good answer. The best solution is to work for a company that encourages ethical behavior, that doesn't put its employees in difficult moral quandaries. And that, I might say, is an excellent lead-in to my next and final point: Is ethical behavior worthwhile for a company?"

Worthwhile for a Company?

"Clarence Walton, widely recognized as *the* pioneer in the field of business ethics, concluded the introduction to his recent book, *The Moral Manager*, with this quotation from a report issued by the American Assembly, a prestigious association connected with Columbia University:

> On the important subject of values, we discern a marked deterioration in traditional values essential to competitiveness. A lack of both individual and institutional leadership has eroded respect for community and nationhood. We conclude that values of integrity, social justice, and moral leadership are not only necessary in themselves, but lead directly to competitive advantage. *Our standard of living and our standard of values are inseparable.*[2]

"I agree with that conclusion, but you will want to know, I am sure, why. A good way, perhaps, to encapsulate it is by reference to a recent article, "Challenging the Egoistic Paradigm,"

---

[2] Running Out of Time: Reversing America's Declining Competitiveness (New York: The American Assembly Report, November 1987), 11, as quoted in Clarence C. Walton, *The Moral Manager* (Cambridge, MA; Ballinger Publishing Company, 1988), 9.

by Norman E. Bowie.[3] Don't let the title turn you off; obviously the article was not written, or captioned, for laypeople, but anyone who is willing to make a little effort can follow the logic. Much of it is based on a fairly recent book, *Passions Within Reason*, by economist Robert Frank.[4] Admittedly, it is hard to do justice, in a few words, to the way Bowie and, presumably, Frank develop the thesis, but I'll try to give you the gist.

"Bowie argues—and demonstrates with some interesting examples—that people, and I'd include companies, do not operate solely out of self-interest. He gets into what I consider particularly interesting when he says that what he calls 'reciprocal altruism' is self-defeating. He goes on—"

"Excuse me, but what is reciprocal altruism?" Stevenson interrupted.

"In simple—I hope not oversimplified—terms, reciprocal altruism amounts to 'I'll scratch your back if you'll scratch mine.' Tit for tat. In business, if you, the employees, will give us loyalty, we'll not close the plant during a downturn in business. The problem is you don't trust a reciprocal altruist because, when push comes to shove, he or she might renege. What we need is what Bowie and Frank call hard-core altruism. An example:

> Suppose a firm is having difficulty with employee morale and management believes that taking steps to increase employee morale will lead to greater profits. What steps do they take? Unless management adopts a strategy that is convincingly altruistic, the employees are likely to treat management overtures cynically and behave accordingly. Any gains in productivity are likely to be suboptimal. Management needs a strategy that represents what Frank calls altruistic commitment. A no-lay-off policy during an economic downturn is an example of such a policy. It communicates to the employees that management is concerned about them even when that concern does

---

[3] Norman E. Bowie, "Challenging the Egoistic Paradigm," *Business Ethics Quarterly* (January 1991), 1–21.
[4] Robert Frank, *Passions Within Reason* (New York: W. W. Norton & Co., 1988).

not yield greater profits. Such a policy would be adopted because it is right rather than because it leads to greater profits.[5]

"Do you buy that?" Hendricks asked skeptically.

"Joe, I have a couple problems with it," Iverson replied. "Up to a point, I think it's quite persuasive if you can put yourself in the proper frame of mind. But there has to be a limit: No company could make an ironclad, forever no-layoff commitment. If the downturn went long enough, it might push the company into bankruptcy. Even profitable operations might get pulled down.

"My other problem is, perhaps, a matter of faith. To operate on the basis of hard-core altruism requires faith, and a person or a company has to be committed before undertaking it. It reminds me—have any of you ever rappelled?"

"What's that?" asked Hauser.

"Rappelling is using a hand-held rope fastened to a tree or rock at the top of a cliff and going over the edge and down backward. I was in survival school in the Air Force, up in the Rockies, and we'd had a demonstration. The instructor turned to me and said, 'Lieutenant, why don't you lead off to show your crew how it's done?' It required me to loop the rope around a stout tree, then wrap it around my body in such a way that holding my end out would permit the rope to pay out, in other words for me to drop. Pulling my end in would stop the descent—so the instructor said. I had to jump off backward into space, then pull on the rope and hope it would halt my fall. And, oh yes, I forgot to mention—going down I had to brace my feet against the cliff face to keep from banging into it, leaning back and keeping my body stiff and horizontal to the ground far below."

"Did you do it?" O'Malley asked.

"What choice did I have? I couldn't chicken out in front of my crew. And yet I would have given a thousand dollars—which was quite a bit more than I had in the bank then—to figure a way out. So I did it, and obviously made it."

---

[5] Bowie, *op. cit.*, 16.

An Act of Faith

"But why do I tell you this? Because, despite the logic behind it, even a demonstration that it worked for someone else, I had to accept on faith that if I pulled down on the rope it would stop my descent. And that keeping my legs stiff and leaning back would keep me from getting bruised and cut up against the face of the cliff. I think that this hard-core altruism Bowie talks about, or altruistic commitment, is something of the same thing."

"I don't think I'd be too comfortable taking the leap of faith," Stevenson said.

"I understand, but just remember that this commitment to employees in the illustration Bowie gave is really part and parcel of the quality circles, management-worker teams, and worker participation that so many people say we need today. I won't pretend to be an expert on what makes Japanese industry so successful, but there seems to be some mutual commitment that we may not have.

"And besides, remember that you don't have to accept all this in order to think that business ethics is worthwhile. It's just another argument. And what's to lose?"

"Nothing, probably. But you'll agree, Carl, that we still have to run a tight ship, won't you?" Hendricks asked. "A spirit of goodwill can only go so far."

"Absolutely," Iverson responded. "As I said earlier, we mustn't confuse being ethical and being sentimental. It has long been recognized in the military that outfits whose officers maintain a strict, but fair and consistent, discipline are happier, more efficient, than lax organizations. Respecting the rights of others as human beings has nothing to do with being sloppy. Disciplining, even firing, an inefficient employee is not, per se, unethical."

"We seem to be focusing on employees," O'Malley observed. "What about suppliers, customers, other stakeholders?"

"Andy," Iverson said, "I think any difference may be only of degree, of closeness. I'd like to read you something I think is quite relevant, something that Kenneth Andrews, a well-known business professor and former editor of the *Harvard Business Review*, wrote. I believe I quoted something he said before dinner, although I may have forgotten to mention his name then—anyway here goes:

> An adequate corporate strategy must include non-economic goals. An economic strategy is the optimal match of a company's product and market opportunities with its resources and distinctive competence. (That both are continually changing is of course true.) But economic strategy is humanized and made attainable by deciding what kind of organization the company will be—its character, the values it espouses, its relationships to customers, employees, communities, and shareholders. . .[6]

"Indeed, it goes beyond business; as we have discussed, doing right in business is just one aspect of ethical behavior, not something apart. In commenting on recent developments in the Soviet Union, Edvard Shevardnadze, the foreign minister who broke with Gorbachev over the slow pace of perestroika, wrote that 'only the policy that is morally right is victorious.'[7] Although this may sound a bit platitudinous, I am convinced that he is right over the long run.

"But I know we have to stop now. Before we do, though, I'd like to emphasize a view I hold strongly—that good ethics is good business but that that is not the sole, even the primary, reason for behaving ethically. I'll read something that ethicist W. Michael Hoffman has written that sums it up for me:

> One thing that the study of ethics has taught us over the past 2,500 years is that being ethical may on occasion require that we place the interests of others ahead of or at least on par with our own interests. And this implies that the ethical thing to do, the morally right thing to do, may not be in our own self-interest. What happens when the right thing is not the best thing for the business?

---

[6] Kenneth R. Andrews, "Ethics in Practice," *Harvard Business Review* (September-October 1989), 103.

[7] Edvard Shevardnadze, *The Future Belongs to Freedom* (New York: The Free Press, 1991), as quoted in *The New York Times Book Review*, September 22, 1991, 7.

Although in most cases good ethics may be good business, it should not be advanced as the only or even the main reason for doing business ethically. When the crunch comes, when ethics conflicts with the firm's interests, any ethics program that has not already faced up to this possibility is doomed to fail because it will undercut the rationale of the program itself. We should promote business ethics, not because good ethics is good business, but because we are morally required to adopt the moral point of view in all our dealings—and business is no exception. In business, as in all other human endeavors, we must be prepared to pay the costs of ethical behavior.[8]

"And that," Iverson said, "brings what I have to say to an end, at least for now."

"Thanks, Carl, from all of us," Hauser said, rising and shaking hands. "This has been great. Give me just a minute, if you will, to talk with the others on the committee."

The committee members stepped out in the hall for a few minutes, then returned. George said with a smile, "Well, Carl, it seems that we all want an ethics program to get started—and as soon as it can be done right. I'll be in touch soon to discuss some details, and we'll be setting a date for an initial implementation meeting in about two months.

With that, everyone said goodnight and left, chatting with one another as they went out the door.

---

[8] W. Michael Hoffman, "Business and Environmental Ethics," *Business Ethics Quarterly* (April 1991), 176.

CHAPTER TEN

The Story's Epilogue

Three Months Later

George Hauser and Stuart Andretti had finished looking over the luncheon menu and had placed their orders. Hauser asked, "Tell me, Stu, how do you think you'll like being the CEO at Hauser-Moore?"

"Give me a little time to get over the shock," Andretti laughed. "When you said that some board representatives wanted to talk to me last week, I had no idea what was in the wind. It even crossed my mind for a moment to wonder if I'd done something wrong or was over the hill—if maybe people wanted to replace me on the board.

"After they talked to me," he continued, "I got the idea why I was asked to take the job. And, of course, I talked it over with you. As an old friend, though, I'd appreciate your filling me in from your perspective, especially since you had to be the moving force."

"There were, of course, a number of reasons, and I'll recap them as best I can," Hauser said. "But first, obviously, we couldn't have even given you a thought if it hadn't occurred to me that you might be available—and willing."

"What ever gave you that idea? It hadn't crossed my mind."

"Well, Stu, you are six years younger than I am—and in good health. I know why you stepped up to board chair and turned the day-to-day running of your company over to your son three years ago. You thought he was ready. And you wanted to do it while you could still be available to him for counsel and advice.

"You may not remember, though, that you told me about six months ago that it had worked almost too well, that you didn't really have enough to do. And I've had a feeling you were getting a bit bored—you'll never be a full-time golfer. So I put two and two together and thought maybe you'd be the answer to our prayers. You've known our family for years, and you've been a Hauser-Moore director for 17 years. Most important, we have compatible philosophies.

"My biggest question—besides, of course, whether you'd even consider the job—was how long you'd be willing to stay. We sure didn't want a series of interim CEOs, people who wouldn't start anything new because they wouldn't be around long enough to see it through. And there's always a lot of jockeying for position underneath when there is a temporary boss. When you told me that you would be willing to give us up to five years barring something unforeseen, it put that concern to rest. I knew we'd have enough time to plan properly for the future. Does that answer that question?"

"Very well. And it makes sense," Stu agreed. "But I'm still surprised you moved so quickly. I thought you'd hold on to the job for a little longer. After all, you were not just another interim CEO."

"But I was," Hauser insisted. "Everyone knew my stay would be quite limited this time. We're still suffering from the trauma of the sudden relocation decision and Dick Bentley's departure. Something had to be done to restore some stability, some sense of continuity. I have been able to tide things over temporarily, but everyone knows it's just that—my age and my heart condition . . . and Jessica's insistence that I take it easier.

"Nothing personal against Bentley," he continued, "but we probably made a mistake bringing him in, especially when we did. It wasn't good for us or fair to him. He was a big company man, from a big city; that's fine, but I think maybe the combination of Hauser-Moore and Janesboro was a culture shock for him—and his wife. They never adjusted.

"And frankly, Stu, I may have been naive. We hadn't hired top people from the outside before, and I looked only at his track record—his technical competence, personality, things like that. I didn't give enough attention to how he'd fit into the company or the community. To refer to something Carl Iverson covered, I perhaps ignored our traditions, our firm culture."

"But we mustn't overdo that culture bit," Andretti broke in, "and overreact. I agree with the importance of tradition, but we mustn't become inbred, parochial. Tradition can be a dead hand on the throttle as well as a positive influence. Any organization needs an infusion of new blood from time to time."

"I know, but carefully planned," Hauser said thoughtfully. "Brought in gradually and at the right levels. And with attention to whether there is a common set of basic values." After a short pause, "But let me go on with the other reasons we asked you to become CEO. I don't see anyone in the company ready to take over, although two or three may be in a few years. That may have been one of my biggest mistakes, acting as if I'd live forever and not considering succession. And none of us wanted to risk rushing outside again and maybe not getting the right person. A company can take only so many of those jolts, especially in a short time."

"I agree with that," Andretti said, "and I can see that I had some of what was needed. One of my biggest challenges will be to build a good management team, most importantly to identify and prepare my possible successors. Of course, I know quite a few of the officers and executives but not well in most cases. You said there are two or three possibilities in the company?"

"Yes, and one of them might surprise you. Do you remember the problem with the relocation cost study? The brush-off young Saunders got from Joe Hendricks—the fact that there were errors in what Hendricks provided?" Andretti nodded, and Hauser continued, "Well, I had a good talk with Hendricks about that, and it may have been one of the few success stories to come out of that fiasco. I told him I liked his hard-nosed approach to management but that he needed to develop more respect for the rights of others. Not to bull his way through life. He seemed to take it pretty well and admitted that he'd given Saunders a rough time—and shouldn't have. He seemed to understand the seriousness of what he had done, that we were lucky the ramifications hadn't been worse. Well, I gambled and put him on the committee to develop the ethics program."

"That's a strange twist," Andretti said with surprise. "How did it work?"

"Better than I could have expected. He has made a real contribution in several key areas as we have been working on implementation. And he told me the other day how much he had gotten out of it . . . seemed to be quite surprised that ethics could be interesting, and relevant to running a business.

"Of course," Hauser went on, "he has a ways to go. But we're keeping our eye on him. And if you agree, I think he's the logical person to be named vice president of manufacturing when Jerry Stratton retires this fall. I don't want, though, to preempt your judgments—that will primarily be your responsibility. Or to imply that Hendricks would be the leading candidate from within the company to be your successor. We have a couple others that are just as likely. You'll be getting to know them."

"And we mustn't ignore the possibility of people who aren't even with the company now," Andretti commented.

"You're absolutely right. We have some gaps in key positions that may have to be filled from the outside. And at least two of these are at rather high levels. These are things we'll have to talk about in some detail when you begin coming in full-time next week.

"By the way," Hauser continued, "I assume you are planning to commute. With only a 20-mile drive—good roads all the way—

I assumed you wouldn't be moving. But I have been remiss in not raising the question—seeing if there is anything we can do."

"That's all right," Andretti replied. "As a matter of fact, Joan probably would have told me to say no to the job if it had required giving up our home. We're both involved in a lot of activities there, too. We'll see—I may decide to take an apartment in Janesboro to use in bad weather or when there are late meetings. And I shall want to get into some community activities here that will probably involve dinners and so forth. We'll have to let that evolve."

"Well, Stu," said Hauser as they rose from the table after running through several other matters, "I know you have to get home to take care of some matters there. I appreciate your coming over to meet with some of the people this morning and to stay for lunch with me. I don't need to tell you how much it means to me to have you fill this gap—it's a lifesaver, maybe literally."

One Year Later

Michael Lerner had come to Stuart Andretti's office to discuss several pending matters. As he sat down, he remarked, "I understand that George and Jessica finally got off on that cruise they had to cancel last year. I'm glad. It was a rough period for him—and for her. But they seem to have adjusted quite well. Is he able to stay away from here as much as he hoped—or at least thought he hoped?"

Andretti smiled, "I know what you mean, but really it's worked beautifully, both for George and for me. Probably the fact that we've been friends for all these years has helped."

"How is the relocation of the small engine line going?" Lerner asked. "Is it almost completed?"

"Yes, and it's going quite smoothly, that is, as such major moves go. But it's a pity it happened the way it did . . . and got off to such a bad start. It was really the right thing to do, as you made us realize when the discussion first came up at the board meeting over a year ago—the one just before Bentley resigned. It would have been a serious mistake, I now see, to have retooled and put the facility here.

"What was wrong," Andretti continued, "was the way it was handled . . . inadequate advance planning . . . no consideration of the people problems . . . lousy PR. The steps we have taken since have, I believe, controlled the damage. There are wounds that will never heal, but even most of the terminated employees can see that Hauser-Moore has done everything it can to fulfill its obligations to them—not just to pay lip service but to be seriously concerned about them as human beings. As a result of the retraining program and placement efforts, most of them now have jobs . . . maybe not exactly what they wanted, maybe not as good as what they lost, but jobs. Termination payments have helped with others. Most of all, efforts at communication have helped. You might call it sensitivity."

"I guess the ethics program is going well from all I hear. Is it all in place?"

"Most of it is, Mike. And I believe it has helped, in the aftermath of the relocation as well as generally. Maybe I'm giving it too much credit, but it seems to have engendered a feeling of goodwill, possibly confidence that the attitudes, the traditions, of the Hauser family will remain."

"It seemed to me from something he said at the last board meeting," Lerner said with a smile, "that even Larry Albertson has mellowed. Or is that wishful thinking?"

"Well," Andretti laughed, "it's been a while since he's lashed out at do-gooders. Seriously, though, Larry's all right. He just wants to make sure the rest of us don't get carried away. In several conversations we've had, he's had good things to say about the ethics initiative, as he calls it. I think what makes him feel best is the improved relationship around the community, at least part of which he acknowledges has come from the company's stepping up to its obligations to stakeholders—although we'll never get him to use that term."

"And our long-range planning committee that you set up right after you came in is a very positive development," Lerner observed. "It's well structured, with representation from both the board and line management. Naturally I'm glad that you selected our Business Research Bureau at the college as consultants; I'm not completely objective, but I think that was a good move. It looks as if Hauser-Moore's taking charge of its own future rather than just reacting. That doesn't mean, of course, that there won't be problems, that we won't suffer setbacks, even that something won't sneak up on us. But we're much better positioned, I think."

"Yes," Andretti replied, "I think we are. The additional work that your Business Research Bureau has done has pretty well confirmed that Janesboro is not the place to continue our heavy manufacturing indefinitely—certainly not the place to expand it. Hendersonville was a good choice for the new line of engines. And it, or some other place, is where we'll gradually relocate our manufacturing. But now we can plan for it. And anticipate the effect on employees, suppliers, other stakeholders.

"It's not all negative for Janesboro, though," he continued. "Our engineering department is developing some exciting new high-tech products, ones that can very well be produced here. We'll have to manage it carefully, but we can probably retain our presence here, possibly even enhance it, while avoiding future problems like last year's relocation."

"Interestingly, like Carl Iverson and other ethicists say," Lerner responded, "this shows that ethics is entwined in good business planning. The two go hand in hand. There has to be some give-and-take, sure, and we can never avoid hurting people occasionally . . . or making mistakes. But at least we can see what we're doing, plan so as to balance the various rights and obligations, and come out with the best answer we can figure under the circumstances."

"Yes," Stuart Andretti said thoughtfully, "at the risk of sounding stuffy, I would say that that is what business ethics is all about—trying to run a profitable business while, at the same time, considering the rights of others . . . being responsibly pragmatic. To steal the title one writer applied to an article, it's "Ethics Without the Sermon."[1]

---

[1] Laura L. Nash, "Ethics Without the Sermon," *Harvard Business Review* (November-December 1981).

How to Get an Ethics Program Started

All that has gone before is important—sound and, it is hoped, interesting—but only groundwork. Chapter 8 dealt generally with the elements of an effective company ethics program. But just how can a company get such a program under way? This conclusion attempts to answer that question, at the same time taking the opportunity to emphasize the importance of, and to throw additional light on, the various elements.

Companies deal with ethics in a variety of ways. Some have formal programs, perhaps headed by full-time persons in management and incorporating all or most of the elements discussed in Chapter 8. Others have less-structured but still well-defined programs, sometimes coordinated through a committee of management and other employees. Still others incorporate some of the elements of an ethics program, but without identifying them as such. Too many, unfortunately, although not denigrating the importance of ethical behavior, take it for granted and do not address training and implementation of ethics as a recognized, integral part of company strategy and operations.

The goal of this "Conclusion: How to Get an Ethics Program Started" is to encourage companies to establish or enhance effective ethics programs by showing how they can begin. It will focus on the following elements described in Chapter 8:

A statement of values
Corporate tradition and culture
Tone at the top
A code of conduct
Established procedures
Training
Hot line
Ongoing oversight

Before these are addressed, however, some broad, general issues require mention.

Company Participation in Design of Ethics Program

The effective design of a new or substantially revised program calls for the active, informed participation of responsible persons within the company, usually through a committee. Whether or not the company retains an ethics consultant to provide counsel and guidance (a matter discussed later), establishment of a steering committee is important for several reasons. It fixes responsibility for getting something done. It sends a message—the commitment of management, evidence that what is being done is really important and has top-level support. The fact that people who will have to live with the results participate actively in developing the program ensures that it will be consistent with the company's operations and style, that it is not a plug-in model, a stereotype, lifted from outside without an understanding of the company's operations and culture. Active involvement generates enthusiasm, making the committee members feel that they have a stake in the results. And it leaves a cadre of informed leaders for the ongoing program.

In the Hauser-Moore case, George Hauser took on the responsibility of heading the committee. This was plausible under the circumstances—the way in which the company's need for an ethics program developed, Hauser's paternalistic interest in the company, and his desire to get an effective program established before withdrawing from active management. Ordinarily we would not find a CEO chairing the steering committee, but the person who does head the steering committee should preferably be an active senior officer—someone whose appointment underscores the importance of the program. That individual should understand the overall role of the program within the structure of the company, should have the "clout" to obtain cooperation and should be able to make commitments for management.

The other committee members should represent a reasonable cross section of skills and disciplines, with the majority consisting of line managers who will be directly affected by whatever they develop. Although human resources people should be represented and play an important part, both substance and perception make it important that the program not be primarily a headquarters or staff project. The individual members must have a genuine interest in and commitment to the effort and should be able to spend whatever time is required. This was evident in the makeup of the Hauser-Moore committee and in its operations described in Chapters 7, 8 and 9.

The role of such a committee cannot be categorized; it will depend on its charge and the timetable given it. These factors, in turn, will depend on whether there is an existing program, what elements the board or management wants to have included in the program, and whether a consultant will be available to provide counsel and guidance.

Is a Consultant Needed?

Beginning in Chapter 2, an ethics consultant, Carl Iverson, played an active role, indeed a central role, in the Hauser-Moore case. He was involved in all aspects. A logical question would be: *Is such an extensive use of an ethics consultant customary? Or necessary?*

Iverson's continuing participation provided an excellent vehicle for showcasing a board of directors' evolving ethical awareness, for depicting a variety of ethical dilemmas, and for portraying, with broad strokes, an approach to developing a company's ethics program. The ethicist's involvement there might be an ideal, especially with a concerned, interested board and a management that has the time, money, and inclination to pursue such a course. But such a major role would not be typical, and no management need have apprehensions about starting an ethics program for fear that anything less than what Hauser-Moore did would be ineffectual.

That leads to another question: *Is it necessary to retain an ethics consultant at all if a company wishes to initiate or to improve an ethics program?* The answer is that it may not be necessary but that it would often be desirable. As could be seen from Hauser-Moore's experience, understanding ethics and knowing how to deal with ethical dilemmas are not always simple, not matters merely of possessing a sense of goodwill and following lessons learned during childhood. Moral reasoning is a sophisticated discipline. And good training also requires the application of specialized skills.

The extent to which a company might wish to use an ethics consultant would depend on a number of factors: whether it has, or plans to have, anyone on its staff with training and experience in ethics—an important consideration; whatever ethics program it might already have; the elements of its existing or contemplated program with respect to which management feels uncertain; its general philosophy toward using outside consultants; and the size of the company, perhaps.

Unless a company already has an established, effective program, it might consider the use of consultants for certain elements. Guidance in developing a statement of values, for example, and a code of conduct that is tailored to a company's own operations and traditions. And training, especially training—a matter discussed in greater detail later. Then, help in designing an effective program for ongoing oversight.

Another question might be: *Where does a company find a consultant?* This is a particularly pertinent question, not because consultants are hard to find but, rather, because there are so many today. According to a recent article, the Chicago-based International Association of Ethicists, a nonprofit research clearinghouse and referral service for ethicists, has identified more than 1,440 organizations and individuals in some way concerned with ethics.[1] But all are not necessarily well qualified. Some may have trouble relating theory to the realities of business. As one CEO said, "I've read so much on this subject by so-called experts who have never set foot in the real business world."[2]

There is no sure, easy way to secure the services of a well-qualified consultant. First, perhaps, a company might wish to talk with qualified persons in a company that has a functioning program, especially one that has used a consultant. Find how they made a selection—what they looked for and how the consultant was used. Decide whether the company's needs are for someone to help with the conceptual foundation, which might suggest an academic, or for system design. Obtain references for anyone under consideration—and check them.

Managements, especially of companies that do not make extensive use of outside consultants, will be concerned about what the services of a consulting ethicist would cost. A precise answer is not possible here, any more than it would be with other providers of professional services—lawyers, accountants, engineers, data processing advisors, or management consultants. Estimates, or perhaps range commitments, can and should be obtained in advance.

Now let us turn to specific suggestions concerning the eight elements of a company program that were identified in Chapter 8. To get the benefit of the experiences of managers, consultants, and professors who have been actively involved in business ethics

---

[1] Tani Maher, "Ethics Entrepreneurs," *Financial World* (June 27, 1989), 84.

[2] John A. Byrne quoting Andrew C. Sigler, chairman of Champion International Corp., in "Businesses Are Signing Up for Ethics 101," *Business Week* (February 15, 1988), 56.

and to convey the flavor of their views, parts of the discussion that follows will draw heavily on quotations from their presentations and writings.

A Statement of Values

Some companies with effective ethics programs do not have statements of values, also characterized as credos or mission statements. Perhaps they regard such statements as window dressing. They may contend that actions speak louder than words. But many people who have worked extensively with business ethics regard credos as the cornerstone of a complete program, a commitment—telling shareholders, employees, customers, vendors, and the public just what the company stands for.

A statement of values should be specific, believable. It should be evident that it is an essential part of the company's operations, integrated into company policies, not something off to one side that can be observed or ignored, as one sees fit. And, although a credo should have the evident support, the commitment, of top management, it should not be perceived as something handed down from on high. The line organization should participate actively in the development of the statement of values, ensuring that it represents what the entire organization believes and the way it intends to operate. As one ethicist who has worked extensively with companies in developing their programs has written:

> [Statements of values] serve as directions to organizational members, as an orientation to new members and as a centralized articulation of the shared values operative in the organization. *Statements which are drafted by means of a survey have the advantage of being more readily acceptable, rather than those which are imposed in a "top-down" manner.* They should express the basic purpose of the organization and the relative value that it places upon its relationships with groups both internal and external to the organization.[3] (Italics added)

---

[3] Peter Madsen, "Managing Ethics," *Executive Excellence* (December 1990), 11.

Any survey should be carefully structured. As part of its work with management change, Andersen Consulting uses an "Organization Values Survey" that lists 33 values and asks each respondent within the organization to rate each value, both as the respondent believes it exists today and as he or she believes it should be. The beginning of that survey follows as an illustration:[4]

It should be noted that ethics considerations are commingled with business values, as is necessary if the survey and conclusions drawn from it are to be effective. Respondents may include the entire organization or be a sample, the only criterion being that the responses should be representative.

The result is an inventory of values—a starting point; there would normally be a considerable interplay of views within a company before a credo would be issued. An important feature is that the result indicates whatever gap may exist between the existing and the desired organizational values and characteristics, providing useful information for developing a new organizational culture. Management should carefully consider, but is not constrained to accept without modifications, what the respondents deem desirable. Because the statement should "stretch," setting forth realistic behavioral goals for the company, the final product might go somewhat beyond what the survey consensus aims for.

No statement of values should be regarded as final. A company should conduct new surveys and revise its credo from time to time, especially when:

There has been a significant strategic redirection.
There has been a transgression of ethics, morals or the law.
Traditional values are inappropriate for the new climate.
Significantly different groups are combined.
Downsizing, layoffs, decline in performance, attrition, or redeployment of the work force is necessary.[5]

---

[4] Reproduced, with permission, from an internal document of Andersen Consulting that is a part of the firm's Change Management Services. Copyright © 1991 by Andersen Consulting, Arthur Andersen & Co, SC.
[5] *Ibid.*

ORGANIZATION VALUES SURVEY

This survey is used to identify the current and desired future values of your organization. To complete the survey, use the set of response codes at the top of each page. In column 1, indicate the degree to which you agree or disagree that the values listed below accurately describe your organization today. In column 2, indicate the degree to which you would *like it* to describe your organization in the future.

CODE
(5=Strongly Agree) (4=Agree) (3=Neutral) (2=Disagree) (1=Strongly Disagree)

Column 1 Today	The organization where I work ...	Column 2 Like it To Be
————	1. Is commited to quality/excellence	———
————	2. Encourages "planned" risk-taking	———
————	3. Is committed to customers	———
————	4. Has management that openly shares information	———
————	5. Is committed to fair profitability	———
————	6. Balances short-term and long-term goals	———
————	7. Rewards people who support change	———
————	8. Is a leader in the marketplace	———
————	9. Allows flexibility in policies and practices when necessary	———
————	10. Has a positive community image	———
————	11. Tolerates the uncertainty that accompanies change	———
————	12. Rewards loyalty	———
————	13. Encourages employee commitment	———
————	14. Emphasizes individual growth and development	———
————	15. Respects the past but is not afraid to change	———
————	16. Encourages bottom-up decision making	———

A company may wish to consider whether it should retain consultants in conducting a values survey and developing a statement of values. This depends on a number of factors, some noted earlier—among others, whether there is an existing credo or ethics program, whether consultants will be retained for other parts of the program and how comfortable management feels in inventorying and summarizing its values without outside assistance. The overriding consideration is that what comes out of the effort must be carefully developed, must reflect shared values held within the organization, and must be set forth in a useful form.

Corporate Tradition and Culture

Companies are molded in large part by their traditions, and they respond almost automatically, especially in times of crisis or stress, from their basis of culture. What one management professor has said about the role of this corporate tradition is instructive:

> Sociologists are keenly studying what they call corporate stories, legends, and heroes as a way organizations have of transmitting the value system. Corporations . . . have even hired consultants to perform an audit of their corporate culture. In a company, the leader is the person who understands, interprets, and manages the corporate value system.[6]

As noted in Chapter 8, a company cannot create an instant tradition or culture. But it has, for better or for worse, an existing culture—one that it must live with and, if necessary, try to change. Maintaining or rebuilding this culture is a long-term, never-ending process, but company management must start somewhere. Developing and issuing a good statement of values is an excellent place to start—then acting in accordance with that statement.

Having an established culture that is known to, and accepted by, the organization though, is not enough. It must be nurtured—made known, publicized. This should not be regarded as a public

---

[6] LaRue Tone Hosmer, *The Ethics of Management* (Homewood, IL: Irwin, 1987),120–121.

relations gimmick, although sound professional advice may enhance the communication. Vehicles for this abound: company histories, orientation sessions for new employees, videotapes of important company events, memoirs of past leaders, memorabilia displayed at headquarters or training centers, celebrations of important anniversaries.

To be effective, these approaches must not focus exclusively on accomplishments or smack of corporate braggadocio. Sometimes, indeed, the most effective messages about corporate culture dwell on what might, at the time, have seemed a failure; for example, loss of a customer or client because of a stand taken in a difficult situation. Even humorous stories about company leaders may add an important aspect to company tradition by revealing their humanness, their approachability.

Tone at the Top

Suggesting how to achieve an ideal "tone at the top" is difficult, since it involves the very essence of the practice of leadership. Tone at the top does not involve procedures; it is not something where anyone in the company—or, for that matter, anyone outside—can make studies, establish procedures, or do anything to make it happen. Tone at the top comes from within the leaders—the personal values of the management team, the belief that these values are important and must be observed, regardless of cost, and the willingness to be an example even when it is difficult or inconvenient. So, what follows comes closer than might be wished to preaching, an exhortation to management to stand up and be counted. As one business school professor has written:

> The way the chief executive exercises moral judgment is universally acknowledged to be more influential than written policy. The CEO who orders the immediate recall of a product, at the cost of millions of dollars in sales because of a quality defect affecting a limited number of untraceable shipments, sends one kind of a message. The executive who suppresses information about a producer's [sic] actual or potential ill ef-

fects or, knowingly or not, condones overcharging sends an-other.

Policy is implicit in behavior. The ethical aspects of prod-uct quality, personnel, advertising, and marketing decisions are immediately plain. CEOs say much more than they know in the most casual contacts with those who watch their every move. Pretense is futile. "Do not *say* things," Emerson once wrote. "What you *are* stands over you the while, and thunders so that I can not hear what you say to the contrary." It follows that "if you would not be known to do anything, never do it."[7]

And it is instructive to note what happens when the CEO evidences interest in an ethics-related issue. "Just ask Bruce W. Karrh, the Du Pont Company's vice president of safety, health and environmental affairs," a newspaper story said. "As a Du Pont officer, Mr. Karrh, who has run the company's environmental operations since 1984, is a honcho in his own right. Even so, plant managers often balked when he advised them to commit resources to environmental projects.

"Then, in May 1989, Du Pont's chairman, Edgar S. Woolard Jr., called for 'corporate environmentalism' and dubbed himself Du Pont's 'chief environmentalist.' All of a sudden, plant people were begging Mr. Karrh for environmental advice.

" 'I used to have to do a real selling job to the line people,' Mr. Karrh said. 'Then suddenly it wasn't just me trying to get the organization to do things, it was Ed. Now they call all the time.' "[8]

That pretty much sums it up. But the emphasis must not be solely on how the CEO handles the major issues, the potentially "big news" or traumatic ones. The little decisions that go into day-to-day management may, in the aggregate, be every bit as important. In Chapter 8 of this book, George Hauser's decision to chair the committee set up to advise on Hauser-Moore's ethics program is a good example. By his actions, he was telling the

---

[7] Kenneth R. Andrews, "Ethics in Practice," *Harvard Business Review* (September/October 1989), 102.

[8] Claudia H. Deutsch, "Giving the Environment Teeth," *The New York Times* (March 4, 1991).

organization what he, the CEO, considered important far more effectively than if he had only created the committee and had then appointed someone else to head it. How this contrasts with the CEO, described in the same chapter, who didn't want to "sit in plastic chairs and drink coffee out of styrofoam cups with all those people"!

Of course, one cannot expect the CEO to be present everywhere, to take the lead in everything. An effective CEO must set priorities, budgeting his or her time. Otherwise the effort becomes fragmented, dissipated; nothing happens, and no message gets sent. And it takes more than just the chief executive to create tone at the top. The CEO may be the most obvious, and what he or she does is likely to influence others in management. But other members of management should remember that they are also part of the "top." It should be the responsibility of every manager—and every supervisor, too—to remember that some people look to them and draw conclusions from their behavior regarding what is acceptable practice within the company.

The importance of tone at the top is so important that it must be nurtured. The character of those considered for employment or promotion should be as important a factor as technical competence. In Hauser-Moore, we saw the damaging results of hiring an outsider who did not fit in with, even understand, the company's traditions—and George Hauser's acknowledgment that he may not have given enough thought to maintaining the culture that had been built up over the years. Tone at the top must be more than skin-deep. A respected business administration professor has captured the ongoing nature of this well, at the same time pointing toward some of the program elements yet to be discussed:

> In a large, decentralized organization, consistently ethical performance requires difficult decisions from not only the current CEO but also a succession of chief executives. Here the board of directors enters the scene. The board has the opportunity to provide for a succession of CEOs whose personal values and characters are consistently adequate for sustaining

and developing established traditions for ethical conduct. Once in place, chief executives must rely on two resources for getting done what they cannot do personally: the character of their associates and the influence of policy and the measures that are taken to make policy effective.[9]

Code of Conduct

Codes of conduct sometimes tend to become confused with statements of values. Indeed, in some companies the two may be the same, or at least overlap. As discussed in Chapter 8, however, they fill different roles. Rather than stating broad values held by the organization, codes of conduct "are specific guidelines that cover the most fundamental areas of concern and should be well circulated throughout the organization. Codes can serve the purpose of mandating behavior standards and of clarifying responsibilities. Clear statements of disciplinary actions in case of violations should also be made in the code.

"Topics which most organizational codes cover include: conflicts of interest, illegal conduct such as bribery or kickbacks, safeguarding company assets, honesty in organizational communications, whistleblowing, gifts, entertainment and travel, proprietary information, governmental contracting responsibilities, drug and alcohol abuse, sexual harassment, etc."[10] The comprehensive nature of one company's code of worldwide business conduct and operating principles is illustrated by the following list of its section headings:

Business Purpose
Business Ethics
Involvement of People
Human Relationships
Privacy of Information about Employees
Ownership and Investment

---

[9] Kenneth R. Andrews, *op. cit.*, 103.
[10] Peter Madsen, *op. cit.*, 11.

Board Stewardship
Corporate Facilities
Disposal of Wastes
Product Quality and Uniformity
Competitive Conduct
Relationships with Suppliers
Sharing of Technology
Accounting Records and Financial Reporting
Intercompany Pricing
Currency Transactions
Differing Business Practices
Public Responsibility
Observance of Local Laws
Relationships with Public Officials
Disclosure of Information
Inside Information
International Information Flow
Free Enterprise, Worldwide
Reporting Code Compliance[11]

A participant described candidly how another company developed, uses, and regularly updates its code:

> *Our first priority was to determine the corporation's practices around the world.* How did we conduct business in places like Korea, Indonesia and Taiwan? How much did we really know about our distributors and agents? And could we live with these "locally accepted business practices" we were learning about? And if not, how would we deal with them? For us, it was a new ball game on a new field. Suffice it to say, the [newly created] business conduct committee made many trips that first year and asked lots of questions.
>
> Following our initiation, *we drafted our global guidelines— which would become our first code of conduct—"A Matter of Integrity."* At the time, we considered it a noble and informed effort.

---

[11] Code of Caterpillar Inc. as reported by Michael R. Lane, "Improving American Business Ethics in Three Steps," *The CPA Journal* (February 1991), 31.

By the early 1980s, however, we had learned enough to know that certain parts of the original code reflected the world the way we felt it *ought* to be, not the way it really was.

The next priority was to assure that all employees received the code, read it and understood it. That was done by mailing the code to each employee's home accompanied by a cover letter from the CEO. We have continued that practice with each revised edition of the code.

The description of this code continues:

Since our first code, we have had four revisions—the first in 1981 and the most recent [in 1990]. We translate our code into seven languages, and believe me, we have learned that preserving the spirit and literal meaning of the code in its many translated versions is a challenge.

From the beginning we have tried to keep the code very visible. You'll see it in our offices, hallways and lobbies. We encourage our people to discuss the code with customers and business contacts. We're continually looking for ways to keep the code visible . . . in company publications and in management presentations.[12]

Later we shall return to this company's experience to learn how understanding of the code is reinforced and how compliance is monitored.

Because every company does not address its code with such a vigorous, continuing focus, it is important to warn against the downside of some code practices. As Carl Iverson acknowledged in Chapter 8:

Too often, they are rather detailed lists of things to be done—or things not to be done. And it is sometimes a mixed bag; for example, it may include such things as a dress code— not very stirring, I'm afraid.

Also, many of the codes tend to be too self-focused. A widely quoted 1983 study of 119 codes seemed, as two critics

---

[12] John E. Swanson, Senior Consultant, Communications and Business Conduct, Dow Corning Corporation, at the Integrating Business Ethics Conference, The Conference Board, April 24, 1991.

put it, "to reflect a more abiding concern for conduct that is directly inimical to a firm's internal operation [for example, a heavy emphasis on conflicts of interest] than for relations in keeping with [its responsibility to the society of which the corporation is a part]."

Sometimes a code emerges as a response to legal or ethical problems that a company or an industry has found itself in. There is nothing wrong with this, but as a result cynics tend to dismiss the effort as PR. It may be written, or at least heavily edited, by house counsel, which is likely to make it rather sterile.

Those who work on codes of conduct should be aware of these pitfalls and attempt to avoid them.

Established Procedures

Nowhere is the interrelationship of ethics with sound business practice more evident than with respect to established procedures.

Even without any consideration of ethics, efficient companies recognize the need for formalizing operating procedures in every area of their business operations. The reasons hardly need listing—improving the efficiency of performance, making supervision easier, ensuring accuracy and consistency, facilitating the training of new employees, avoiding duplications of effort, leaving "tracks"—to cite just a few that come readily to mind.

What may not be as widely recognized is that having formal, written procedures is conducive to ethical behavior. Their existence reduces sloppiness, which in turn can lead to improper shortcuts and abuses. An awareness that there is a record of what has been done, and that it may be checked, sometimes removes temptation. There is less opportunity for someone caught in a misdeed to plead that he or she "didn't know."

The new Federal Sentencing Guidelines used by Federal judges to levy fines against business defendant organizations were discussed in Chapter 2. These included seven key elements, two of which are:

- Establish compliance standards and procedures to be followed by company employees and other agents.
- Communicate the standards and procedures to all employees and other agents through training programs and/or printed materials.

Compliance with these and the other five elements is a matter for a company's legal counsel to consider. As part of any program to help ensure compliance, managements may also want to have accounting or other consultants review their procedures and the manner in which they are disseminated and documented.

Training

Training lies at the heart of any effective ethics program—and may well require greater, and more sophisticated, effort than any other part.

Surveys have indicated that between 35 and 45 percent of respondent companies (presumably larger ones) provide employees with some kind of ethics training, although great variations in scope and quality are probably buried in those broad responses. As a pair of writers have noted, some programs "easily lend themselves to a focus on the 'thou shalt nots.' Employees learn what they should not do in specific situations. But they may not be equipped to make decisions in situations that are less clear-cut or not explicitly covered by 'the rules.' "[13]

Rather than being strictly compliance-oriented, the goals of effective training should be to:

- Increase awareness of ethical consequences of business decisions.
- Develop a decision model for managers that includes a consideration of ethical ramifications of their decisions.

---

[13] Dan Rice and Craig Drellinger, "Rights and Wrongs of Ethics Training," *Training & Development Journal* (May 1990), 103.

■   Integrate relevant cases and vignettes that reinforce the organization's code.[14]

Also, as one writer has noted, "Since policy cannot be effective unless it is understood, some companies use corporate training sessions to discuss the problems of applying their ethical standards. In difficult situations, judgment in making the leap from general policy statements to situationally specific action can be informed by discussion. Such discussion, if carefully conducted, can reveal the inadequacy or ambiguity of present policy, new areas in which the company must take a unified stand, and new ways to support individuals in making the right decisions."[15]

Ethicist Peter Madsen has set forth the way in which training should be designed in a clear way that deserves quoting:

> Once the subject matter of an ethics training program has been identified . . . , then the best approach is to structure the session so that general ethical concepts, principles and theories are introduced early to provide an analytic framework participants can use when addressing the ethical questions they find bothersome in their professional lives. This general-to-specifics approach provides a natural order to the session and offers participants a useful skill they can take back to the workingplace with them.
>
> Ethical precepts (e.g., the Golden Rule, utilitarianism, rights theory, theories of justice, the concepts of responsibility and obligations, fairness) provide common standards of behavior or suggest ways to judge and think through issues that have an ethical dimension. They can be reviewed in almost any basic introductory text on ethics.

Continuing, Madsen writes:

> Once an appropriate analytic framework is identified, participants should apply these concepts in discussions of case studies appropriate to the subject matter of the session. The

---

[14] Michael R. Lane, "Improving American Business Ethics in Three Steps," *The CPA Journal* (February 1991), 31.
[15] Kenneth R. Andrews, *op. cit.*, 102.

case study method is the preferable instructional style in ethics education. Almost all ethics training done today has some case analysis built into it. Ethics cases present objective situations with real life implications for users. They are more desirable as instructional tools than lectures or stand-up presentations which run the risk of sounding like holier-than-thou moralizing and preaching to listeners.

Cases stimulate interactive learning by drawing participants into a dialog that allows for the exchange of ideas and viewpoints and provides the context within which participants can apply the precepts and rules that formed the analytic framework developed for them initially in the session.

There are several good collections in book form in the field of business ethics. Ethics cases vary in length, depth, and complexity, so choosing appropriate cases for a training session will be a matter of individual taste. Experience, however, suggests that short cases that present readers with a dilemma or quandary they must solve have the best educational impact in a training setting since they lend themselves nicely to dialog and discussion.[16]

This provides an excellent overall blueprint—an outline for initiating an ethics training program. Most large companies will have in-house training specialists; many will also have persons qualified in ethical analysis. These companies will be able to design and present competent ethics training programs. Also, they will be in a position to retain outside consultants to advise them in their efforts.

But what about medium-sized and small companies, many of which will lack either training specialists or persons with ethics skills—or both? They may be the very ones who most need the training. The greatest difficulty they may face is finding someone who will be sufficiently qualified to present the theoretical foundation—and is comfortable in doing so. There is broad agreement

---

[16] Peter Madsen, "An Ounce of Prevention: Designing Ethics Training Programs," *The Human Resources Professional* (September/October 1989), 33–34.

that trying to address ethics training without this conceptual underpinning is likely to be ineffectual, possibly even misleading.

There is no single best answer, but one or a combination of these may serve their purposes:

- Retaining a qualified ethicist to consult on the structure of a training program—possibly to assist in at least the initial sessions.
- Sending one or more persons with some training skills to seminars on business ethics so that they will be qualified to prepare and conduct company training sessions.
- Having someone within the company, using a book such as this one, lead discussion seminars with presentations of dilemmas prepared personally or selected from available books.

Consideration must be given to the levels of employees to which the training should be directed. Ultimately some form of training might well encompass all employees. At the outset, however, as discussed in Chapter 7, it would probably be best to cover managers and supervisors.

Plans should also be made for continuing sessions. Again as noted in Chapter 7, training of any type requires reinforcement. Also, turnover and promotions change the makeup of many organizations in a surprisingly short time. The results of one-shot efforts, therefore, are likely to be short-lived.

Hot Line

In Chapter 8, the Hauser-Moore committee debated what kind of system or procedure a company might install that would provide employees with a means to raise ethics questions or to report known or suspected transgressions. The approach that seemed to have the most appeal was creating the position of ombudsman, described by a management professor as follows:

> An ombudsman is a person within an organization, often an older and respected manager, close to retirement, who has been relieved of operating responsibilities and assigned the

task of counseling younger employees on career problems, organizational difficulties, and ethical issues. ... Often the ombudsman can go considerably beyond counseling and investigation and is able to act informally to resolve problems . . .

But the same writer dashed cold water on the idea, going on to say:

> Does the position of ombudsman work? Again, not really. The problem is that the person reporting the incident is not truly "not implicated in any way." We can assume that ombudsmen are generally discrete [sic] in talking with an offender, but the source of information for the ombudsman—the originator of the complaint—is usually awkwardly clear. It has to be a person within the organization who has a source of information about the practice and the moral scruples to report it. It generally is someone who has spoken to the guilty person about the practice within the past 30 days. It almost inevitably is someone who is easy to identify. The ombudsman does not have to be concerned about retribution; his or her contact generally does.[17]

The criticism is valid, certainly. This is a difficult area in which there is no completely satisfactory solution. As Carl Iverson observed, "If there is a good, generally applicable answer, whoever has found it has certainly kept it secret. Much of how a company handles this problem depends on its tradition, its structure, a whole lot of intangibles. What works in one place may not in another."

And yet some measures are necessary: Employees cannot be left with nowhere to go with their concerns. Iverson pointed this out, saying, "Although it's no panacea, I believe the ombudsman approach probably has the most to offer. Quite a few companies have adopted it. It is certainly better than leaving the employees on their own. If you're going to tell your people that ethics is important—that you want and expect them to behave ethically—

---

[17] LaRue Tone Hosmer, *op. cit.*, 158.

you owe it to them to open a channel for dealing with their problems."

The manager quoted earlier who participated in setting up his company's business conduct committee summed it up:

> Another role—albeit not a primary one—of the committee is to serve as an ombudsman. We encourage our people to go through their normal channels, but sometimes that's awkward or even impossible. So, we—either individually or as a committee—act as the "source of last resort."[18]

Ongoing Oversight

The importance of ongoing oversight, continuing attention to an ethics program, cannot be overemphasized. It cannot be perceived as management's fad for today, destined for tomorrow's scrap heap when something more trendy comes along. As Carl Iverson told the Hauser-Moore committee:

- It must be clearly evident that the program has the continuing attention and commitment of the board of directors and top management.
- The program must be kept up-to-date.
- There should be an effective system for reviewing compliance.

Common sense and the experience of companies with effective ethics programs indicate that designating some person, committee, or other group to head the program on a continuing basis is essential. For convenience here, the term "committee" will be used to identify this leadership. It must have recognized authority, credibility, and access to the CEO and the board. Depending on the size, structure, and traditions of the organization, the person who chairs the committee may devote full time to its activities; in any event, it should be apparent that he or she is handling it on more than a casual, when-time-is-available basis.

---

[18] John E. Swanson, *op. cit.*

The committee, which should meet at frequent intervals, should be responsible for maintaining the program, either by making changes on its own initiative or by submitting recommendations to management and the board. Although its head may report operationally to the CEO or another senior member of top management, it should have access to and should meet periodically with the audit committee or another designated committee of the board.

The scope of compliance reviews and the way in which they are conducted can vary greatly. In one company that was a pioneer in designing and installing a comprehensive process, the committee members have handled a major part of the reviews themselves. Although this approach differs from what others might wish to follow, learning how they went about this conveys the enthusiasm, the dedication, with which they addressed the job. In the words of one committee member:

> The [next] priority was the establishment of an ongoing procedure to continuously monitor our global conduct, and to interpret and clarify the code. In my opinion, this was the single most important decision the committee made in its first year. We first looked at what other companies were doing. There were a few training programs at the time—and we found a couple of interesting executive ethics conferences. Several companies simply required their managers outside the United States to sign a compliance form annually. There were some excellent new initiatives, but we decided on another way.
>
> We wanted our process to be highly involving and participative throughout the entire organization. We also wanted employees to see our initiative as a *permanent* commitment, not just another program that would have a brief moment in the sun and then fade away. We were not thinking in terms of six months, or a year. We were thinking more in terms of an endless journey, a way of life.

Continuing, he has described the resulting approach:

> We decided to do face-to-face compliance reviews on a regular basis. Small group sessions—heavy on dialogue—that would be

held periodically and repeatedly at our locations around the world, which today number about 80. For the first few years, a limited number of reviews were conducted at our area head-quarters. . . . Today, 25 to 35 reviews are conducted annually, about one-half outside the United States.

Two of the four committee members will typically conduct each session. Discussions are guided by the relevance of specific code of conduct items to a particular audience. These are our code headings:

> Responsibilities to employees
> Responsibilities as employees
> Relations with customers, distributors, suppliers
> Social responsibilities, conservation, environment, and
> product stewardship
> International business guidelines
> Financial responsibilities

Under each there are several separate items.

Our production people, for example, have a major stake in code guidelines about waste materials and the disposal of hazardous materials. Salespeople are interested in how far they can go to obtain competitive information or the permissible limits to gift giving or customer entertainment. (Although I would add that our salespeople have become much more in-terested in our commitment to safeguarding the environment in recent years.)

We also set aside enough time to talk about ethical issues and situations that are *not* covered in the code—or in some cases may not be covered well enough. I should also point out that the discussions are two-way, not one-way presentations or inquisitions. The committee's role is to *facilitate* the discussions, to provide examples based on past . . . experience or to clarify particular code statements when necessary.

In conclusion, he said:

Over the past 15 years—which have to date included over 400 reviews—the committee has received an education, as have our people around the world.[19]

---

[19] *Ibid.*

A more common approach would be to have a group such as the internal audit department conduct the reviews, in accordance, of course, with a scope designed and agreed upon with the committee. The advantage of using internal auditors is their training, their acceptance by the organization as objective fact-finders and the structure of their process: maintaining continuing files, following specific programs, documenting their findings, and making and following up on recommendations. To avoid the problem envisioned by Joe Hendricks in Chapter 8 of having "bean counters" review areas like engineering and manufacturing that might be outside their technical competence, their work should be coordinated with senior persons with expertise in the area being reviewed.

Some companies ask their independent auditors to help with the design of their compliance reviews, and in some cases they are asked to conduct the reviews.

Regardless of who conducts the compliance reviews, the results must be reported to the appropriate levels within the organization. The committee should certainly receive detailed reports, but it would also be desirable for the CEO and the appropriate board committee to receive summaries and to have the opportunity to question those who conducted the reviews.

All the foregoing is meaningless, possibly worse, without prompt, fair follow-up on the findings. Weaknesses in procedures should be promptly remedied. Derelictions on the part of individuals must be disciplined as appropriate. The Federal Sentencing Guidelines address this, stating that companies should "install monitoring and auditing systems" and:

- Reinforce standards consistently through appropriate disciplinary mechanisms.
- Respond appropriately to reported offenses and take action to prevent recurrence.

As Peter Madsen has written:

> If an organization takes the time and effort to devise an ethics program, it should take the time and effort to adequately enforce any infractions of the policies or code that it devises.

Nothing sends the wrong signal to employees like unenforced policies or codes. Violations are sure to increase, if management "looks the other way" when wrongdoing takes place. This is not to suggest, however, that executives enforce its ethics program without due process. Enforcement must be firm, but fair.[20]

Will a sound program, with effective procedures and ongoing oversight, provide assurance that a company will not experience ethical lapses? No. It's a tough world in business today. Systems and transactions are increasingly complex. Companies are under intense pressure to compete, even to survive. Managers and other employees may feel driven to produce results—to gain advancement, even to hang on. Companies with impeccable reputations for their leadership role in business ethics, built up with care and pride over the years, are sometimes embarrassed to find their names in the headlines. Bribing government officials, perhaps. Making kickbacks. Disposing improperly of hazardous material. Overcharging customers. Selling flawed products. And when this happens, someone is likely to ask: What good can an ethics program be if things like that still happen?

The answer is that no organization can be immune to human error, even deliberate transgressions, by employees, agents, and sometimes officers. With thousands, often tens of thousands of individuals involved, something can slip through even the best of systems. And yet for every miss, there are probably scores of success stories that go untold, lapses that are avoided by a good program. People are reminded of what can happen. Controls are built into the system that make intentional or careless violations more difficult. The corporate culture discourages actions that can damage the company's reputation.

No, in summary, an ethics program does not provide an absolute guarantee against moral failures. But it greatly improves the odds against their occurrence, certainly against their magni-

---

[20] Peter Madsen, "Managing Ethics," *Executive Excellence* (December 1990), 12.

tude or frequency. The payoff in human values and, often, in dollars and cents is real.

Selected Reading List

The following books have proved to be particularly informative, stimulating and interesting as background for the writing of this book. Not having been able to read everything, or even a major portion, of what has been published with respect to business ethics, the author is sure that there are many others as useful as those that have been identified. A sampling from the following list, however, will challenge your thinking; this, in turn, may lead you to some of the other publications that these authors cite.

Thomas Donaldson, *Corporations and Morality* (Englewood Cliffs, NJ: Prentice Hall, 1982).

R. Edward Freeman and Daniel R. Gilbert, Jr., *Corporate Strategy and the Search for Ethics* (Englewood Cliffs, NJ: Prentice-Hall, 1988).

W. Michael Hoffman and Jennifer Mills Moore, editors, *Business Ethics: Reading and Cases in Corporate Morality* (New York: McGraw-Hill Publishing Company, 1990).

LaRue Tone Hosmer, *The Ethics of Management* (Homewood, IL: Richard D. Irwin, Inc., 1987).

Donald G. Jones, *Doing Ethics in Business* (Cambridge, MA: Oelgeschlager, Gunn & Hain, Publishers, Inc., 1982).

Alan M. Kantrow, *The Constraints of Corporate Tradition*, first Perennial Library edition (New York: Harper & Row, Publishers, 1988).

Charles M. Kelly, *The Destructive Achiever: Power and Ethics in the American Corporation* (Reading, MA: Addison-Wesley Publishing Company, Inc., 1988).

Peter Madsen and Jay M. Shafritz, editors, *Essentials of Business Ethics* (New York: Meridian, 1990).

Jack Mahoney, *Teaching Business Ethics in the UK, Europe and the USA* (London and Atlantic Highlands, NJ: The Athlone Press, 1990).

John B. Matthews, Kenneth E. Goodpaster, and Laura L. Nash, *Policies and Persons: A Casebook in Business Ethics* (New York: McGraw-Hill Book Company, 1985).

Michael Rion, *The Responsible Manager: Practical Strategies for Ethical Decision Making* (San Francisco: Harper & Row, Publishers, 1990).

N. Craig Smith, *Morality and the Market: Consumer Pressure for Corporate Accountability* (London and New York: Routledge, 1990).

Barbara Ley Toffler, *Tough Choices: Manager's Talk Ethics* (New York: John Wiley & Sons, 1986).

Clarence C. Walton, *The Moral Manager* (Cambridge, MA: Ballinger Publishing Company, 1988).

Patricia Werhane and Kendall D'Andrade, editors, *Profit and Responsibility* (New York and Toronto: The Edwin Mellen Press, 1985).

Manuel G. Velasquez, *Business Ethics: Concepts and Cases* (Englewood Cliffs, NJ: Prentice-Hall. 1988).